best wishes,

Spinwars

Politics and New Media

Bill Fox

KEY PORTER BOOKS

Canadian Cataloging in Publication Data

Fox, William J. (William John), 1947-
    Spinwars : politics and new media

Includes index.
ISBN 1-55263-037-4

1. Journalism – Political aspects. 2. Journalistic ethics. 3. Sensationalism in journalism. I. Title.

PN4781.F69 1999   070.4   C98-931557-6

THE CANADA COUNCIL | LE CONSEIL DES ARTS
FOR THE ARTS | DU CANADA
SINCE 1957 | DEPUIS 1957

The publisher gratefully acknowledges the support of the Canada Council for the Arts and the Ontario Arts Council for its publishing program.

Canada

We acknowledge the financial support of the Government of Canada through the Book Publishing Industry Development Program (BPIDP) for our publishing activities.

Key Porter Books Limited
70 The Esplanade
Toronto, Ontario
Canada M5E 1R2

www.keyporter.com

Electronic formatting: Heidy Lawrance Associates
Design: Peter Maher

Printed and bound in Canada

99 00 01 02 6 5 4 3 2 1

To Bonnie

Contents

Acknowledgments

This project began as a preoccupation, evolved to an obsession, and remains as a convenient excuse for procrastination. Some day soon I will have to decide what I want to do with the next phase of my professional life.

The book has its genesis in an old-style newsroom on Queen Street in Ottawa and draws its spirit from the boys and girls on campaign press buses careening along highways across Canada and the United States. I miss the energy, the enlightenment, the nights, the tunes, and souls like Hubert Bauch.

The Ottawa bureau of the *Toronto Star* in the early 1980s was a magical place to be. The *Star* experience taught me what political journalism can be, mostly because I got to work for Lou Clancy, a superior editor and an even better friend. Friendships forged with Pamela Wallin, Carol Goar, and John Honderich have stood the tests of time, distance, and the odd disagreement. Each excels in the field.

To political colleagues from campaigns past and present my unreserved admiration. And I will always guard a special place for those who served in "PMO One"—Brian Mulroney's first Langevin Bloc.

When a period of introspection seemed appropriate, former Carleton Journalism School director Anthony Westell opened a door. Professor Paul Atallah's intellect and acumen provided a necessary kick start. Stuart Adam and Michael Whittington ensured my graduate school sojourn was both enriching and rewarding. I want to thank Peter Johansen, Christopher Dornan, and their colleagues for their scholarship and their friendship.

Former Trudeau adviser Tom Axworthy was the catalyst for extending my academic walkabout, providing me with the excuse to drop in on Marvin Kalb, director of the Shorenstein Center on Press, Politics and Public Policy, John F. Kennedy School of Government, Harvard University. Kalb's generous invitation to apply for a fellowship at the center fundamentally changed my life. To my colleagues Claude Moisy, Dr. Lance Jefferies, Maimouna Mills, Colin Seymour Ure, and Warren Mitofsky, my appreciation and admiration for creating an atmosphere of collegiality and rigor that broadened horizons well beyond anything I could have imagined. My thanks to Fred Schauer, Pippa Norris, and especially Richard Parker for their guidance and insights. To Julie Felt, Nancy Palmer, Edy Holway, Jennifer Quinlan, and Michelle Johnson, "merci" for a thousand kindnesses.

Charles Overby and the people at the Freedom Forum Media Studies Center in New York proved lightning can strike twice, especially if a redirecting hand intervenes at an appropriate moment.

My colleagues Lord Asa Briggs, Michael Janeway, Al Gollin, Orville Schell, Jeffrey Toobin, Mitchell Stephens, Hank Klibanoff, David Shenk, Margaret Usdansky, and fellow Canadians Marjorie Ferguson and Edna Einsiedel moved me from the camp of the "declinists" at the start of our shared experience to the ranks of the "neo-Pollyannists" by year's end. Ev Dennis, our mentor and spiritual leader, is, at once, a scholar and a gentleman. Rob Snyder, Adam Clayton Powell, III, and Larry McGill were particularly supportive of my research, and Jessiman Reich and Valerie Keane sat perched outside my office door, the better to ensure I had everything I needed to work. My graduate assistant Antonius Porch, a brilliant graduate from Yale and Columbia's law school, taught me much about life south of the 49th. I miss his insight, and his infectious good humor, and know his career will be marked by a series of triumphs.

My former partners at the Earnscliffe Strategy Group—Harry J. Near, Michael Robinson, Bruce Anderson, Elly Alboim, and David Herle—are the best business partners, and friends, a body could hope for. My personal assistants over the years, in particular Cathy Duff, Linda Campbell, Sabrina Berry, office manager Terry Stephen, and Shirley Harris, will recognize much of this work.

Hugh Segal ensured that the Harvard and Columbia years would serve some broader purpose by introducing me to the School of Policy Studies at Queen's University. His loyalty and friendship are a critical component of my daily life, further enriched by his wife, Donna, and daughter, Jacqueline.

My friends at Aalpha Business Services, Peter Somerville and Rosemary Paquette, deserve special recognition. Their grace under fire is nothing short of remarkable. A special thanks as well to Jack Fleischmann, Rick Muller, and the folks at News Theatre.

My parents, Bill Sr. and the late Jessie Fox, taught all the Fox boys and girls the value of community and public service. To my dad's dismay, his efforts produced more socialists than Grits, but, to his intense relief, only one Tory. Graham, Christiane, and Martin have been rooting for their old dad to reach the finish line for years. I am delighted in their company, and am in awe of their discipline and determination. I say without qualification that they have been a constant source of pride and inspiration. Graham's stint as press secretary to Hugh Segal's leadership campaign introduced him to the world of spin. Wisely, he is pursuing postgraduate studies at the London School of Economics.

Because much of this work revolves around my thoughts about the Rt. Hon. Brian Mulroney, his wife, Mila, and their children, I will not go into any detail here except to say thanks for an experience that has shaped so much of my life.

Garth Turner's interest in this initiative led me to Anna Porter's door. The team at Key Porter, led by Susan Renouf, were unfailingly supportive and nurturing of a first-time author, encouraging me to find my own voice.

Editor Andrea Bock's clarity and creativity helped me work through the clutter and confusion. Her infectious good humor and drill sergeant's adherence to an editorial timetable were dispensed in equal measure. The work is immeasurably better for her effort; any shortcomings are mine.

And then there is Bonnie.

Bonnie Brownlee is my life partner, an indomitable spirit whose strength of character carries many of us along. Bonnie has lived every moment of the experiences set out in these pages, tempering the euphoria, coping with the brooding Celt, nurturing the nomadic tendencies, accepting the lifestyle adjustments that are the inevitable consequence of Quixote-like forays into the demimonde of black-tee-shirt-clad *artistes*. I may never get life right, but, if I ever do, Bonnie will be the reason. In the spirit of my old craft of newspapering, this book carries a double byline.

1

From Declinist to
Neo-Pollyannist

As a senior fellow at the Freedom Forum Media Studies Center at Columbia University during the 1995–96 academic year, I would meet weekly with my colleagues to discuss the great journalistic issues of our time. We tended to break into two camps, dubbed the "declinists" and the "neo-Pollyannists" by colleague Mitchell Stephens, a professor at New York University.[1]

The declinists would argue all is not well in the media Land of Oz. Today's political journalism is less substantive than it was twenty years ago, preoccupied as it is with lifestyle trivia at the expense of detailed analysis of policy options. The irony inherent in this is readily acknowledged, given that today's journalists are better educated, better paid, and have access to technological advances that facilitate the timely delivery of editorial content to the marketplace of ideas.

News managers, say the declinists, are largely reactive. As colleague Michael Janeway observed, they are "preoccupied with what to do with the flight of the audience."[2]

The fact that corporate ownership of media outlets is incompatible with good journalism is an article of faith for declinists. They believe the concept of "social responsibility" for newspaper ownership is lost on the suspender-snapping fund managers that hold the lion's share of publicly traded media companies. They are preoccupied with mergers and takeovers, and worry that concentration of ownership in a few publicly traded global giants will maximize pressure for quarterly results at the expense of quality editorial content. They predict this concentration of ownership will result in silenced voices, especially voices of dissent. The declinists fear a world of newspeak, though they tend to characterize the threat as the more benign version of Aldous Huxley's *Brave New World* rather than that of *1984*, George Orwell's more authoritarian take.

Market-driven journalism, with its roots in the world of entertainment and its trend toward trivialization and tabloidization, is cited as an inevitable, if regrettable, response to this paradigm shift in ownership from Main Street to Wall Street.

The declinists see the mainstream media as having moved away from their traditional mandate—that of establishing and communicating matters of importance—to the more commercially viable mandate of communicating matters of interest. The broader the range of issues, the more emotional, diverse, entertaining, and interesting those issues are, the better the prospects are of assembling new coalitions as audiences.

Elly Alboim, a professor at Carleton University, says that, as a direct consequence of this shift, survival strategies are paramount, particularly for network television. What viewers and readers want to know has increasingly become an important test of its newsworthiness. To reduce the discussion to the rhetoric of a bumper sticker, the *Pathfinder* mission to Mars may be important, but O.J. Simpson's murder trial is interesting.

To students of government the implications of this analysis are as obvious as they are unsettling: what happens to society's ability to organize itself when commercial considerations clash with the concept of journalism as a public service? Bluntly put, can healthy self-government survive on a steady diet of editorial "junk food"?

News, at least in theory, sets both the political and the public policy agenda. News determines the context within which political events will be perceived, and assigns responsibility to political leaders for resolving, or failing to resolve, policy problems.

The declinists are on solid ground when arguing that, in recent years, media and politicians alike have conducted themselves in a manner unbecoming such a custodial relationship.

Television's emergence as the primary vehicle for political communication established the importance of a leader's ability to "perform." Political events were "staged," and policies were "packaged." Political journalists became "critics." And the pundits among them became a part of the show itself.

Analysis replaced the straightforward reporting of fact, which in turn made "managing expectations" a key component of campaign strategy. "Spin" is all about managing expectations. A candidate who finishes second in a primary race isn't a loser if he or she was only expected to finish no better than third. "Spin" became an important part of campaign strategy, whether the campaign involved getting a candidate elected or getting public support for a policy initiative. In the broader context of politics and public policy, the "spin" wars are a battle to shape congenial truths, and to control the dominant news frame. "War" is the accurate term, not only because of the intensity with which the issue is contested by media advisers for political leaders and journalists alike, but also because it involves numerous skirmishes and battles before the outcome is determined.

Political discourse today is too often about loud and angry voices. Assertion takes precedence over reason, and spin is at the root cause of much of this rhetorical excess. Candidates for office succumb to the lure of the killer quote, only to find themselves victims of their foolishness later. Just ask Preston Manning what time bingo starts at Stornoway tonight.

Too often politicians and reporters engage in what is the political equivalent of insider baseball—a dialogue that excludes the very public both are dependent upon.

But in recent years, having spent the better part of a generation consciously or unconsciously excluding the public from their world, politicians and press alike have finally tumbled to the fact that the public, in the end, actually did get the message. Seizing opportunities presented by new media, the public is starting to move on.

Therein lies the flicker of hope.

I began the year at Columbia in the declinist camp, troubled by the down-market reporting practices of recent years. Somehow "gotcha" journalism had usurped solid investigative reporting. Even journalistic heavyweights seemed preoccupied with gossip rather than governance. Celebrity emerged as the ultimate test for both the politician and the journalist.

This dumbing-down of public discourse meant serious issues were being ignored. The size of prime-ministerial clothes closets was the stuff of the front page, the tainted-blood scandal wasn't. Presidential dalliances were news, the savings-and-loan scandal wasn't.

The diversionary nature of much of today's political coverage promotes government by risk avoidance. Today's cabinet is being ruled by the doctrine of "plausible deniability"—a direct consequence of Watergate.

An unsettling hypothesis advanced by communications scholar Neil Postman struck a particular chord. Postman believes that, in today's world of "news assembly," reporters can apply the professional conventions and rules of their craft and yet deliver an editorial product analogous to Potemkin's village—artificial, even surreal, and largely unconnected to the truth.[3]

Over the course of my year at Columbia, however, I slowly converted to neo-Pollyannism. Intrigued by colleague Mitchell Stephens's excitement at the innovative programming being done in Toronto at Citytv, I somewhat sheepishly began to wonder what I was missing in my own backyard and I began to pay more attention to deconstructionist advertising as indicative of the future of news. I was further inspired by Canadian communications scholar Marshall McLuhan's admonition that the medium is critical to the message. If an exciting new medium was emerging, there was every reason to be hopeful about the next generation of messages as well. I was also seduced by *Newsweek* technology columnist Steven Levy's assertion that the Internet is the most empowering of media technologies, both in terms of creating editorial products and as a consumer of those products; the Net has the power to turn us all into digital pamphleteers. A.J. Liebling, recognized as the great media critic of his time, used to argue that freedom of the press extends only to those individuals who own one. Levy seemed to be suggesting that, with digital technology, anyone could be a publisher, filmmaker, or electronic-newsletter editor.

Omar Wasow is the kind of person Levy is talking about. Wasow produces New York Online from his Brooklyn apartment. He employs seven people, was grossing $400,000 a year in 1997, and is a featured New Age pundit on MSNBC, the self-declared cradle of new commentary.

Wasow was a featured speaker at a conference on new media organized by Harvard's Neiman Foundation in May 1995. He projected self-confidence without the attitude, and communicated a cool awareness of the enormous potential inherent in new media, a sense that was infectious.

Wasow represented the personification of Levy's message to aging Boomers that they need not worry about corporate concentration in media because the "propeller heads" have already stolen the revolution, or at least the electronic future. The neo-Pollyannists could listen to someone like Wasow and get excited about a new era of communication.

The neo-Pollyannists see audience fragmentation as liberation theology. Magazines may have pioneered the move away from the law of "large" numbers to the law of "right" numbers, but the neo-Pollyannists have taken the trend to its logical conclusion. They have redefined community, moving away from the geographic boundaries to embrace the virtual community.

In this new configuration, the "product" in media companies is no longer the assembled audience, as it is for the mass media. The new media model ascribes more value to editorial content. Though advertising will continue to be critical to the revenue base, the editorial content itself will generate revenue as well.

Levy points to a future information Nirvana through the World Wide Web, a world where individuals will be able to access the best editorial products in the world. Stuck with a local newspaper that maximizes profit at the expense of editorial content? Subscribe to the *Guardian* or the *New York Times*.

The passive world, the hallmark of the television era, will give way to a new interactive public discourse that will challenge the "top-down" news approach of the past thirty years. News consumers will have more control over how much information they can access on any given subject, even from the mainstream media. An all-news-headline service may draw your attention to a news development in the Middle East, for example. But a point-and-click process will allow you to access a ninety-second news report fleshing out the details. Viewers interested in more information can then access a five-minute background piece offering some context, a newsmagazine-length takeout exploring the positions of each of the interested parties, or an hour-long documentary exploring the broader geopolitical issues at stake. Individuals looking for more can keep working their way through newsmagazine articles, essays in learned journals, or books written on the subject.

Communication technologies, therefore, will prove to be every bit as emancipating for the mainstream media as they are empowering for new and emerging media.

The media, in their various forms, remain the most effective and efficient forum for political discourse in our increasingly complex world. There is a tendency to dismiss the mainstream media as dinosaurs, but, as one communications adviser to Bill Clinton observed, even if you accept the analogy, that just means the establishment media are big, fast, and likely to last a million years.

The cornerstone for my newfound optimism is a premise first articulated by Bernard C. Cohen in his work *The Press and Foreign Policy*, published in 1963. Cohen argued that media coverage matters, not because the media tell us what to think, but more precisely because the media tell us what to think about.[4] What will be radically different in the Internet Age is the number of media voices telling us what to think about. Communication between electors and the elected will reflect that radical change.

My perspective on these issues is somewhat unique in that I have spent more than thirty years working each point of the press/politics/public policy triangle. I have held senior reporting positions at Canada's largest newspaper and appeared frequently on radio and television public-affairs programs. More recently, I have advised prime ministers, presidents, and captains of industry on the occasionally arcane art of political communication. In the shorthand of colloquial speech, I am a "spin doctor."

My career choice always seemed serendipitous, but may have been preordained, or at least the direct consequence of an accident of urban geography.

Born in the Northern Ontario gold-mining town of Timmins, I grew up across the dirt lane from the Art Deco building that housed the *Daily Press*, Lord Thomson of Fleet's first newspaper. Kids could buy the newspaper for a nickel a copy at the pressroom door and hawk it on the streets and in the taverns for seven cents. When making change you learned to fumble for the pennies in your jeans, hoping the hardrock miners coming off the day shift at the Hollinger or the Aunor would be so anxious to quaff a couple at the Lady Laurier that they would wave you off rather than wait for the three cents owed.

Summer nights, our revered sports columnist Doug McLellan could be found at Hollinger Park, home of the Mercantile Fastball League. For the people of Timmins, Schumacher, and South Porcupine, players such as pitcher Luke Lefevre, shortstop Lyle Porter, and my personal favorite, third baseman Danny Belisle, were as special as Mays, Mantle, and the Duke of Flatbush. Chomping on an ever-present cigar, with reporter Reg Noble often at his side, Doug offered up insight and conversation as compelling as the action on the field. McLellan's patience and tolerance of my thousand and one questions suggested he was a first cousin to Job.

A desultory undergraduate experience with grades numerically comparable to outdoor temperatures in March was interrupted early in 1967 when a copy-boy position opened up at the *Ottawa Citizen*. My job was to run to the corner coffee shop umpteen times a day, trying to remember whether the late Eddie Morris wanted his tea with the bag in or out. An extraordinary journalist and teacher named Lindsay Crysler, then the *Citizen*'s newly minted city editor, provided the proverbial break of a lifetime. The ensuing apprenticeship followed the tradition of the craft: citydesk clerk, night police beat, courts, suburban school boards, then suburban councils, City Hall, a provincial election campaign, and on to Parliament Hill. By the time Timothy Crouse penned *The Boys on the Bus*, I had finally become one. What I didn't realize at the time was that I was learning my craft in the period media analyst Ellen Hume would describe as the "golden era of noncommercialized news."

I first met Brian Mulroney in a turnover note. In the spring of 1973, following a self-financed sabbatical year at the Sorbonne, I returned to Canada as Quebec correspondent for Southam News. My predecessor, Jim Ferrabee, had thoughtfully developed a lengthy contact list of Montreal movers and shakers he thought might be helpful to me; Mulroney's name was near the top.

If information is the currency of journalism, Mulroney's, that of a political activist and labor lawyer, was platinum; he was an excellent source, with extensive contacts in virtually all segments of Quebec society. We quickly discovered that we had certain shared experiences and sufficiently striking differences to keep the lunchtime conversation interesting. A more personal relationship began to develop after his unsuccessful 1976 bid for the leadership of the Progressive-Conservative party.

After a four-year stint in Quebec covering stories as varied and exciting as the 1976 Summer Olympics, the election of the René Lévesque–led Parti Québécois government, prison riots, and gang wars, I was transferred to Ottawa to cover federal politics.

The transition proved more difficult than I expected. Some years later, a former CBC correspondent helped explain the reasons why when he said that correspondents—either foreign or regional—look at life through a telescope, but Ottawa reporters look at life through a microscope.

Political coverage in any national newspaper is the world of the wall poster: every utterance by a public figure is carefully parsed, every shading in language or nuance of phrase signals something of significance.

I was most at home on the campaign plane—an unsettling thought, given the surreal nature of that world.

A move to the *Toronto Star*'s parliamentary bureau in 1980 was without doubt the best professional decision of my life. I got to work with an exceptional group of reporters and editors in the toughest, most competitive newspaper market in North America.

By the time Joe Clark, the once and future leader of the Conservative party, decided he would prefer to fight his leadership battles in the open, I had succeeded John Honderich as the *Star*'s Washington bureau chief. That post is one of the best jobs in Canadian journalism, and to this day my explanation for why I voluntarily gave it up needs work.

Suffice to say that, by February 1984, I had evolved from hack to flack. Hired as a solution to a perceived problem in then Conservative party leader Brian Mulroney's media-relations operation, I served first as press secretary to the Leader of the Official Opposition, then as press secretary and later director of communications in the Prime Minister's Office.

Having covered hundreds of scrums, I was now giving them. Political cartoonist Terry Mosher reduced me to the role of the Herve Villechaize character in the television series *Fantasy Island*.

After three years of front-line service, I emerged a battle-scarred veteran of the early years of the Mulroney government. No longer part of the solution, I had become part of the problem. Even a casual review of old newspaper clippings will reveal that I have far more experience in dealing with crises than was good for me or the government I sought to serve. To this day, the word "tuna" causes my anxiety level to shoot upward—the lingering effects of a media-driven "crisis" over some suspect fish at a Starkist plant in New Brunswick.

The years since my government experience have included long periods of reflection in an ongoing attempt to reach a better understanding of the nature of the relationship between the press and politicians, and the impact this relationship has on public opinion and, by extension, on public policy. This search led me to the halls of academia: along the Rideau River, the Charles River, and the Harlem River.

A lifelong practitioner, I was introduced to the theoretical world of media scholars Herb Gans and Leon Sigal, of Tom Patterson and Robert Entman. Mentors such as Marvin Kalb, at the Shorenstein Center, and Ev Dennis, at the Freedom Forum Media Studies Center, helped me connect the dots between Shanto Iyengar's explanations of dominant news frames and Andie Tucher's concept of congenial truth. And as I read Larry Sabato's description of media feeding frenzies, I rubbed emotional scar tissue formed from frenzies I'd survived.

I spoke with Neil Postman about the kind of television-inspired journalism that stripped the news of all context, either historical or ideological. I listened attentively as Jim Fallows decried the media's pervasive tendency toward tabloidization and titillation. I heard people express their concerns about what happens to public policy when the communication vehicle of choice—the media—presents a world of refracted reality on nightly television newscasts. And I got to have a drink with Tom Leonard. Unfortunately by that point in my life I'd hung up my flagon, and the cranberry juice and soda seemed woefully inadequate for the occasion.

Leonard's premise that the media are a primary site of political discourse in any liberal democracy and that journalism is therefore responsible for much of the vernacular for the dialogue between the electors and the elected is critical to any appreciation of the importance of media coverage in today's world.[5]

Journalists, as Leonard explains, are prime suppliers of information about society. In fact, the media are, arguably, the central nervous system of today's wired world.

2

Where the Rubber
Meets the Road

Journalism and government have more interests in common than professionals in either discipline are inclined to admit, though reporters and politicians tend to trumpet their differences. Former Liberal campaign guru Senator Keith Davey says flatly: "I honestly believe that a healthy, wholesome tension between politicians and the fourth estate is the essence of democracy."[1]

Politics and public policy are an exercise in accommodation, the search for the common denominator of agreement. For reporters, the basic quest is to discover and highlight disunity. The reporter is Hegelian, says author Douglas Cater; he or she thinks in terms of thesis and antithesis.

These differences notwithstanding, journalism is an integral part of the government process, a reality confirmed in historic references to the media as the "fourth estate." The business of governing would be impossible without the news media; journalists and politicians, figuratively speaking, are joined at the hip.

A cynic—or a Marxist-Leninist—might argue that both make constant references to their differences to divert public attention away from the fact that both institutions are dedicated to the preservation of the socioeconomic status quo. Journalists and politicians, typically, are both part of the new ruling class, members of an intellectual, technological elite. They have attended the same institutions of higher learning, studied the same philosophies and social sciences, and are each dedicated to the preservation of Western liberal-democratic systems of government.

Political revolutionaries might argue the media–government relationship is symbiotic; clashes between the two are little more than an affectation to allow members on each side to sleep better at night, secure in the knowledge that their daily activities make any possibility of dramatic change to society or its institutions less likely. If journalism and government are mutually dependent on each other, then communications and policy are similarly dependent within government—an assertion that strikes most policy wonks as a reach. Policy types tend to dismiss the communications component of a major government initiative as the stuff of charlatans, the jingoistic machinations of folks who call a meeting to get IQ totals into three figures.

The government–media two-step is essentially a twentieth-century phenomenon, although both sides began to bunk together here in Canada in the late nineteenth century, when the Speaker of the House of Commons first set aside space for the distinguished members of the parliamentary press gallery. In Washington, William Price, a reporter with the now defunct *Washington Star*, began stationing himself outside the White House in 1896 so he could interview Grover Cleveland's visitors.

Woodrow Wilson was the first U.S. president to hold regular press conferences. Throughout the Western democracies, the press corps in national capitals grew only because the government grew. And as the press corps grew, government press operations grew. Franklin Delano Roosevelt held news conferences, but didn't want to be quoted directly, so he set his own ground rules, providing only "background" information to reporters.

John F. Kennedy was the first president to hold live televised news conferences. Lyndon B. Johnson gave us the "credibility gap," and Richard M. Nixon taught us the importance of the qualifier "at this point in time," as well as coining the term "inoperative" to describe previous statements proven to be false.

Mike McCurry was the first White House spokesperson to allow his entire daily briefing to be televised, a briefing he had taken to calling the "gaggle." His former boss, Bill Clinton, raised precision of language to an art form.

Most government press officers, known as flacks, are seen by reporters as first cousins to a snake-oil salesperson; yet Stephen Hess, a distinguished observer of media operations in Washington, discovered that Washington-based reporters covering the federal government contacted press officers on more than half their stories. Hess penned a portrait of the career press officer as "semi-bureaucrat, semi-reporter; in the bureaucracy, but not truly of it, tainted by association with the press, yet not of the press."[2]

There are certain organizational issues of significance involved in government–media relations. In Ottawa and Washington the rubber meets the road at the parliamentary press gallery, the Prime Minister's Office, the White House, and on Capitol Hill. The press secretary is the front man for the press office, the access point for reporters covering the head of state or government. And as the designated spokesperson, he or she is the government's connection to the world of mass communication.

On the government side, a press secretary is the operational individual whose primary responsibility involves tactical execution. A director of communications, however, typically attends to the strategy, and restricts his or her direct dealings with working journalists to an "A" list.

A press secretary need not be a substantive expert, but he or she had better be a quick study. The press secretaries have to be even-handed, though not necessarily egalitarian. They are advocates, but they can't ever lie, even in a matter of national security.

The litmus test for press secretaries, as applied by working reporters, is the test of access. A press secretary who doesn't have it simply isn't a player. Prime Minister Chrétien's press secretary Patrick Parisot, for example, suffers from the media perception that he isn't always in the loop.

Ottawa "Bigfoots" in particular believe that if they want to know what is really going on in the Chrétien government they had best speak to communications director Peter Donolo.

If *access* is what reporters want from press secretaries, *responsiveness* is what they want from press officers. Press officers function on three distinct planes. First, they are the point of contact for government reporters. Probably half a press secretary's working day is spent working the phones. Second, they prepare and distribute background and supportive material on government announcements. Third, they assume responsibility for media logistics. Press-office personnel are responsible for the care and feeding of journalists accompanying a touring president or prime minister. Known as "wagon masters," they make flight arrangements, organize ground transportation, book hotel rooms, set up media working rooms on the road, provide sound systems, and operate as den mothers. The media, in turn, pay for their travel, usually a figure that reflects commercial rates plus a premium in the order of 15 percent.

The director of communications, as the ranking media strategist, also plays a pivotal role in the senior management group of any government organization. Recent history is replete with examples of the disasters that ensue when senior staff members, without media expertise, decide what the press should or should not be told.

In 1983, White House spokesperson Larry Speakes was told to dismiss as "preposterous" reports that the United States was about to invade Grenada. Hours later, the Marines hit the beach. Fortunately for Speakes, White House correspondents knew he'd been lied to by the national security advisers.

Any spokesperson for a head of state or government has had to deal with this "curse of the gifted amateur." Foreign-policy experts who bristle whenever a press officer offers a view on a policy position routinely offer advice on an appropriate media strategy without the benefit of any media experience, training, or even the briefest exposure to basic mass-communication theory. Their views are invariably expressed in a dismissive, even condescending, tone, as if the exercise of media relations in a crisis is the least of the government's worries.

The position of press secretary as we've come to know it was pioneered by James Hagerty, who served former president Dwight D. Eisenhower and to this day is considered perhaps the best ever to fill the position. In his book, *Call the Briefing*, former Reagan and Bush press secretary Marlin Fitzwater wrote: "The press secretary to the president stands between the opposing forces, explaining, cajoling, begging, sometimes pushing both sides to a better understanding of each other."[3]

The terminology is somewhat different in Washington and Ottawa, but the core message is the same. Fitzwater refers to the need to "feed the lions." We, in turn, use the old reporter's adage about the need to "feed the goat." Fitzwater refers to "dancing," which occurs "when a spokesman isn't quite sure of his facts but wants to sound authoritative." Here in Canada, reflecting our passion for hockey, we describe the same situation as "going for a skate."

There is no one model or experience set that suggests one individual will make a better press secretary than another. My own sense is that remaining unflappable may be more important than any other skill, at least in a "government context." A different skill set is definitely required in a campaign setting. Good or successful reporters do not necessarily make the best press secretaries, for a number of reasons. For starters, there is the general stigma of having "gone over the wall." Then there is the further complication that many of the reporters with whom a journalist-turned-press secretary will have to deal are friends, former colleagues, or competitors. Journalists, almost without exception, do make good political advisers, however, as their antennae tend to twitch at all the right times.

During a long bus ride at a 1995 conference on government–press relations in Mexico City, sponsored by the newspaper *El Universal*, Fitzwater and former Gorbachev spokesperson Gennadi Gerasimov were swapping "Cold War" stories of the Reagan–Gorbachev summits and leading a small group of us in a "Hot Stove" discussion about life as a press secretary.

As we compared notes, I was struck by the similarity between George Bush and Brian Mulroney's attitude toward the media. Bush believed "friendships" were a factor in presidential press relations. Fitzwater begged to differ. "Treat them like professionals," Fitzwater advised, "and they will be your friends. But treat them like friends and they will betray you every time."[4] Mulroney also believed personal relationships could help shape media coverage. Before winning the Conservative party leadership, Mulroney enjoyed extensive and largely positive relations with many reporters, in part because he cultivated them, but mostly because he was that valuable journalistic commodity —a well-informed source. Mulroney's professional, political, and social circles in Montreal and across Canada put him in the position of having quality information. His outgoing personality meant he was predisposed to share it. As a political reporter, I had been a regular recipient of Mulroney's insights, observations, and information. Later, as his press secretary, I had to contend with Mulroney's irritation at what he perceived as "churlishness" on the part of reporters he had befriended in the past. Mulroney further believed my personal relationship with certain national reporters should have been an important part of the media-relations equation. The former prime minister understood and supported the theory that a reporter is neither friend nor foe, but rather a professional intermediary between the electors and those who would lead them. But whenever a problem arose, Mulroney still had a tendency to believe a personal call from me to *Globe and Mail* columnist Jeffrey Simpson or the *Toronto Star*'s Carol Goar would suffice to move the columnist to a more supportive position.

Any reluctance on my part to play the personal card triggered a search for alternative messengers. In a political office, there is never any shortage of senior staff people who *know* they would be better at media relations than the press secretary. And they are always ready to volunteer their services as intermediaries. Mulroney seemed particularly "blessed" in this regard.

Depending on my humor on any given day, I would be amused or enraged to watch a carefully considered media strategy rendered meaningless when a colleague would acquiesce to a prime-ministerial request and slide Val Sears of the *Toronto Star* or Mike Duffy, then with the CBC, in a side door of Mulroney's Centre Block office for a "background" briefing. Perhaps it is endemic to high office. The *Washington Post*'s Howard Kurtz reports President Clinton operates under the mistaken assumption that good personal relations should somehow pay a dividend in coverage terms.

President Bush was often irritated by unauthorized leaks and the media's appetite for information attributed to unidentified "sources." Says Fitzwater, "If we would all talk on the record, everyone would be better off."[5] Mulroney shared Bush's frustration. In 1985, responding in part to a gag order imposed at External Affairs by Joe Clark, Mulroney instructed Privy Council clerk Paul Tellier to issue a set of guidelines for media relations that essentially instructed Canada's public servants to stay "on the record." The guidelines were as unworkable as they were unenforceable. And a substantive point in terms of the latter's belief in the need for the government to explain itself clearly to the public was lost in the ensuing public furor. Tellier had informed deputy ministers that the public communication of government policy and programs was an important part of the job jar, and their performance evaluations would reflect that fact. The "gag order" spin reduced the guidelines to a subject of ridicule which allowed Ottawa mandarins to ignore its more constructive elements.

In his days as a Trudeau cabinet minister, Prime Minister Jean Chrétien made himself available to reporters, and even listed his home phone number in the telephone book. "It is not unusual for a reporter to call me on a Sunday night, often after failing to reach anybody else. Naturally, I see some reporters more than others, because of their specialization or personality, but I have not gone out of my way to be buddy buddy with any of them."[6]

The Age of Television

When we swept into our offices in the Langevin Block in September 1984, following Mulroney's historic election victory, I was struck by how different the approach to government communications and press relations was than had been the case either in Opposition or on the campaign trail.

The explanation lies in the fact that the Government of Canada as an institution simply hadn't kept pace with the evolution of the media through the 1980s. Howard Kurtz says the modern presidency is a media presidency, and over the past twenty years in particular, that means a television presidency. In Canada in the early 1980s, government communication was still largely print-oriented. Departmental communications divisions produced impressive newsletters, fact sheets, pamphlets, and every other manner of printed material. Communications products rarely, if ever, included anything in the way of visual material. Civil servants who would spend hours talking to a columnist at the *Globe and Mail* or a reporter from *La Presse* would recoil in horror at the suggestion of an on-camera interview. Given that television was far and away the information source of choice for most Canadians, this institutional pro-print bias was problematic. Some years later, former CBC Ottawa bureau chief Elly Alboim, who would leave Holy Mother Corp. to join the Earnscliffe Strategy Group, literally revolutionized the game with communications strategies for Finance minister Paul Martin that reflected a fundamental shift in orientation toward the electronic age. Alboim and his associate David Herle more or less dragged the government into the television era, even as the television era itself was in the process of being overtaken by new media.

Our parliamentary system of responsible government, we learned, is ill-suited to an information distribution paradigm that focuses on television.

As media advisers to Mulroney, we were often accused of affecting a presidential style. In fact, this perception was a direct consequence of television's emergence as our information medium of choice. Television is geared toward an executive model of government. The notion of a prime minister as first among a party of equals does not translate to the television screen. Television focuses on a central actor—in our case, the prime minister.

Television is best suited to a presidential system. Appointed cabinet secretaries tend to "stay on message." The entire media strategy can be controlled from the White House, with the Oval Office or the Rose Garden providing an appropriate backdrop.

A parliamentary system may be more democratic, but from a communications perspective it is unwieldy. Daily, prime ministers must face their political opponents in Question Period. There is a provision for Opposition MPs to provide notice, but most days there is no advance warning. Questions are put in both official languages by Members of Parliament whose political ideologies span the spectrum.

There were also certain operational difficulties to our communications efforts. Some were attitudinal. Our deputy prime minister, Erik Nielsen, was known as "Velcro Lips," a nickname as accurate as it was deserved. Others were operational. The Privy Council Office, as the prime minister's "department," had skilled advisers in their communications shop, but their activities, in the main, were geared toward serving as the secretariat for the cabinet committee on communications, a body convened to coordinate the government's communications activities.

Cater argues a government's failure to explain itself clearly and candidly to its citizens is a failure for democracy. The philosopher and educator John Dewey believed no policy, however sound, could survive a flawed "process," and the communication of the policy is central to that process. If journalism and government are mutually dependent, then communications and policy are similarly interdependent within government. In the Opposition days, there was no person that I worked more closely with than our senior policy adviser, Charles McMillan. Government policy makers, however, always left me with the impression that their calling was decidedly above ours.

Government communication should be the result of careful, comprehensive planning. A properly researched and executed communications plan should include a detailed assessment of the public environment that situates any policy initiative in a local, then regional, then national, and, finally, global context. Even the most noble cause can be ill-fated if the timing of the initiative is out of sync with current events.

The plan must also have simple thematic messages, a point of constant irritation for the policy wonks. They will insist you can't sell freetrade in an eight-second clip, or that a fundamental reform of the tax system such as the Goods and Services Tax (GST) cannot be explained in a few sentences. Their solution, invariably, is to produce highly technical printed material couched in the arcane language of the expert.

The Department of Finance for years had been pushing for a fundamental overhaul of the federal tax system, urging a shift away from exclusive dependency on corporate and personal income tax to a blended system that would include a consumption tax. Finance wanted a single tax rate to be applied indiscriminately to all sales and business transactions—no exemptions. The political staff, particularly certain of us in the Prime Minister's Office, balked at the notion of taxing the basic essentials of life: food and shelter.

Following a meeting of cabinet's priorities and planning committee in the summer of 1986, a group that included Finance deputy minister Stanley Hartt convened over drinks in a hotel suite to kick around the idea of exemptions. Hartt, a true intellectual with the wit of a Catskills comic, was articulating Finance's "no exemptions" position. At one point in the conversation, I picked up a cocktail napkin with the hotel's insignia on it, turned it over, and drew a cross with a felt-tip pen. I then wrote the words *food, tax* and *reform*, and *tax* in each quadrant, as follows:

food	tax
tax	reform

I said to Hartt, "Stanley, it comes down to four words, two of them are the same. Food tax and tax reform: which two do you want to campaign on?" The Mulroney government could either face the electorate as a government that overhauled an antiquated tax system or as a government that decided, literally, to tax their daily bread.

My simplistic reduction of a substantive policy initiative to four simple words triggered some good-natured derision from senior policy adviser Charles McMillan, who, with his infectious laughter, denounced my "bumper-sticker mentality." The decision, in the end, was to proceed with what is now the infamous Goods and Services Tax, with exemptions. Finance didn't approve, and the GST issue was oft cited as yet another example of how "the gang that couldn't shoot straight" in the PMO had screwed up a perfectly rational policy initiative. In the decade since, however, Canada's federal government has managed to move out of a deficit situation without forcing seniors and others on fixed incomes to pay tax on the staples of life. And, as we used to intone in the Latin mass of my youth: *Et dignum et iustum est*— it is both right and just. Had I kept the hotel napkin, I would have framed it.

A communications plan must identify target audiences. It is important to identify the various "constituencies" for a particular initiative while identifying the appropriate medium with which to connect with them. A provincial government contemplating a change in fishing seasons will be better served with an in-depth interview on the sports-channel fishing shows than with a front-page piece in the *National Post*.

One of the target audiences most often overlooked in communications planning is the internal audience, the people in the organization itself.

Finally, you have to figure out who the other participants in the debate are likely to be and what their line of attack might be. Interest groups should be a primary focus. Back in 1990, for example, Greenpeace activist Gordon Perks was credited with setting the tone for the Ontario provincial election that saw then premier David Peterson defeated by Bob Rae's New Democrats. To describe the result as unexpected is to understate the case. Perks effectively crashed Peterson's launch, hijacked the media agenda, and derailed the Liberal campaign with his guerrilla media tactics.

Ours is a parliamentary democracy, with a cabinet comprising individuals elected in their own right, but media coverage patterns do not respect such constitutional niceties. The leader of a government, as Columbia University sociologist Herbert Gans established, is the dominant newsmaker in any country. And ministers of the Crown, however able, will be by definition afforded secondary status, a reality that never sits well with either the minister's political staff or department officials. This reality was compounded in our case by the fact that our distinguished Secretary of State for External Affairs, Joe Clark, was himself a former prime minister. Other senior ministers, such as Finance minister Michael Wilson and Transport minister John Crosbie, had been strong candidates for the party leadership, were experienced parliamentarians, and had longer and more extensive relationships with correspondents in the parliamentary press gallery than Mulroney did. As a result, tensions would invariably surface at major international events, such as economic summits or gatherings of the Commonwealth nations, despite everyone's best efforts to avoid stepping on anyone's toes.

There were also occasions when the agenda of "the center"—read: the Prime Minister's Office or the Privy Council Office—might not coincide with a line department's agenda. An incident prior to the 1986 economic summit in Tokyo illustrates this difficulty. Canada's farmers were increasingly concerned over subsidy practices in other countries that were distorting the international marketplace, a particular problem for Western grain producers. Mulroney had promised to raise the issue at the summit, but before leaving for Tokyo, at the behest of Don Mazankowski, the prime minister announced an aid package at a news conference in Ottawa. The purpose was to generate a good-news headline prior to a scheduled meeting with agricultural-sector leaders in Vancouver just before the flight to Tokyo. As the Armed Forces 707 winged across the prairies, Finance minister Wilson's staff on the plane began circulating the press section, in effect deflating the subsidy announcement. The Jesuits over at Finance decided to let the world know that, while Mulroney might lack resolve on restraining government spending, they were determined to hold the line on the deficit. Wilson's staffers characterized the Ottawa announcement as mostly blue smoke and mirrors, served up for political consumption. Their "spin" was reflected in the coverage.

By midterm in the first mandate, everyone was talking communications, and not in a positive way. Ministers were convinced the government's policies were sound, and therefore concluded the problem had to be communications.

The problem, in part, flowed from the ministers' predisposition to what I describe as the "Moses" school of communication. You remember the biblical references to Moses' journey to the top of the mountain, the burning bush, the two tablets, and the ten rules—the ones we call "the commandments"? Moses came down from the mountain and read out the rules. So it is with too many cabinet ministers. They think if they table a piece of legislation, follow up with a news conference, do a quick round of *Canada AM*, *The National*, *As It Happens*, and maybe *Le Point*, Canadians will see the wisdom of the policy and embrace it enthusiastically. Well, that approach didn't work for Moses either. The biblical account of Moses coming down from the mountain suggests his people kept partying, leaving him to wander the desert for forty years.

There is a serious challenge in communicating policy. Howard Kurtz says the press has a limited appetite for ideas. As Thomas Patterson explains: "Policy problems lack the novelty that the journalist seeks." Patterson notes that the first time a leader or a candidate for office takes a position on a policy issue, it is deemed newsworthy. However, "further statements on the same issue become progressively less newsworthy unless a new wrinkle is added."[7]

Because most reporters lack the expertise to assess policy issues on their merits, they tend to shape their coverage to focus on the element of a policy they are expert in—the politics of it. Finance minister Martin's deficit-reduction campaign, therefore, is rarely addressed in the context of being good or bad public policy, but is more often addressed in the context of the "politics" of deficit reduction. These days the assessment tends to be made in the context of whether Martin's decisions help or hinder an anticipated candidacy for the Liberal leadership if and when Jean Chrétien decides to step aside. Similarly, Health minister Allan Rock's handling of policy issues, from the future of home care to compensation for hepatitis-C victims, is measured against the standard of assumed leadership aspirations.

Fallows maintains that the media are simply copping out by insisting viewers/listeners/readers are not interested in substantive policy news. "Issues that matter to people can always be made interesting. That is simply the challenge of execution."[8] These kinds of communications challenges are significant in any Western liberal democracy. They are even more daunting for emerging nations expected to communicate their political agenda instantly to all corners of today's wired world.

Consider the case of the Democratic Republic of the Congo (DRC). The flickering flames from oil-burning lamps provide the only light along Kinshasa's main thoroughfare. Aging trucks with metal sides spewing noxious black fumes from corroded tailpipes are the only form of public transit. Young people, wedged in like sardines, turn their heads toward postage-stamp-size windows in the unlikely event a breath of air will offer some relief from the stifling heat. The capital of the DRC has been ravaged by thirty years of corruption and neglect. There are few traffic lights in this city of 5 million, and it is virtually impossible to find a street or road that isn't pockmarked with crater-size potholes.

President Laurent Kabila "liberated" the DRC in May 1997 after thirty years of bloody struggle against the dictatorial regime of the late Joseph Mobutu. Kabila and his forces swept out of the wilderness one week, and were expected to get a coherent media message out on the Web the next week. New governments, such as Kabila's, are confronted with the reality that news, particularly in North America and Western Europe, has become a powerful political and diplomatic force. Television images of starving Somali mothers and children had such an immediate impact on public opinion in the United States that the president was forced to approve an emergency humanitarian aid program.

The rapid transmission of information by journalists with hand-held camcorders, Comsat cell phones, and laptop computers now serves as a sort of central nervous system for the world. The explosion of information technologies and the creation of twenty-four-hour news services such as CNN means "live" coverage from the world's hot spots. E-mail, faxes, Web sites, cell phones, and satellites mean information is circulated instantaneously. The world, as former U.S. secretary of state George Schultz once put it, is now on real time—especially on the campaign trail.

If governments are slow to embrace emerging communications technologies, campaigns celebrate their arrival. In fact, the leaders' tour, as we know it, coincided with the coming of age of transcontinental trains.

For the better part of fifty years, the routine on either side of the 49th parallel hardly changed. At each "whistle stop" (a term campaigners gave to the vernacular) a gaggle of fedora'd reporters would pile out of a train, stand on the tracks, record the "bon mots" of the candidate, count the crowd, clamber back on the train, and write a piece that was then handed over to the telegraph operator to file. The reporters, for the most part, were interchangeable drones. Edward T. Folliard, once the *Washington Post*'s chief campaign reporter, said, "It was all very friendly and romantic ... the men wrote what they heard and damn little about what they thought."[9]

But political reporting, both the campaign and the government variety, began to change in the late 1960s and early 1970s. As Canadian communications theorist Marshall McLuhan observed, there was an element of technological determination to the shift, linked to the emergence of television as our information medium of choice. Television, as Columbia University sociologist Paul Lazarsfeld suspected, trumped his "two-step" flow theory of political communications. In an earlier print-dominated time, Lazarsfeld concluded that most of us received our information about politics or public policy from family, friends, or acquaintances whose news-consumption habits were more developed than our own. Our information, therefore, had been processed through the personal filter of the individual passing on the information. By definition, the information was altered by the interests, and even biases, of the primary news consumer. Lazarsfeld's study included a prophetic footnote. He noted that a new medium—television—had recently been introduced to postwar America, and he predicted that television might change the equation.

Not surprisingly, the science of communicating public policies and the candidates advancing these ideas had to evolve to reflect the new medium.

The assassination of John F. Kennedy in Dallas on November 23, 1963, is generally regarded as the moment in history that signaled television's ascendancy. Two days later, millions of viewers watched the live coverage as Dallas night-club owner Jack Ruby shot alleged assassin Lee Harvey Oswald in the basement of police headquarters.

On the "content" side of the newspaper, the trinity of Vietnam, Chappaquiddick, and Watergate heralded a sea change in American journalism. Vietnam and Watergate publicly established that successive holders of the highest elected office in the land had proved to be less than trustworthy. The fact that the two perpetrators in this case were from each of the established parties lent a wonderfully bipartisan note to the situation. Chappaquiddick, on the other hand, caused journalists who had been overly deferential to the privacy of public figures to conclude that this treatment was undeserved. The result of these debacles, says University of Virginia professor Larry Sabato, was the emergence of "character" as a defining feature of political coverage, and a shift in the orientation of the editorial product from *description* to *prescription*.

The distinguished Harvard historian Theodore H. White ushered in the era of insider coverage with his breakthrough book on the 1960 presidential campaign, *The Making of the President*. White took readers behind the scenes for a look at how presidential campaigns are conducted, won, and lost. In fact, White's friend and former *CBS News* anchor Walter Cronkite, as guest speaker at the First Annual Theodore H. White lecture sponsored by the Kennedy School's Shorenstein Center, told the assembly, "Teddy White ... almost ruined political reporting." Cronkite says it really wasn't White's fault that the press read his work and concluded it should concentrate on the sizzle instead of the steak of political campaigns, but he does believe that "in emphasizing political manipulation rather than issues, we of the press probably have contributed to the public cynicism about the political process."[10]

The Kennedy campaign also established the imperative of understanding the new medium's properties for candidates seeking high office. Kennedy's triumph over Richard Nixon in the televised debate was identified subsequently as a defining moment in the campaign. Kennedy and his advisers had figured out the debate wasn't about Nixon, it was about the assembled television audience. Kennedy basically ignored his Republican opponent, focusing instead on establishing a bond with the viewers. Presidential politics would never be the same.

One of the journalists present at the Kennedy–Nixon debate was CBS executive producer Don Hewitt, who would later go on to revolutionize television news and current-affairs journalism by inventing the award-winning public-affairs program *60 Minutes*. "When it was over, I remember thinking there is something wrong there," Hewitt said in an interview with the *New York Times*. "We're electing a president by how he performs on television. We may have made a right choice, but it worried me that it might be for the wrong reason. We were electing a matinée idol."[11]

White, in turn, begat Joe McGinniss's study of Richard Nixon's successful resurrection in 1968. Building on his innovative 1952 "Checkers" speech, Nixon discovered he could use television to go directly over the head of Washington reporters, who didn't like him much anyway, and establish a direct link with the electorate. Of equal significance was the conclusion by Nixon staffers that communications techniques which had been used for decades in television advertising could be adapted for politics. McGinniss believes that politics, in a sense, "has always been a con game. Advertising, in many ways, is a con game too."[12] McGinniss says it was hardly surprising, therefore, that politicians and advertising people would discover one another.

Tim Crouse argues McGinniss's success with *The Selling of the President 1968* embarrassed journalists into examining candidates' use of media. By the time reporters set out for New Hampshire and the 1972 presidential primary, Abe Rosenthal, managing editor of the prestigious *New York Times*, was telling his campaign reporters: "We aren't going to wait until a year after the election to read in Teddy White's book what we should have reported ourselves."[13]

The Campaign Tour

The 1972 presidential campaign in the United States ushered in a new era of the leader's tour—an era marked by a press corps that openly chafed at the media-manipulation tactics of party leaders, tactics that had their genesis in the graphic revolution of the mid-nineteenth century, tactics built around the "pseudo-event."

In his book *The Image*, Daniel Boorstin says the pseudo-event must be distinguished from propaganda. "A pseudo-event is an ambiguous truth; propaganda is an appealing falsehood." Boorstin states a pseudo-event is "not created by demagogues or crooks. It is the daily product of men of goodwill." Pseudo-events by their very nature are more compelling than natural events. "The American citizen thus lives in a world where fantasy is more real than reality, where the image has more dignity than its original," Boorstin adds.[14]

Reporters themselves can be principal players in the production of this synthetic commodity known as the pseudo-event. An interview, for example, is a pseudo-event, and so is a news conference or a press release. A news "leak" is a form of pseudo-event, and proves the axiom that pseudo-events produce more pseudo-events in geometric progression. By way of example, in the 1997 federal election campaign, the Liberal policy document known as "Red Book II" was leaked to Reform party leader Preston Manning prior to its official release. Manning used the leak to stage an event, and then other campaign events flowed from Manning's news conference.

Franklin Delano Roosevelt is credited by Boorstin as being the first modern political master of the creation of the pseudo-event: "On his production team, in addition to newspapermen, there were poets, playwrights, and a regular corps of speech writers."[15] Boorstin believes the rise in the power of the presidency, or in Canada the increased focus on the leader, coincides with the growing use of the pseudo-event, a tactic that is particularly pronounced in television journalism.

Television, of course, is the ideal medium for pseudo-events, and the staging of politics for television's purposes has fundamentally altered the role of the candidate, as well as the role of the reporter assigned to cover him or her.

The leader's political tour is the ultimate pseudo-event, in part because of what *Globe and Mail* reporter Graham Fraser describes as the "campaign correlative." The correlative holds that if a political formation cannot run an efficient campaign tour, then it probably cannot run an efficient government either. Says Fraser: "In this analogy, the campaign tour becomes a metaphor for government."[16]

The leader's tour, if flawed conceptually, can have a devastatingly negative impact on a national campaign. Consider the case of the 1988 free-trade election, when the Mulroney-led Conservatives were seeking a second mandate with a tour strategy that was a variation on the old Holiday Inn motto "No surprises."

The campaign was carefully scripted; voters were being offered a safer, blander Mulroney. The problem, however, was that the pablum campaign provided no focus for the media. For want of anything else, reporters began to file pieces about Mulroney's "Boy in the Bubble" campaign style, highlighting Mulroney's perceived lack of accessibility.

In his bestseller, *One Hundred Monkeys: The Triumph of Popular Wisdom in Canadian Politics*, Robert Mason Lee argues the lack-of-accessibility charge leveled by campaign reporters does not stand up to very much scrutiny. Putting a stopwatch on Mulroney, Lee states, would show that the Conservative leader was available to reporters in question-and-answer sessions for more than twenty minutes each day for three of the first four days of the campaign. Lee's investigation led him to conclude the "Boy in the Bubble" accusation had its genesis in three, seemingly minor, facts, specifically:

- Mulroney's campaign plane was configured in such a way as to keep him screened off from the reporters at the back of the plane.
- RCMP dogs were called in to sniff reporters' luggage, officially for bombs. But who knew what a well-trained dog might find in someone's Samsonite, as my friend Hubert Bauch discovered in 1993.
- The white-rope-and-chain barriers designed for use in the 1984 Papal tour of Canada had magically reappeared and were being used to restrict reporters' movements at Mulroney's events.

Tory strategists, for their part, were convinced their approach would allow Mulroney to cruise to a majority victory. Whenever anyone would point to Liberal leader Turner's more rough-and-tumble campaign style and draw comparisons, Tory strategists would scoff and suggest that the only reason Turner was exposing himself to the open-line shows was that he could not draw flies to a staged campaign event. So confident were Tory campaign advisers that their strategy was sound, they would get apoplectic whenever Mulroney removed his bifocals during a speech —a telltale sign he was about to depart from the prepared text. Like the crew of the ill-fated *Titanic*, Tory campaign organizers were convinced of their infallibility even as they steamed toward disaster.

Tory pollster Allan Gregg says: "This initial strategy turned out, in retrospect, to have been a colossal error. It cast the prime minister in a low-key, technocratic role, completely unsuited to the electorate. It had the effect of reminding people of their own worst fear—change."[17]

Gregg told Robert Mason Lee that voters no longer respond to staged television clips; they dismiss the product as the end result of image makers, pollsters, and spin doctors. "They love the scrums, because they are spontaneous. They love to see the politician cornered, questioned, sweating. What they are looking for is what I call the glimpse of the soul."[18] The Tory pollster's views seem to be at variance with Daniel Boorstin's theories, at least on the surface. Boorstin recognizes a lurking desire for real events, in part explaining our fascination with crime and sports news. But Boorstin's theories do not preclude a carefully nurtured image crafted to strike the very chords Gregg has identified. The Tory pollster says the watchwords for the politicians of the 1990s are *spontaneity, emotion*, and *motive*. John Turner's 1988 "Fight of My Life" approach effectively communicated these messages. Mulroney's "Boy in the Bubble" campaign decidedly did not.

The metaphor, as used by a campaign strategist, signals an approach to politics and political campaigning that has come, in Lee's words, "to distinguish campaigns in the postliterate age. It was a way of talking about things by describing what they were like rather than what they were. In the modern campaign, a black rapist becomes the metaphor for the Dukakis record on law enforcement, just as a disgraced minister becomes the metaphor for Tory avarice."[19]

The semiotician Christian Metz identified Hollywood cinema as a multilayered sign system integrating five channels of communication—

image, written language, voice, music, and sound effects. Television and cinema are neighboring sign systems, and as leaders' tours are made-for-television, they can be analyzed in a similar fashion as a semiotic system.

Politicians whose electoral careers span several decades tend to be dismissive of the complete integration of all five channels of communication and consistency in the image message. Erik Nielsen was derisive and dismissive of what he described as the photo-op mentality of Mulroney's Prime Minister's Office. Nielsen either never understood or totally rejected Boorstin's theories of "image" and "celebrity" and the "pseudo-event."

As political advisers knew and political reporters came to understand, the "message" is that any text is lost if it is contradicted by the visuals. Political advisers spend time identifying arresting visuals, not as a substitute for a substantive message, as Nielsen always suspected, but to ensure there was nothing in the visual that distracted from the substantive message.

Virtually no one can recall the subject of John Turner's speech the day he was photographed with the pitchfork that appeared to be growing from the top of his head. Similarly, Mulroney's attempt before a high-school audience to convince Canadians that the free-trade agreement with the Americans was nothing to fear suffered considerably when photographs appeared in the press of Mulroney against the backdrop of a screaming eagle (painted on the wall behind him) that seemed set to carry him off.

In the 1988 federal election campaign, Conservative strategists devised an integrated set of television signs that were structured to portray Mulroney as the reassuring figure who could help Canadians cope with millennial anxiety by effectively managing inevitable change. At the ideological level, the connotative meaning of Mulroney's tour was a portrait of a new, highly competitive society, a society of winners and losers. As much as we wanted to be winners, we feared we might end up losers in this new order. And we wondered why Mulroney was pushing this new order so hard. Even as he sought to portray himself as reassuring, he was widening the gulf with most of the electorate.

Television images of other elements of Mulroney's 1988 tour—the brute-force tactics of police who hauled away protesters at public events; the Tory youth brigade, or "white shirts," as they became known, who followed Mulroney on tour; the overall emphasis on the controlled event—conveyed a message at the connotative level that distanced Mulroney from the very people he was trying to connect with: the electorate.

Mulroney, in person, has the qualities Gregg identified as central to the postliterate campaign—spontaneity, emotion, and motive. But these had been drilled out of him by campaign advisers who wanted to run a "Holiday Inn" campaign featuring no surprises.

Granted, there is a very fine line between media management and media manipulation. A political leader cannot allow the boys and girls on the bus to control the agenda. A leader's message on evening newscasts is lost if he or she is constantly reacting to developments in other campaigns, or indeed in the world. But having said that, a leader cannot be seen to be ducking the press, and for that reason the "cocoon" strategy that followed the early days of the 1988 campaign was fatally flawed. Instead of compensating for a perceived weakness, it magnified the weakness by communicating at the connotative level a lack of trust between the leader and his advisers.

The implications of this in political communication terms are devastating and can be reduced to a single question: If the people who know the leader best do not trust him or her, why should you?

The television debate between Turner and Mulroney resulted in a radical displacement of the connotations the Tories were hoping to ascribe to Mulroney. In a heated exchange that lasted but two minutes and thirty-eight seconds, Turner succeeded in connecting with the electorate, despite the fact that the Liberal leader did not utter a single substantial line in the exchange not already used in earlier campaign appearances.

Mulroney's handlers, for their part, were not at all dismayed with the prime minister's performance in the debate. They were convinced Turner had failed to land a knockout punch, and that Mulroney would continue to cruise to a majority victory. The pundits were split on the issue, their reviews ranging from neutral to Turner by a decision. But a *CBC Television News* panel modeled on a focus group provided the first hint that the people had come to a collective conclusion that had escaped the pundits. As the Gallup organization began its sounding, the results were dramatically at variance with the views of the self-styled experts. Fully 72 percent of respondents to the Gallup poll declared Turner the winner; only 17 percent thought the prime minister had emerged the victor.

The debate triggered a dramatic slide in expressed support for the Conservatives. Similarly, support for the Canada–United States free-trade agreement softened appreciably. As Liberal senator Keith Davey is fond of saying, in politics, perception—or image—is reality. If the voters think the candidate's political opponent has won an exchange, he or she has but two choices: the candidate can waste time trying to convince anyone who will listen that he or she did not do that badly, or the candidate can respond.

New Democratic Party leader Ed Broadbent, who was also kicked around by Turner in their segment of the televised debate, was "Dukakisized." For ten days following the debate, Broadbent's campaign lost its focus. His message was confused; he could not settle on a target; he seemed hesitant and uncertain and looked that way on television. Like a deer caught in the headlights, Broadbent was paralyzed in terms of political communication. Democratic presidential hopeful Michael Dukakis was similarly frozen when the late Lee Atwater unleashed the infamous "Willie Horton" ads against him in 1988.

The prime minister, by contrast, knew intuitively the ground had shifted, and he adopted a new tour strategy immediately following the 1988 debates. Ensconced in a suite at the Royal York the night after the debate, while his pollster pored over the entrails of the overnights, Mulroney knew the "High Road" speech that had been crafted for him days earlier would no longer suffice. Since John Turner had decided the free-trade debate constituted the fight of his life, Mulroney decided to respond accordingly. He, too, would show spontaneity, emotion, motive. Robert Mason Lee wrote that the subsequent battle over the free-trade agreement allowed Mulroney to take off his bifocals "in a very compelling kind of way."

The television footage that best signaled the change was shot at a luncheon speech in Victoria, on November 2. Three members of the audience—John Wilcox, Dave Szollosy, and John Lewis Orr—interrupted Mulroney repeatedly to challenge certain of his assertions regarding the free-trade pact. Instead of having the police haul the trio off, as would have been the case in the early weeks of the campaign, Mulroney invited all three to discuss the issues with him after the speech. Mulroney also invited the television networks to record the exchange.

Alan Fryer's item on the CTV *National News* that night ran almost four minutes. Coverage on other networks followed suit. Tory strategists in Ottawa were ecstatic. Said director of operations Harry Near: "I think it was a turnaround point. Mulroney was saying in effect, I believe in this thing, I know this thing. I'll debate this thing."[20]

Mulroney was more comfortable with the more combative persona he intuitively reverted to following the debate, an image that was more consistent with the real Brian Mulroney. Ironically, that persona turned out to be close to what Canadians were looking for in a leader all along. Three weeks later, the Conservatives won a plurality of votes and a majority of seats in the House of Commons.

On today's campaign plane this kind of staged drama unfolds on fast-forward. New technologies, from laptops to faxes to cell phones, made the traditional news cycle of campaigns obsolete.

The leader's tour is still an exercise in semiotics, a communication tool to foster an image, which in turn is created to affect public opinion. But today's leader's tour must reflect a "total" media environment, everything from news to current affairs, to late-night talk and MTV. The expression of public opinion, particularly in a campaign context, is "one of the most powerful, most interesting, and the most mysterious of pseudo-events," according to Boorstin.[21]

American journalist Walter Lippmann recognized long ago there were political operatives skilled at organizing public opinion in support of candidates or causes, particularly during election campaigns.

The creation of public opinion, expressed through public-opinion research, is the crux of any political campaign. Modern scientific sampling techniques of how to measure public opinion grew out of research in marketing and advertising. By 1935 individuals such as Elmo Roper and George Gallup began to apply these techniques to politics and to sell these survey services to daily newspapers. The net effect, says Boorstin, is that public expression becomes more and more an image into which the public fits its expression: "It is the people looking in a mirror."

There has, however, been a dangerous mutation in the press–politician–public triangle over the past thirty years that can be traced to the emergence of certain reporting practices over that period. First among these conventions is the fact that reporters and voters view politics from different perspectives. The public sees politics as a matter of how it will be governed, and by whom. The reporter approaches politics as a strategic game. As media analyst Paul Weaver notes, this game is played out against a backdrop of governmental institutions and public policies, and it is played before an audience, the electorate. Therefore, the players are constantly trying to create a good impression. "In consequence, there is an endemic tendency for players to exaggerate their good qualities and minimize the bad ones, to be deceitful or engage in hypocrisies, to manipulate appearances,"[22] says Weaver.

ABC News anchor Peter Jennings said he was struck by the divergence between the mainstream media and the public it allegedly seeks to inform during the 1992 presidential race. "It hit me in New Hampshire," Jennings said, "when I realized the press only cared about Gennifer Flowers and the voters only cared about the economy."[23]

This focus on the game schema explains the Canadian media's reluctance to cover the number-one issue for the public in the 1997 campaign—persistently high unemployment levels. The Ottawa scribes cannot work up enthusiasm for the jobs issue. Unity is the "master narrative" of Canadian politics. It is sexier, has more potential for conflict and confrontation, and plays to Canada's historic cleavage—language. NDP leader Alexa McDonough was determined to talk jobs throughout the 1997 campaign, which was one of the reasons she had trouble making the national network news.

Journalists apply a dominant game schema to their campaign coverage, a decision with predictable consequences. For starters, there is no ultimate meaning to any campaign because it really doesn't matter who wins or loses. Strategy is everything, conflict is essential, and there is a systemic tolerance of hype. Former *U.S. News and World Report* editor James Fallows argues that the media show their independence from the campaign with "attitude" rather than intellect. There is no real consideration of whether or not society will be improved if one candidate or one policy platform prevails. There is no real analysis of the policy *specifics* of an initiative, except in the context of the *politics* of the issue.

Marshall McLuhan once observed that issues are useless for election purposes, because they are too "hot." The result is a predisposition to focus on a candidate's image instead. McLuhan said television, therefore, is particularly useful to the politician who can be charming but lacks ideas.

Political scientist Thomas E. Patterson says electors are defenseless against the treachery of broken campaign promises that he says such candidates never have any intention of fulfilling. They are simply lies. Such tactics, if commonplace, turn free and fair elections into a show, says Patterson.[24]

Canadians know of what Patterson speaks. In the 1993 federal election, Jean Chrétien's Liberals promised to scrap the Goods and Services Tax—the most unpopular federal tax since income tax was introduced in 1917. The public furor over the imposition of the tax, fanned by Mulroney's decision to effectively pack the Senate to ensure the enabling legislation's passage in the face of a Liberal filibuster, made the GST a key campaign issue. The Liberal undertaking was as predictable as it was unequivocal: the tax would be scrapped as soon as the Liberals were in office.

From the long-standing promise to scrap the despised Goods and Services Tax to the commitment to tear up the North America Free-Trade Agreement, Chrétien and Liberal colleagues have systematically set aside virtually every major carrot from the 1993 campaign. And it is important to remember that several of these undertakings were pledged when the election outcome was still in some doubt. With the January 1998 announcement that Canada would indeed purchase a rechristened EH-101 helicopter, *Toronto Star* columnist Carol Goar wrote: "The last of Jean Chrétien's crowd-pleasing election promises toppled like a lonely bowling pin this week."[25]

In fairness to Chrétien, policy reversals have been a pattern in Liberal politics since the Trudeau years. In the 1974 federal election, the Liberals aggressively campaigned against a Conservative platform promise to introduce wage and price controls to help curb inflationary pressures. Pierre Trudeau criss-crossed the country, mocking Tory leader Robert

Stanfield's argument with a snappy putdown: "Zap! You're frozen." Trudeau won a majority in that summer campaign. And on Thanksgiving Day weekend a year later, he exercised his prime-ministerial prerogative to ask for time on the public broadcaster to announce the imposition of wage and price controls. Trudeau resisted the temptation to open his address with the news "Zap! You're frozen."

One could argue, therefore, that Chrétien's promises should be considered against recent history. Certainly, in the case of the GST, anyone who thought about the promise for a nanosecond would understand any government determined to tackle the federal deficit could not forgo a $15-billion-plus revenue stream without introducing some other offsetting income stream that would likely be every bit as unpopular.

But Goar offers a different perspective of Chrétien's broken promises. She writes: "Most had little to do with Liberal principles. They were designed chiefly to grab headlines, provide good television footage, or exploit public apathy toward former prime minister Brian Mulroney."[26]

Goar went on to argue that the temptation "to resort to this kind of showmanship" is increased as the ideological differences between most political parties are indecipherable to all but the most rabid of partisans. This point leads me directly to Patterson's premise that the only phenomenon a population cannot protect itself against in a democracy is a bold-faced lie.

So how do we explain Chrétien? How do we explain public-approval ratings in the province of Ontario that reached 75 percent in January 1998—more than four years after the Liberal leader took office and well after it was widely reported that he had reversed himself on virtually every major 1993 campaign promise?

Patterson notes that when the public sees images of candidates unmediated by the press, as is the case with televised leader debates, they tend to like what they see. Yet when the images are restricted to those that air during newscasts, the public comes away with a decidedly more negative impression.

A survey of 1,000 registered voters from across the U.S. conducted by the Freedom Forum's Media Studies Center during the 1996 presidential race concluded the voters heard too much commentary and not enough candidate. Respondents rated the debates—where candidates engage each other with little interference from journalists—as the single most important source of information in the campaign.

Television is still the information source of choice for a majority of voters, with 56 percent of respondents saying the tube is where they get most of their information about a presidential campaign, compared with 17 percent from newspapers, 11 percent from radio, and 2 percent from magazines.

In terms of new media, 27 percent of respondents reported they had access to on-line services, but only 6 percent said they'd ever visited any politically oriented Internet sites. Less than 1 percent cited the Internet as the medium most relied on for campaign information.

By way of reinforcing their message of "more candidate, less commentator," fully two-thirds of respondents said they thought a proposal to give the major presidential candidates free airtime on network television would be useful. Not surprisingly, President Clinton made a specific pledge to increase candidates' access to free airtime during his 1998 State of the Union address.

Patterson argues that, as late as 1960, the news was a forum for a candidate's ideas. "Looking back at election coverage in 1960, one is struck by the straightforward reporting of the candidates' arguments," he stated. Even television news items usually included significant clips from the candidate articulating his or her policy position. The pattern, however, didn't hold. In the intervening years, the candidate's voice has been all but silenced in television campaign coverage. Harvard researcher Kiku Adatto has charted the shrinking sound bite, from an average of forty-two seconds in the 1968 campaign to less than ten seconds by 1988 and 1992. Today, in fact, reporters do most of the candidates' talking for them. An analysis of the 1997 federal campaign in Canada by the University of Toronto's Stephen Clarkson concluded that leaders' sound bites clocked in at between two and three seconds, "leaving the bulk of the television news item to the editorial whim of the particular reporter."[27]

The embrace of the dominant "game" made a preoccupation with "insider baseball"-type coverage inevitable. The chattering classes in Washington gave rise to the term "inside the beltway" to describe opinion among the capital's movers and shakers. Party apparatchiks, from the advertising types to pollsters to spin doctors, acquired higher public profiles than many of the candidates they served. The Mulroney government, for example, included as many as forty ministers and ministers of state at one point, the majority of whom had no significant public profile compared with the prime minister's pollster, or even his press secretary. Pundits panels were all the rage. I had the pleasure of filling in for Hugh Segal on CTV's pundits panel for three seasons while Hugh answered the country's call, serving as chief of staff in the Prime Minister's Office. Every Thursday morning I would troop onto the set at *Canada AM* to trade quips with Liberal senator Michael Kirby and New Democratic Party strategist Gerry Caplan. I say, without equivocation, that the experience was one of the most enjoyable of my life, in addition to giving me a higher public profile than most ministers of the crown.

The rise of the apparatchik spawned a trend known as "revolving door" journalism, where former political aides became syndicated columnists, and former political reporters became political assistants. This is obviously an issue of deep personal interest to me. The practice has been denounced by more than a few political commentators, including Montreal *Gazette* editorial cartoonist Terry Mosher, who has questioned whether individuals who cross the street, such as myself, should ever have been allowed in journalism in the first place. As a traditionalist, I lean toward the you-can't-go-home-again school, but with one important caveat. As long as news organizations insist on offering news consumers "insider"-style coverage, it is only logical to conclude that they are going to reach out to insiders. If the purpose is to explain how the rabbit disappeared, it is hardly surprising that news organizations will seek out the views of the people schooled in the art of making the rabbit disappear.

The media's strict adherence to the "game" schema has also led to a reliance on "horse race"-style reporting, both in the United States and in Canada. Campaign reporting evolved to coverage of politics as a strategic game.

Interestingly enough, in each presidential cycle, reporters take the pledge and promise not to lapse into horse-race journalism. However, the Center for Media and Public Affairs says the habit is more ingrained than ever. The center monitored television coverage of the emerging presidential campaign on the three major American networks in 1995. Some 174 stories had at least twenty seconds of content devoted to who was ahead and who was behind in the race. The comparable figure for 1991 was 36 stories. Even in 1987, the number was 83—and that was the presidential campaign that caused everyone to declare the preoccupation with horse-race coverage had spun out of control.

As mentioned previously, the news media function on two operational tracks: one professional, the other market-driven. The first treats journalism as something akin to a religious vocation: a business, but a business with a sense of purpose. The second approach is more consistent with the traditions of the penny press—overstated assertions, highlighting conflict, controversy, human frailty, and clashes of personality. With the exception of Canada's public broadcaster, media organizations are dependent on the number of readers, listeners, and viewers they attract.

An election result that is a foregone conclusion is bad for business. A competitive campaign, conversely, is more likely to attract and retain audience interest. When the Progressive Conservative party leadership campaign began in the spring of 1998, reporters declared it strictly no-contest, asserting that former prime minister and party leader Joe Clark would win in a week, and the story was relegated to back-page status. Other candidates, such as Hugh Segal and Brian Pallister, tried in vain to get the media to pay attention to their policy pronouncements. David Orchard's antifree-trade campaign was afforded novelty treatment. For the most part of the six months the campaign lasted, journalists wrote about the lack of interest in the campaign, when they bothered to cover the campaign at all. In November, when Clark regained the leadership Mulroney wrestled from him in 1983, the pundits declared it the prize nobody wanted.

In the previous federal election, despite certain difficulties, from the prime minister's town hall appearance on the CBC just before Christmas 1996 to the Somalia inquiry and the Airbus affair, the national media fully expected a Liberal victory, likely a majority victory. Much of the media coverage, therefore, focused on what *Toronto Star* columnist Richard Gwyn dubbed "the race for second place."

Reform leader Preston Manning, despite a slow start, emerged the victor in that race, in no small measure because of a successful "earned" media strategy executed in the days immediately following the nationally televised leaders' debate.

Reform party strategist Rick Anderson believes the media's preoccupation with horse-race coverage, coupled with its predisposition to seek a "congenial truth," had a significant effect on the outcome of the 1997 federal election campaign. Anderson readily acknowledges his frustration with the media bias that suggested the election outcome was entirely predictable and that the only issue to be decided was which party would form the official Opposition. He notes that when the results were finally posted June 2, 1997, the Liberals had garnered only 38 percent of the votes cast, were defeated in four of five regions and in nine of ten provinces, and prevailed only because of an extraordinary result in Ontario that saw the Grits win 102 of 103 seats. Anderson, a former Liberal, can't help but wonder what might have happened had voters in Ontario been told something other than the pundits' unanimous opinion that a Liberal majority was inevitable. "They [the media] gave the Liberals a free pass in the eyes of the electorate and diminished everybody else," Anderson says. "The media put too much stock in pre-election polls; they invented a race for second place."[28]

The strategist says pre-election polls in Canada have proved to be suspect, at best, over the past ten years, at both the federal and the provincial levels. John Turner was thought to be competitive in 1984, yet in the end, Mulroney won by a landslide. The free-trade election of 1988 showed extraordinary volatility in voter preference; and in 1993 Kim Campbell went into the campaign in a dead heat with the Chrétien-led Liberals, only to see her party reduced to rubble. Even in Ontario the pollsters have had some "'splainin'" to do. David Peterson was supposed to be re-elected in 1990. He was not. Liberal Lyn McLeod was supposed to carry the day in 1995. She did not.

Anderson says the premise of pre-election campaign polling—"if a federal election were held today how would you vote?"—is artificial, "and people are smart enough to understand that."[29]

The problem with horse-race journalism and its preoccupation with polls is found in UCLA political scientist Shanto Iyengar's theories of dominant news frames. By being cast in terms of who is winning and who isn't, campaign news coverage sets winning as the agenda. News consumers are then "primed" to consider a party leader in the context of whether he or she is helping or hurting the party's chances of winning. And finally the "bandwagon" effect kicks in when the public begins to fit itself into expressed opinion—previously published polls. If the Liberals are positioned as winners, a percentage of the electorate will gravitate toward them precisely because they are positioned as winners. Conversely, if published polls suggest the electoral tide is going out for a political party, the news stories reporting those findings compound the problem. Ask Kim Campbell. Anderson's argument that the election outcome might have been even closer had the public been told for six weeks that there was a genuine race is not without merit.

Chrétien firmly believes in the bandwagon effect of media coverage, in particular news coverage of opinion polls. "While it is still debatable whether they [polls] reflect instability or cause it, no one can doubt that they have changed the electoral process," Chrétien has written. "Every time they fluctuate, great careers and important polices go up and down with them. The media distribute them as news items, yet their effect is incredible."[30]

The reason television has had a disproportionate influence on politics through the last three decades is that television has given politicians and low-involvement viewers access to each other. And as Kathleen Hall Jamieson explains, "Television made it possible for campaigners to address individuals who were more likely than the highly-involved to be persuaded by such peripheral cues."[31]

Traditionally, the campaign plane has been dismissed as an "Animal House" with wings. The *Toronto Star*'s executive managing editor Jim Travers once likened a visit from a campaign press corps to a "semi-civilized visit from the Hells Angels." But, in truth, the comportment on the campaign bus has evolved significantly since the 1970s; reporters today are a more disciplined lot. In fact the "quiche-eaters'" bus, where mineral water is the libation of choice, now accounts for most of the media entourage.

The seeds of difficulty, if not destruction, for newly elected governments are invariably sown in the hot-house atmosphere of the campaign bus. Rhetorical excess on the hustings tends to be rewarded with serious coverage. At each campaign stop, the pressure to hype the issue of the day grows as the party leader or candidate for office strives to emerge as the "lead" in the next news cycle. The problem with this tactic for the candidate is that the electorate is actually listening.

In the 1984 federal campaign, a sharp exchange between then prime minister Turner and Tory leader Mulroney on the issue of patronage is now considered a defining moment. Turner was forced to defend a patronage binge by his predecessor, Pierre Trudeau, in the final days of Trudeau's stewardship. Turner was attempting to finesse Mulroney's attack with the argument that, while the appointments may have occurred on his watch, they were Trudeau's handiwork. He, Turner, "had no option" but to rubber-stamp the Orders-in-Council. Mulroney struck with deadly precision, arguing that Turner had an option, that as leader he could have refused to enact or endorse Trudeau's patronage binge. It is important to recall that, in the "instant analysis" provided from "ringside," the political pundits did not see the exchange as the proverbial "knockout blow" they look for in each debate. The television audience, however, begged to differ. Once the "overnights" established the fact that the exchange had registered with voters, the "clip" was repeated on every radio and television newscast for days. Mulroney, in turn, developed a full-blown standup routine for subsequent campaign appearances. Inspired by comedian Flip Wilson's humorous Geraldine routine, Mulroney usurped his celebrated line "The devil made me do it."

The nationally televised leaders' debate set the agenda, establishing patronage as an important campaign issue for the electorate. Interestingly enough, Mulroney himself believes the exchange was really about leadership, that patronage was a subtext. The ensuing news reports primed news consumers to consider Turner and Mulroney in the context of their perceived positions on patronage. Television's dominant news frame established patronage as a "problem" and positioned Turner and Mulroney as individuals with the power to either alleviate or forestall alleviation of the problem. Television news stories trumpeted Mulroney's promise to end patronage abuses while "objectively" reporting the fact that when John Turner was presented with the opportunity to take a stand against patronage abuse, he took a pass. These news stories met every journalistic convention of objectivity and fairness. Yet the structure of the news story led viewers to the inescapable conclusion that Turner had dropped the ball. The results of this construct, in terms of public opinion, were devastating for Turner and the Liberal party. The reporting of that expression of public opinion created Iyengar's "bandwagon" effect. On September 4, 1984, Mulroney led his Conservatives to one of the largest majorities in federal electoral history.

Once in office, Mulroney's government began to replace Liberal appointees on the boards, agencies, Crown corporations, and commissions of the federal government with Conservatives. The move was predictable; after all, Canadians had voted for change in 1984 and it was logical to expect that change would be reflected throughout the government. Mulroney took pains to nominate supporters of other political formations to prestigious posts, former Ontario NDP leader Stephen Lewis's appointment as Canada's ambassador to the United Nations being one high-profile example. The Canadian electorate, however, judged Mulroney harshly on the patronage issue. The message voters took away from the TV debate was that Mulroney *personally* was going to clean up past patronage practices. In their opinion, voters upheld their part of the bargain by tossing the Liberals out of office. When, in their view, Mulroney failed to live up to his end of the deal, the electorate held him *personally* accountable.

Mulroney's appointments secretariat spent years pumping out statistical data to support the argument that the Conservative government had appointed more women, more visible minorities, more non-partisans or supporters of other parties to federal posts than had any other government in history. These efforts were doomed from the get-go. The efforts could not overcome the dominant news frame created around the patronage issue during the 1984 campaign. Mulroney's supporters may argue that the former prime minister was being held to an unreasonable standard, but it was a standard Mulroney himself created.

Candidates and their advisers understand the imperative of communicating ideas in truncated, declarative statements in a campaign setting —former prime minister Kim Campbell being a notable exception. Because television connects candidates with low-involvement voters, the rhetoric necessary to get the message across must be as assertive and unqualified as a bumper sticker. These sweeping pronouncements can serve an important political purpose at a particular time. In 1988, for example, then vice-president George Bush decided he had to reassure the right that he wasn't soft on taxes if he was to secure the Republican nomination. At the convention in Houston, Bush looked directly into the television camera and declared, "Read my lips, no new taxes." The promise served its immediate purpose: Bush emerged as the GOP nominee and easily defeated Democratic challenger Michael Dukakis in the November election. Once in office, Bush realized the promise made no sense as public policy. Faced with a serious deficit—a deficit Ronald Reagan helped create—Bush was forced to recant. The electorate neither forgot nor forgave. Bush the president was held accountable for the actions of Bush the candidate.

Candidates for office invariably deal in the simple declarative. Officeholders invariably want to engage the public in a dialogue of nuance. The public appreciates the difference, but it doesn't always accept it.

Chrétien created similar problems for his Liberal government during the 1993 federal campaign on a series of issues—from his pledge to scrap the Goods and Services Tax, to his decision to cancel the purchase of the EH-101 helicopters, to his denouncing plans to turn Pearson International Airport into a private consortium.

On occasion, party leaders can be forced to adopt Bush-style promises for defensive purposes, to seal off a line of attack from the opposition.

Deborah Tannen, in her book *You Just Don't Understand*, examines the difficulties men and women experience in communicating with each other. A parallel may be drawn with the difficulties between reporters and voters.

Obviously, the press must have a story to tell—that is their bias. Because news reporting is a literary art, predicated on a need for novelty, it amounts to a continuous search for storylines. As the situation changes, so does the storyline, and, with it, the news image in which the press envelops its candidate. What is said about the candidate must fit the plot. The voters, in this drama, are spectators, not participants.[32]

In an earlier time, policy problems were far and away the top issues of campaign coverage; now at best they share top billing with campaign controversies. That change reflects the media's increased influence, because, for reporters, controversy is the real "stuff" of campaign politics.

Campaign coverage highlights sharp differences between candidates; nuance is lost. In a leaders' debate, a candidate gets an opportunity to spell out a policy position in some detail. Candidates can even identify policy areas where there is a large measure of agreement.

The problem for candidates during the rest of the campaign, however, is the fundamental requirement to "define" themselves against other candidates, a challenge in a country like Canada, where much of our politics is that of the radical middle. Invariably, the instrument of choice for politicians and their handlers is a confrontation over an issue of substance. The campaign degenerates into a battle for a kicker clip, which is about heat, not light, in terms of policy.

Perhaps the most unsettling statistic of the 1997 campaign should stand as the final comment on politics as played for, and played in, the press: since the Second World War three in four Canadians have exercised their right to vote on federal election day. In 1993, the turnout slipped to 70 percent. In June 1997, it slipped further, to 67 percent of eligible voters—two in three Canadians.

In short, we are slowly starting to tune out and disengage from a dialogue that treats the voter as an outsider.

As technology has changed life on the campaign plane, emerging technologies will change the government–press relationship. Web-based communication has the potential to trigger a renaissance for government information officers, who will have an enhanced capability of communicating directly with taxpayers. If the mainstream media are moving toward "News You Can Use," government information departments can more readily and easily assemble interactive communication packages that can provide interested citizens with all the detail they will need on any initiative, policy, or program. Similar opportunities exist for political communication.

The White House Web site posts texts of presidential speeches, and excerpts from interviews; they make expert spokespersons available, and even set up a presidential "chat room." These opportunities will be interpreted by the mainstream media as just another attempt to out-flank them. And while they are a benefit to citizens, these opportunities aren't likely to lessen appreciably the paranoia for the press for politicians.

In his latest book, *Spin Cycle*, Howard Kurtz says President Clinton believes the press is engaging in a "global conspiracy" to ruin his life. Kurtz provides a compelling look at the daily struggle to control the news agenda. The White House staff, he says, have "to manage the news, to package the presidency in a way that people would buy the product."[33] The media, in turn, have a very different agenda. "They were focused, almost fixated, on scandal, on the malfeasance and misfeasance and plain old embarrassments that had seemed to envelop this administration from the very start." Kurtz said reporters saw it as their job to report what the president said, "but increasingly they saw it as their mission to explain why he said it and what seedy political purpose he was trying to accomplish along the way."[34]

The White House press corps was determined to air the administration's dirty linen, says Kurtz. The White House staff saw it as their job to launder the news.

Former *Wichita Eagle* editor Davis "Buzz" Merritt says an improved government–press relationship is critically important: "In a society of scattered individuals, glutted with contextless information, effective public life must have shared relevant information and a place to discuss its implications. Only free and independent journalists can—but usually do not—provide those things."[35]

Tom Rosenstiel, the *Los Angeles Times* media critic, says: "Democratic theory tells us that an informed and interested public is the key to self-governance."[36] Ben Bagdikian, in *The Media Monopoly*, states that the Age of Enlightenment "acknowledged that the democratic consent of the governed is meaningless unless the consent is informed consent."[37] And the news is where politics and the media come together, in an effort to forge an informed consent.

Which begs the question: What's news?

3

News

That news is an essential component of public discourse in any Western liberal democracy is a given for students of government. The German philosopher Jürgen Habermas argues that the daily newspaper is essential to the effective functioning of the public sphere. But if there is a consensus on the central role of news in political life, the definition of what constitutes news is more elusive.

Professors of journalism have attempted definitions: The scholar Wilbur Schramm, the godfather of the academic field of communications, defined news as "an attempt to reconstruct the essential framework of an event."[1] Practitioners of journalism have come up with more flexible formulas. And the wags hanging off the press-club bar have argued for years that news is mostly about proclaiming the significance of Lord Acton's death to people blissfully unaware that Lord Acton was even alive.

Walter Lippmann was careful to distinguish between news and truth, suggesting the two could coincide only in a few limited areas, such as box scores. Edward Jay Epstein argues that journalists are rarely, if ever, in a position to establish the truth about an issue, that, in fact, the gathering of news is a very different enterprise. He suggests journalists would be better off if they gave up the pretense of being the establishers of truth.

Former *Toronto Star* editor Borden Spears once said the marvel of newspapers is not that reporters get some things wrong, but rather that they get so many things right. "The mistake is to believe that any one

news report or any one newspaper contains the final truth. Every journalist knows that truth is cumulative."[2]

As in a court of law, it is the weight of evidence that finally determines what is news. Richard Nixon's operatives may have been able to
challenge the accuracy of certain details in stories filed by *Washington
Post* reporters Bob Woodward and Carl Bernstein, but the exposé
following the break-in at Watergate stood the test of time.

Journalism operates out of its own conventions and understandings,
and within its own set of sociological, ideological, and literary restraints.
News reporting is conducted within a set of rules and structures that
dictate the organization and production of news, and in particular the
point–counterpoint structure of television news.

Most news-gathering and reporting institutions have formulated
lofty statements of purpose defining their aims in terms of honesty,
accuracy, avoidance of sensationalism and service to the public good.[3]

Journalists, when challenged to provide a definition other than the
Lord Acton version, have been known to advance the view that news is
simply a mirror placed before reality. Media scholars, however, argue
news is anything but.

Columbia University sociologist Herb Gans studied news operations
at four national news organizations—*Time*, *Newsweek*, the *CBS
Evening News,* and the *NBC Nightly News*—to determine how they
decide what is and is not news. A key finding, in this multimedia age,
was Gans's assertion that "Marshall McLuhan notwithstanding,
despite the differences between the electronic and print media, the similarities were more decisive."[4]

Journalists in all media have power, yet in the main they use that
power to support the dominant economic, political, and social ideas of
the day. Journalists, then, are essentially small "c" conservatives,
despite their tendency to affect the look, language, and lifestyle of the
avant-garde. "Objectivity" and "fairness" are the overarching tenets of
North American journalism. Reporters maintain a degree of professional detachment from the subjects they cover and strive for balance
or even-handedness in their copy.

Journalism's embrace of objectivity was, in part, to signal a move *away*
from the era of a partisan press and, in part, to appease anticipated

public concerns about concentration of ownership. Readers in a one-newspaper town might have cause for concern if the paper in question espoused a particular political line in its news columns.

While individual journalists deem themselves to be objective and nonideological, journalism itself is far from ideologically neutral. Journalism has a value set, shaped in no small measure by the Progressive Movement of the early twentieth century.

Journalism is ethnocentric. News organizations value their own "nation" above all else, whether that nation is defined by country or, in the case of Quebec, a people. News promotes a belief in altruistic democracy, that politics should follow a course based on public interest and public service. This position allows the media to be supportive and protective of our democratic institution, particularly the office of the president or prime minister, while being sharply critical of individual office holders, from Lyndon B. Johnson to Richard Nixon or Bill Clinton.

During the crucial week of the Meech Lake constitutional talks in June 1990, the Canadian Broadcasting Corporation's television coverage reflected a determination to keep Canada together, even if the CBC's political reporters had grave reservations about certain of the specifics in the constitutional-reform package and certain of the first ministers crafting it.

Journalism treats politics as a contest but insists all participants be scrupulously honest; in short, a model that is close to the Progressive ideal of government. Reflecting the fact that news is a business, American journalism embraces the notion of responsible capitalism, that business people compete to create increased prosperity for all and will refrain from unreasonable profits and gross exploitation of workers. The media have no quarrel with capitalists or "inventors," like Microsoft chair Bill Gates, who succeed in garnering staggering returns on their intellectual capital. But when Hillary Rodham Clinton turns a $1,000 investment into a $100,000 windfall in hog futures, or Jean Chrétien makes a $45,000 profit in a week on stock he picked up from a friend (Ross Fitzpatrick) he later named to the Senate, that's news.

These kinds of "character" issues are relevant to the emergence of "lifestyle" reporting. The lobbying industry is also a prime news target for political reporters because reporters believe lobbyists earn fees that are unacceptably high relative to the perceived value of their work. Similarly, travel expenses are subject to scrutiny to determine if a public figure is enjoying the high life at the taxpayers' expense.

There are decided differences in the journalism of French-language and English-language reporters. French-language journalists at the elite level are very much a part of Quebec's intelligentsia and have a long and proud tradition of stepping down from their journalistic perches to join the fray as political combatants. From Henri Bourassa to Gérard Pelletier, from Claude Ryan to Lise Payette, Quebec's leading journalistic voices have crossed the journalistic divide to assume leadership roles in political formations and movements. Pierre Trudeau, while trained in the law, established a public profile at *Cité libre* and as a television commentator of note. René Lévesque, the spiritual leader of the modern independence movement, first addressed a broader public from a studio at Radio-Canada. Canada's current governor general, Roméo LeBlanc, began his professional career as a correspondent for Radio-Canada, as did former Conservative cabinet minister and Quebec diplomat Gilles Loiselle.

English Canada's journalism, on the other hand, reflected a British "craft" approach for many years. Newsrooms were staffed by two types of souls. The majority were high-school or university dropouts who, like carnie barkers in an earlier time, ran away to the newspapers. They worked their way up from copyboy, through a semiformal apprenticeship, including stops on the police beat, courts, suburban schoolboards, and municipal councils, a provincial legislature, and finally, for political reporters, the Valhalla of Parliament Hill. The second type was the "gifted amateur," a university-educated person with a major in history, or political science, and all too rarely, economics.

However, in the past thirty years, an increasing number of journalists in both English and French Canada have been formally trained at a journalism school, either at a university or at the community-college level. A journalism degree in the 1960s was rare; a journalism degree in the 1990s is virtually a prerequisite. This move toward a more structured, professional culture has resulted in a pool of journalists who have read the same texts, considered the same theories, discussed the same conventions and mores of the trade, read and/or subscribed to the *American Journalism Review* or the *Columbia Journalism Review,* and who, consequently, tend to view the world through the same panel of the prism.

Harvard University professor Thomas Patterson is heading up a five-country study on the impact a professional journalism education has on the product we call news. Ironically, Patterson discovered that, in the news, the higher the degree of professionalism, the lower the degree of diversity. Professionalism, says Patterson, narrows the vision of the journalist; shared-decision rules drive diversity *out* of journalism and the news process.[5]

While there are differences in the news-gathering process between print and electronic journalism, in part because of television's dependence on pictures, the similarities are more decisive. So it is with Canadian and American journalism—especially with the emergence of journalism schools.

In its specific expression, news is usually about people, as distinct from groups or social processes. And it is mostly about certain people: white, upper–middle–class people; mostly male and, more often than not, in government; people described as "knowns." If the media do not have a "known" for their standard point–counterpoint structure of a news story, they will invent one. Antifree-trade activist Maude Barlow is an excellent example. University professors are useful in this role as well.

Certain people who play important roles in the life of the nation actually don't appear in the news very often. Until recently, the military leadership was rarely in the media spotlight. Through the 1970s and 1980s, big business did not get the media scrutiny it deserved. Nor did the wealthy, except on the society pages in flattering terms.

In recent years, coverage of business reporting has increased markedly, but the coverage continues to focus on the financial equivalent of baseball's box score: annual sales, pretax profit, and comparisons with last year's performance. What remains troublingly inadequate is media coverage of transnational corporations as a major force in public policy.

"Unknowns" tend only to show up in the mainstream media mix in certain defined roles. Protesters can make news; so can rioters or strikers. Victims, of either a crime or a natural catastrophe, are favored news subjects. So are alleged or actual violators of the law. A participant in an unusual activity, like taking Niagara Falls in a barrel, can make the news, especially on a slow news day. Finally, unknowns can make the news in their "vox populi" configuration, as survey respondents, or as participants in a "streeter."

For years the suburbs weren't considered newsworthy in large metropolitan dailies, at least until newspapers discovered zone pages. Young people were considered newsworthy only in the context of behavior patterns deemed deviant by their elders. The economically disadvantaged or the electorally disenfranchised rarely rated a mention. In fact, the poor had basically dropped out of the news except as law violators. News, therefore, was largely by, for, and about the elites.

This predisposition on the part of the mainstream media throughout the 1970s and early 1980s to ignore entire segments of society provided at least part of the impetus for new media voices. Community newspapers filled the void in the suburbs; urban weeklies reached out to the hip. MTV connected to the young on their terms. Specialty channels helped define communities based on something other than geography.

Journalists write news for an audience they largely do not know. Until quite recently, journalists rejected feedback from their audience for fear of compromising their news judgment and professional autonomy. A quote from one senior television producer is most revealing: "You do the show for a cell of people—the office staff, the wife, the kids. I know we have 20 million viewers but I don't know who they are. I don't know what the audience wants and I don't care. I can't know, so I can't care."[6] Actually, they could know with the same research methods employed by advertisers. The substantive point is that journalists, historically, *chose* not to know. In a *Toronto Life* takeout on the newspaper war triggered by the launch of the *National Post*, *Globe and Mail* editor William Thorsell actually made a reference to feedback his paper had received from focus groups, an admission that is still deemed newsworthy.

Reporters also advance certain hypotheses as "given" in news coverage; the west coast as home of the bizarre is one example of a prevailing media view. As coverage patterns in the American press during the O.J. Simpson trial revealed, the primary societal division in the news in the United States is race. In Canada, it would be language, although in the near future race will emerge as a more significant issue, particularly in major multicultural metropolitan centers such as Toronto.

Former *ABC News* executive Ed Fouhy says the press, like William Shakespeare, thrives on conflict—conflict as an element of drama. News, therefore, is increasingly about drama.

The media assessment of what constitutes "news" may not have a solid foundation in fact. *New Republic* writer Michael Massing, at a Harvard brown-bag luncheon discussion, said that in recent years crime has been featured prominently in local news coverage, even though there has been a significant decrease in crime in America. Crime rates in New York City, for example, are at their lowest level in fifteen years. Through the mid-1990s, subway felonies in New York were down 47 percent. Yet these falling crime rates have been offset by news coverage that created fears about crime being on the rise. Former *Boston Globe* ombudsman Mark Jurkowitz describes the phenomenon as "the mean world syndrome."

The media also "tire" of certain stories. Society's drug problem, for example, is a tired story, except in unusual subcategories, such as middle-class heroin addiction. And do you ever wonder what happened to those pit bulls that were such a menace a few years ago?

McLuhan believed technology is the determinant in news selection, but, in fact, a reporter's requirement to meet a rigid deadline may be more decisive.

Because of the limitations of news-gathering resources, both human and financial, journalism is organized more often than not around the beat system, the dominant mode of news coverage for most North American dailies. Beats are a remarkably efficient method for deploying personnel and gathering information. As media scholars James Ettema and Theodore Glasser observe, "If reporters cannot know what will be the news each day, they can at least know where and when to find it."[7]

They can be organized around a physical space—Houses of Parliament or the legislature, the police station, the courthouse—or around subject areas such as medicine, real estate, or technology. Leon

Sigal, who did a study of the origins of 2,859 domestic and foreign stories that appeared in the *New York Times* and *Washington Post*, says that what a journalist knows depends on whom he or she knows, which in turn depends on where those people are. Think about photo opportunities in the Oval Office or press conferences at the National Press Club in Ottawa.

Interest groups have long understood the principle of the bureaucratic organization of news. The fact that journalists know where and how to reach Maude Barlow on deadline contributes to her effectiveness as a spokesperson for the Council of Canadians.

Television journalism has enthusiastically embraced the world of semiotics—the use of music, re-creations, ambush interviews, and walk-and-talk stand-ups.

In the age of show business and image politics, news tends to be emptied not only of ideological, but also of historical, context. New York University scholar Neil Postman writes: "By ushering in the Age of Television, America has given the world its clearest available glimpse of the Huxleyan future."[8]

Network newsmagazines blow up pickup trucks, hire actors to articulate imagined conversations between people in the news, and feature closeups of top secret documents that are neither top secret nor the documents the reporters are talking about. Yet *ABC News* correspondents squawk when the network hires Academy Award-winning director Oliver Stone to develop a prime-time special on the mysterious explosion that downed TWA Flight 800 off Long Island, New York, in 1995, saying Stone would blur the lines between news and drama. CNN correspondent Jeff Greenfield is correct when he states: "The techniques of the dramatist cannot come first when it comes to the work of informing the public."[9] The problem, as Greenfield readily admits, is that television journalism has already blurred that line so thoroughly as to eliminate any trace of it.

This reliance on pseudo-events is particularly pronounced in television journalism. Postman says that the consequences for what we consider "news" are troubling. In his book *Amusing Ourselves to Death* Postman writes, "Television speaks with only one persistent voice—the voice of entertainment."[10] A television news show, he says, is about entertainment, not education, reflection, or catharsis, a problem compounded by the print media's predisposition to ape television.

Sources are a key component of news gathering, and Herb Gans of Columbia University likens the relationship between sources and journalists to a dance. "More often than not, the sources do the leading," he says.[11] For that reason, news is weighted toward sources eager to provide information.

As Leon Sigal's study suggests, journalists operate within a relatively narrow range of sources. Fully 78 percent of the stories Sigal analyzed originated with public officials. The news, therefore, is weighted toward sources with a track record of reliability and trustworthiness eager to provide suitable information on an ongoing basis.

Sigal takes the point a step further with his assertion that news isn't what reporters think, but what their sources say. "News is not what happens, but what someone says has happened or will happen."[12] Because reporters are rarely in a position to witness events firsthand, they must rely on others for information. They must rely on sources. Therefore, who a reporter talks to—the source—has a lot to do with news.

The loneliest transfer in the news business is from the parliamentary bureau in Ottawa to the White House in Washington. As the Ottawa bureau chief of the *Toronto Star*—Canada's largest newspaper—I could count on my calls being returned. The fact that a Liberal government was in power made access for *Star* reporters that much easier.

Washington is another story. With the exception of the Canadian embassy staff, there is no imperative for anyone in Washington to return your call. Even a stringer for the *East McKeesport World Review* has a member of Congress or two who has an interest in getting back to them. Not so for the *Toronto Star*. However, correspondents can be summoned to the White House for specific purposes. Prior to the 1983 economic summit at Williamsburg, Virginia, hosted by President Ronald Reagan, I was granted an Oval Office interview with the president. Reagan had a postsummit message for the Trudeau government. The *Toronto Star* was the administration's print vehicle of choice.

In the days leading up to the interview, I affected cynical detachment. The morning of, I was up by 5:00 a.m., ran a bunch of miles along the towpath for the C and O canal, shaved, showered, gulped black coffee, and was ready to go—by 6:30 a.m., plenty early for the late morning appointment.

A year later, as Mulroney's press secretary, I was back in the Oval Office to meet my counterpart, Larry Speakes.

Journalists have no authority to compel a source to furnish them with an account of an event. Indeed, a source need tell reporters only what the source deems to be in his or her own self-interest. Because of the voluntary nature of the source–reporter relationship, the supply of information continues only if the source is satisfied with the way the journalist uses the information. Journalists must protect their sources if the relationship is to develop.

There are characteristics that are common to good sources. Past suitability is one criterion: a source is more suitable if he or she provided good information in the past. Productivity is an issue: a source needs to provide a lot of information. Reliability is important: is the information any good? Trustworthiness is essential: the information cannot be simply self-serving. Authoritativeness is important: information from individuals in positions of authority. And finally, articulateness: it helps if the source can "give good clip."

Beat reporters, whether at the White House or on Parliament Hill, the courthouse or city hall, tend to be close to their sources and, in the case of political reporting, are often of the same chattering class as the people they cover. Other beat reporters, such as medical writers, can be *de facto* ambassadors to the lay world for the beat they cover.

Investigative reporting is a whole other world. Gans concludes: "Most news media resort to investigative reporting only when they cannot obtain access any other way or equally often, when they need a circulation or ratings boost."[13] It is no coincidence that the Tunagate caper, which resulted in John Fraser's resignation from the Mulroney cabinet in September 1985, was featured on the season opener of the CBC's *the fifth estate*.

Investigative reporters are a very different breed from their "daily" colleagues. While both groups concern themselves with "hard news," the characteristics of hard news are very different for each group. Edward Jay Epstein says, "Despite the more heroic public claims of the news media, daily journalism is largely concerned with finding and retaining profitable sources of pre-packaged stories."[14] Epstein adds that much of what passes for investigative reporting is really just the development of sources "within the counter-elite" or among government "dissidents."[15] Epstein's analysis would seem to apply to both the Pearson International Airport saga and the Airbus scandals.

Both stories were based on "leaks": the anonymous, unauthorized release of information. Leaks are a major commodity in the world of news gathering. And by way of illustrating where leaks often originate, legendary *New York Times* columnist James "Scotty" Reston once observed, "a government is the only known vessel that leaks from the top."[16]

Brookings Institute fellow Stephen Hess has developed a typology of leaks. There is the "ego" leak, which involves giving a reporter information primarily to satisfy a sense of self-importance. There is the "goodwill" leak, which Hess describes as a play for future favor, a leak whose primary purpose is to accumulate credit. There is the "policy" leak, a straightforward pitch for or against a proposal using some document containing inside information. An "animus" leak is simply used to settle grudges. A "trial balloon" leak is used to reveal a policy or program proposal that is under consideration in order to assess its assets and liabilities. The "whistle blower" leak is usually employed by, and is the last resort of, frustrated civil servants.

The Pearson puzzle is the story of an animus leak, or a "whistle blower" leak, depending on one's perspective. But the saga most certainly reflects the priorities of the people doing the leaking. And the leaks had the most profound impact on a major public-policy initiative in the way it shaped the news.

Most journalists prefer not to have to vouch for the veracity of what is reported, opting instead for accuracy. The investigative reporter, on the other hand, not only shoulders the burden of justification for his or her facts, but creates a method for doing so. Investigative reporting typically focuses on wrongdoing of various sorts and often must rely on sources that—in bureaucratic terms—are incredible.

The investigative reporter, therefore, must establish credibility through a series of intellectual exercises—often in concert with colleagues, including those who may work for other media outlets—that includes screening the tips, weighing the evidence, fitting the pieces together, and evaluating the story.

The relationship between an investigative reporter and a source was at the heart of the 1998 controversy between the CBC, its Gemini Award-winning reporter Terry Milewski, and the Prime Minister's Office.

Milewski won the award for reporting the ugly confrontation between pepper-spray-wielding RCMP officers and student protesters at the APEC conference in November 1997. Peter Donolo, director of communication in the PMO, accused Milewski of bias, insisting the reporter's objectivity had been compromised in an e-mail message he'd sent to student protester Craig Jones. In it, Milewski referred to the federal government as "the forces of darkness."

CBC News officials defended Milewski from the charge of bias, noting the PMO did not challenge the facts in any of Milewski's on-air reports. Privately, however, they bemoaned his use of the term "forces of darkness" in the e-mail sent to Jones.

While many of us tend to view e-mail as electronic conversation, with the tendency to familiar language inherent in such an assumption, the fact is that e-mail is still written communication. Milewski adopted a collaborative tone with Craig Jones that reporters—in particular investigative reporters—use in dealing with sources every day. The CBC correspondent's only "problem" was that he got caught.

Donolo, for all his self-righteous indignation, has had scores of similar conversations with reporters himself, particularly when the Liberals were in Opposition. Opposition MPs and their staff routinely collaborate with journalists to organize a line of attack for the daily Question Period. And reporters, who do not enjoy parliamentary immunity, will readily share information with an MP that they couldn't prove to the satisfaction of a libel lawyer.

During the early Mulroney years, the Liberal Opposition's celebrated "Rat Pack"—Don Boudria, Sheila Copps, John Nunziata, and Brian Tobin—worked closely with reporters in the parliamentary press gallery. And you can take it to the bank that both sides shared opinions and characterizations similar to Milewski's exchange with Craig Jones.

Investigative reporting is unabashedly moralistic, highly personalized, even idiosyncratic. Investigative reporters have an aversion to the methods of daily reporting and the standard definitions of news.

Elm Street editor Stevie Cameron is described by *Maclean's* columnist Allan Fotheringham as Canada's best investigative reporter. Cameron's exposé on the Mulroney government, including this writer, underscores the difference between an investigative reporter and a regular reporter. Cameron's writing is based on varied sources, ranging from senior RCMP officers to a disgruntled chef. Certain of her sources, such as François Martin, the aforementioned chef, would certainly qualify as "bureaucratically incredible." Investigative reporters use specific cases or incidents to establish a "larger truth."

Reporters, particularly investigative reporters, can never be certain of the interests they are serving or what will be the eventual outcome of leaks or sourced information. In his bestseller *No Holds Barred*, former Tory cabinet minister John Crosbie is unequivocal in his assertion that the Airbus "scandal" was "concocted by Boeing, a sore loser, which spread baseless rumors about its rival's sales tactics." Crosbie says these rumors were seized on by "certain investigative journalists who were not prepared to let the truth interfere with their single-minded pursuit of the Mulroneys."[17]

The Pearson International Airport affair is one example of a larger truth that did not stand up to the exacting test of a court of law. Cameron describes the proposed $700-million redevelopment of Terminals 1 and 2 at the country's busiest airport as "one of the sleaziest affairs" of the Mulroney years in office. The *Ottawa Citizen*'s Greg Weston and the *Toronto Star* team of Bruce Campion-Smith and David Lewis Stein were nominated for print journalism's highest honors, the National Newspaper Awards, for their stories on this debacle. The *Ottawa Citizen* was even given Canada's prestigious Michener Award, the newspaper industry's acknowledgment of work deemed to be of significant public service.

The headlines in these two leading newspapers told of cronyism and sweetheart deals, conveying the sense that Mulroney and his cabinet colleagues were going to literally give Pearson airport to their political friends.

Specifically, the media portrayed the deal as being loaded in favor of private interests poised to proceed with the airport's redevelopment. Focusing on Paxport principal Don Matthews, invariably described as a former president of the PC Party of Canada and co-chairman of Mulroney's 1983 leadership campaign, the coverage trumpeted the fact that federal bureaucrats in the Department of Transportation were opposed to the idea of privatizing Pearson. Therein lies the key to the Pearson saga.

In the late 1980s, Pearson International, in the opinion of the deputy minister of transportation at the time, was a disgrace, an airport that simply wasn't working. The airport handles one-third of all passenger flights in Canada each day, and 40 percent of all cargo traffic. It was operating way beyond capacity, and Terminal 1 was literally falling down. In the early years of the Mulroney government, a new terminal, Terminal 3, was built with $53 million in private funds, a terminal that would ultimately be owned by Charles Bronfman's Claridge Inc. Matthews's group had been an unsuccessful bidder for Terminal 3, but was determined to bid on any future privatizations.

My first involvement in the Pearson issue was in 1990, when I was contacted by Ray Hession, president of Paxport Inc. Hession, a likable former deputy minister of supply and services, asked if we could meet for lunch at the Rideau Club, home away from home for Ottawa's mandarins. Hession explained that the policy issue of further privatization at the Toronto airport was meeting resistance within the Department of Transportation itself. Hession wanted to take the case for further privatization to media opinion leaders. We agreed on a short-term contract that called for my company, Fox Communications Consultants Ltd., to advise on the initiative. The assignment was straightforward. Like an architect on a construction project, my job was to design the media-relations initiative, identify key media opinion leaders among the nation's columnists and commentators, and work with Hession to craft supporting materials, from talking points to background papers.

Through 1991 and 1992, cabinet considered a range of options for Pearson: to proceed with redevelopment itself, privatize the entire airport, or call for proposals to have private interests proceed with redevelopment on a lease-back arrangement. In March 1992, after seventeen months of preparation, which included input from interested parties, cabinet decided to issue a request for proposals.

Within hours of the cabinet decision, Gardner Church, Ontario's deputy minister for the greater Toronto area, confirmed that he and his colleagues at Queen's Park had received a "brown envelope" from a disgruntled employee in Transportation Canada that stated a call for proposals was about to hit the street.

From that point on, a steady stream of brown envelopes found their way to the *Citizen* and the *Star*. Greg Weston, in journalistic competitive terms, had the early "lead" on the story. The information being leaked to him in dribs and drabs raised questions about the probability of the deal, but lacked—in media terms—a definitive answer. Weston, as a columnist, had the luxury of a prime piece of journalistic real estate on page 2 of the paper. He wrote a column one day that basically said the proposed redevelopment plan didn't make sense. "What it [the column] was, frankly, was an invitation to sources,"[18] Weston said later.

The invitation was accepted, and another key brown envelope found its way to Weston. This one contained a cabinet document. As Weston notes, even in Ottawa "getting a cabinet document is not a common occurrence." The document included an analysis by Price Waterhouse that, in Weston's view, made the case that the Pearson redevelopment deal wasn't a good deal for the Crown. The cabinet document, a submission to the Treasury Board, seemed to suggest the government was proceeding with the redevelopment against contrary advice. "That's what all those stories were about," Weston says. An accounting firm had been paid to crunch the numbers and, according to Weston, "no journalist is in a position to authenticate that." The chartered accountants, in other words, are "competent knowers" in this area, and a journalist will accept their professional opinion. Weston notes there was a decided absence of factual response to his stories, except for an ill-considered attempt by Transport minister Jean Corbeil's staff to discredit him personally.

The Pearson International Airport story was "framed" by "sources" from three dissenting groups—federal civil servants in Ottawa, civil servants at the airport itself, and Metro Toronto officials who wanted the airport turned over to a local airport authority. In December 1992, the federal government announced that an evaluation committee, which included representatives from Transport, Justice, the National Transportation Agency, Richardson Greenshields, Price Waterhouse, Deloitte & Touche, and Raymond Chabot Martin and Paré, had deemed Paxport's to be the most attractive bid. Negotiations began. Some weeks later, Paxport and Claridge combined forces and formed a new company called Pearson Development Corporation (PDC).

News announcements concerning the project rolled out regularly through early 1993. PDC even offered to brief the then Opposition Liberal caucus on all details of the redevelopment plan.

On August 27, 1993, an Order-in-Council was passed following Treasury Board approval, authorizing the parties into lease and development agreements. The deal was formally announced on August 30, 1993. By then, the brown envelopes were flying through newsroom transoms. The Toronto Star headlines in particular suggested the deal was unacceptable. When then prime minister Kim Campbell called an election on September 8, the airport redevelopment story had become a major election issue.

The "sources" were equally active. Robert Bandeen, head of the Greater Toronto Regional Airport Authority, a local authority that wanted to run the airport itself, went to the Star and described the federal government's handling of the airport as "really scandalous." Later, when testifying under oath at the Senate inquiry into Pearson, under questioning from Senator Marjory LeBreton, Bandeen acknowledged the phrase may have reflected a degree of "overexuberance."

Chrétien's communications director Peter Donolo encouraged his leader to take an aggressive stance against the airport deal during the 1993 federal election campaign. Flanked by Toronto area MPs Dennis Mills and former Liberal leadership candidate John Nunziata, Chrétien attacked the proposed privatization as symbolic of the excess and cronyism of the Mulroney era. The fact the developers had kept Chrétien and his caucus colleagues apprised of the various twists and turns of the negotiations in some detail was never mentioned. Nor was the fact that Chrétien left his Toronto rallies to attend a fundraising event hosted by Senator Leo Kolber, a Claridge principal.

While Chrétien was blasting the deal, preparations were well advanced to sign the final, formal agreement on October 7. Because an election had been called, senior public servants sought direction from Campbell as to whether she wanted the signing to proceed or be delayed. Campbell decided to proceed. Liberal MPP Mike Colle, a former corner line-backer for his college football team, disrupted a news conference by Transport minister Doug Lewis, shouting his condemnation of the deal.

Toronto Star science reporter Peter Calamai, then editorial-page editor of the *Ottawa Citizen*, says the Pearson redevelopment deal was a preoccupation at his paper. Calamai says his position, that if you sign a contract you are bound by the contract, was the minority view on the newspaper's editorial board. However, Calamai insists he did not consider the ideological differences between him and his colleagues on Pearson International Airport sufficiently important to attempt to exercise a veto. "You pick and choose the mountains you are going to die on," Calamai said, adding, "[editor in chief] Jim Travers would have overruled me anyway."[19]

Some members of the *Citizen*'s editorial board, Calamai says, suspected "venial culpability" in the case.

Jim Travers also believed the Pearson story "was something the *Citizen* could ride to some prestige," Calamai says. Travers's attitude is typical of crusading editors. As former *Wichita Eagle* editor Buzz Merritt wrote: "Scalps on the belt, particularly government scalps, were the sign of rank and the measure of testosterone at gatherings of the tribe."[20]

The fact that Gordon Baker, lead counsel for Don Matthews's Paxport Group, was "an old university chum" of Calamai's certainly was a factor for the editorial-page editor. Calamai arranged for Baker to start sending him background material on the case directly. Calamai was and remains convinced there were legitimate questions to ask about the Pearson development plan. "I never felt in the whole time that our house was built on a foundation of sand," Calamai said. "I always thought that there were legitimate public policy questions to be asked. Further, we honestly believed these were questions that needed to be answered."[21]

After Chrétien's victory, his Ontario leadership campaign co-chair Robert Nixon quickly produced a report that provided the rationale for canceling the contract. The government then moved to introduce legislation intended to prevent developers from seeking any compensation beyond out-of-pocket expenses incurred during the bidding process—pegged at $30 million. The Pearson Development Corporation countered with a lawsuit challenging the constitutionality of the bill. On three separate occasions, the government had opportunities to present evidence of Tory malfeasance to the court, such evidence constituting "cause" to cancel the contract. The federal government declined. In addition, at extensive public hearings conducted by the Senate—at which this writer appeared as a witness—literally scores of public servants appeared and swore under oath that the Pearson process was completely aboveboard. A settlement was inevitable. Donolo responded with a series of well-placed, well-timed leaks and disclosures.

Calamai says the *Citizen* always opposed the idea of a court case, preferring a political inquiry, although a Senate inquiry was not their first choice because the paper "was against the Senate as an institution."

Calamai rejects the argument that the federal government's failure to ever produce any evidence of wrongdoing in a court of law raises questions as to the legitimacy of the news story in the first place. The courts, says Calamai, will not allow the introduction of "hearsay" evidence. Journalism, on the other hand, is "based on hearsay. All sorts of things that go into framing a story are things that wouldn't even be germane in a court case," he says. "That doesn't mean that there wasn't compelling journalistic evidence."

The *Ottawa Citizen*'s coverage, says Calamai, was valid "by modern journalistic standards." Travers, he says, pushed the story quite hard, "never to the point of ordering up an editorial, but he expected advances when developments occurred. Travers wanted the story to be true. There is nothing wrong with that."

Calamai believes an editorial board should be inspired by Ibsen's *Enemy of the People* and "speak truth unto power." An editorial board, he says, has a "counterflow responsibility" and should avoid a rush to judgment on an issue.

The governing Liberals managed their retreat on Pearson as carefully as they had orchestrated the media "crisis" in the first instance. "Despite the noise and fury of the Senate and the legalistic argument of the court case, people never wavered from their core belief that there was something fishy about that deal in the first place," Donolo said in an interview. "The key period was Easter Week, April 1997. We positioned it—through some leaks and stuff—in a way that maximized the money the airport authority was getting." The prime minister's spin doctor's strategy was crafted to make Pearson a "good news" story for Toronto press: highlighting the fact that the airport would be turned over to a local authority and trumpeting the infusion of federal cash.

Prime Minister's Office staff also used selective leaks to buttress Chrétien's personal standing on the issue. Reporters were fed a steady diet of "insider" information about how determined Chrétien was to fight the developers. A school of thought subsequently emerged that suggests Chrétien's stubbornness cost the Canadian taxpayers many millions extra, that the federal Liberals should have reached an out-of-court settlement earlier. Donolo disagrees. "The prime minister couldn't look eager to be giving money to developers," Donolo says. "The stories that got out, that Chrétien was being tight-fisted, worked for us." That these stories got out is no accident. These "insider" disclosures were part of a carefully orchestrated campaign by Chrétien's media advisers.

By the time the 1997 federal election was called, "Pearson Airport was not an issue, period," the prime minister's communications adviser says, despite efforts by Preston Manning to draw attention to the issue with a campaign news conference on site. In the spin war over Pearson airport, Donolo had emerged the undisputed victor. However, a look at the headlines in the Toronto media in the fall of 1998 reporting Air Canada's increasing unhappiness with the cost of the Liberal redevelopment strategy suggests the Liberals may not have heard the last about Pearson airport.

What is particularly significant in the Pearson case is the complete about-face in the shaping of the story by "sources." The late Scotty Reston, *New York Times* columnist and a Washington institution, advised young reporters to seek out the disgruntled party, believing as he did that "people who are disenchanted are more likely to speak candidly."[22] The dominant news frame, through the early phases, was set by protected "whistle-blower" sources warning an unsuspecting public of cronyism and patronage. Later, when summoned to testify before a Senate inquiry, many of these sources swore under oath that the process of awarding the redevelopment was squeaky clean and aboveboard. And then, incredibly, government officials planned a defense against PDC's court case predicated on the assertion that there wasn't any need to pay damages because the developers weren't likely to make any money on the deal anyway. Where once they claimed Mulroney was in the process of giving away the crown jewel of Canada's airport system to his friends, the "sources" were now arguing that Ottawa had to cancel the deal to protect the developers from themselves, that the agreement as negotiated was so favorable to Ottawa that the developers would never have realized any profit, and therefore weren't entitled to any payment.

By May 12, 1997, the *Globe and Mail* was reporting on its front pages that the cost of getting out of the Pearson airport deal "will approach $1 billion over 20 years, according to an analysis of federal documents." Greg Weston of the *Citizen* says, "I was fascinated after the fact to watch a lot of these same bureaucrats back-pedal."[23]

The Conservative majority on the Senate inquiry denounced the decision to cancel the original agreement with PDC on the basis of Nixon's report. "We note as well that Mr. Nixon's findings are not supported in the position now taken by the federal government itself. The government is arguing before the Ontario court adjudicating a suit brought against it by the developer that, based on sworn affidavits by Mr. Jean Desmarais, the return to the developers would have been negligible, and that therefore there is no need to provide the developers with compensation for the cancellation of the deal."[24]

Globe and Mail columnist Terence Corcoran says that the "Pearson scandal" began "during the last federal election as a cynically clever Liberal campaign exercise. It looms today as a financial mega-disaster."[25] Jeffrey Simpson summarized the saga in early 1998 as follows: "Finally, four years later, Pearson will get a more expensive overhaul than the one originally cancelled."[26]

The final chapter of the Pearson airport saga is yet to be written. In April 1998, *Financial Post* columnist Neville Nankivell cited a study by Stephen Lerner, a lawyer in McCarthy Tétrault's London, England, office, that appeared in the *Annals of Air and Space Law*. Lerner's paper states: "Mr. [Robert] Nixon's handling of this issue is very troubling." Lerner says the cancellation will cost Canadian taxpayers some $873 million over twenty years, a far cry from the $60 million trumpeted in the headlines of the day. Lerner further described the Chrétien government's cancellation rationale as "a maze designed to confuse."[27]

The purpose here is not to determine which of these "story lines" has merit, but rather to illustrate graphically how sources, not journalists, can shape a story.

All too often, in political coverage in particular, the compulsive-greed explanation is offered up as the prime motive for anything a public officeholder might do, thereby excluding the possibility that anyone can be motivated by the common good or the public interest.

Journalists, myself included in my reporting days, rarely write about the motives of their sources. In 1975, while working in Quebec as correspondent for Southam News, the late Kendall Windeyer and I conducted an investigation into questionable property transactions in Barbados involving Air Canada executives. The story triggered a royal commission of inquiry, headed by Mr. Justice Willard Estey. The presumed motive—greed—was readily accepted by us and by the readers.

This predisposition to assume the worst leads to a journalism defined by cynicism rather than skepticism, journalism that triggers the declinist in us all, journalism that actually threatens the very future of reporting.

Journalists use competition to evaluate their own performance. A competitor's reaction is the only feedback a journalist tends to take seriously, and, in a curious way, it can lead to a "consensus" that is often an expression of pack journalism. A story's credibility is created by the "pack" as the central thesis is advanced, whether that consensus forms up around the notion of Trudeau's urbanity, Mulroney as *arriviste*, Chrétien as nice guy, or Clinton as philanderer.

Reporters invariably believe they are fair and objective in their approach to their work. But the fact is, reality in a news context is a prism, and reporters can be looking through different panels, each convinced he or she is seeing the truth. Like the rest of us, a reporter's "objectivity" reflects their education, socioeconomic background, experience, and individual values. What that means, in the Canadian context, is that a news story on a dispute between Ottawa and Quebec can be radically different if the reporter writing the story is a federalist or an *indépendantiste*. News, therefore, is influenced by what Gans describes as a "weave of conscious and unconscious opinion."

Opinion is expressed in news coverage through pejorative words or phrases, and those phrases can change in the wake of highly visible or traumatic events. "Rebel insurgents," for example, tend to become an "army of liberation" when they reach the outskirts of the capital. The key to understanding the importance of these traumatic events in terms of news coverage is that they allow reporters to fundamentally alter their position on a person or institution without a loss of credibility.

The Cult of Celebrity Journalism

The impact of market pressure is not restricted to down-market journalism, described colloquially as the "dumbing-down" of the news.

In a bid to build audience share, news and current-affairs programs have embraced celebrity journalism. Morning-show hosts such as Katie Couric of NBC seem to be on some sort of network loop: she fronts the *Today* show in the morning and magazine-format current-affairs programs in later time slots. *Canada AM* host Valerie Pringle and *CTV National News* anchor Lloyd Robertson also host the network's flagship public-affairs program, *W5*. The attraction of this opportunity to broaden the scope of their work for both Pringle and Robertson is self-evident. Furthermore, the attraction to the network to feature their highest-profile hosts in an increasing number of journalistic settings is equally self-evident. But how much journalism can be involved in this game of musical chairs? Can these personalities do much more than "front" the items they are presenting?

Print reporters are also lured into the celebrity circus. Writers for serious publications—Fred Barnes of the *Weekly Standard* comes to mind—are expected to crank up the volume, and the outrage, for weekly appearances on the *McLaughlin Group*. Recently, *McLaughlin Group* panelists have even appeared in a number of feature films.

Print journalists eyeing the celebrity gravy train must cultivate a public persona. One effective way to develop such a persona is to insert yourself and your views into your copy. A marked increase in "interpretive reporting" follows. One survey revealed a tenfold increase in the number of interpretive political stories run on the front page of the *New York Times* through the 1980s. James Fallows is a particularly vocal critic of celebrity journalism. "The more prominent today's star journalists become, the more they are forced to give up the essence of real journalism, which is the search for information of use to the public," Fallows states.[28]

Veteran political journalists such as the *Washington Post*'s David Broder bemoan a second celebrity-inspired trend, the trend to revolving-door journalism—the practice of allowing individuals who have gone over the wall to government service to return to daily journalism. My own interest in this debate is obvious. Yet the very news organizations that employ the Broders or the Jules Witcovers or the Jeffrey Simpsons reach out to the Jody Powells or the Chris Matthewses or the Giles Ghersons precisely for their insider status and potential star appeal.

George Will used the back page of *Newsweek* to launch a lucrative career as a television talking head. Will reportedly earns in excess of $1 million a year. Fallows refers to the pundit class, including Will, as a "pestilence. They drive home the idea that journalist as performer is more important than the topic." As far back as 1975, Will "had deduced the fundamental logic of modern journalistic careers," Fallows says.[29] Will understood his column was important because it got him on television. And television was important because it got him on the lecture circuit.

Canadian journalistic legend Charles Lynch, the former chief of Southam News, had figured the same thing out long before George Will came along. And the chief could play the harmonica to boot.

Even allowing for the difference in exchange rates, Canada's celebrity journalists work for cents on the dollar compared with the "bigfoot" media stars in the United States. It's like playing major-league baseball for the Montreal Expos. But the pattern stands up. The *Globe*'s Jeffrey Simpson was the panelist of choice for CBC television for years. The launch of the *National Post* will make a multimedia star of Paul Wells. And one wonders what public-affairs show producers in English Canada would do if *La Presse* correspondent Chantal Hébert ever decides to retire.

Too often the insertion of "self" is wrapped in negativity and cynicism. Spiro Agnew, one-time vice-president and convicted felon, did succeed in articulating a Pat Buchanan–penned denunciation of journalists as "nattering nabobs of negativism" in the early 1970s. But the negativity seems even more pronounced today.

Commenting on the scene in a press room where briefings were being conducted for the Persian Gulf War, *Washington Post* writer Henry Allen said the sessions "are making reporters look like fools, nitpickers and ego-maniacs; like dilettantes who have spent exactly none of their lives on the end of a gun or even a shovel; dinner party commandos, slouching inquisitors, collegiate spit-ball artists, people who have never been in a fist fight, much less combat; a whining self-righteous, upper middle class mob jostling for whatever tiny flakes of fame might settle on their shoulders." Allen insists: "The horse race, insider baseball, gotcha question, the feeding frenzy, cult of toughness—these ought to be seen as unsustainable practices."[30]

Allen's prognosis was intended primarily for the salonistas of political journalism. But journalism with an attitude isn't restricted to the political pages.

The flaw in the celebrity approach—whether adopted by the candidate, or by the people who write about candidates—is revealed in Boorstin's comparison of the celebrity and the heroes of antiquity. Political figures who seek to establish themselves with image will, throughout their political career, be judged against that image. And when those political figures, having achieved high office based on an image, then wish to be measured like the heroes of antiquity by accomplishment, they are doomed to failure unless accomplishment is part of the image.

Pierre Trudeau fashioned himself the philosopher king. Brian Mulroney, the boy from Baie Comeau, epitomized upward mobility.

Jean Chrétien carefully cultivated the little-guy-from-Shawinigan persona. And, in the end, each was judged by the electors against the image he had fashioned, not the policies he put in place.

Political journalism in the 1990s is journalism with an attitude. At gatherings of the learned where the journalistic issues of the time are discussed, the role model for this new school is Maureen Dowd of the *New York Times*. Leads that raise the putdown to an art form are referred to as "Dowdisms."

Dowd's coverage of former Rhodes scholar Bill Clinton's return to Oxford is illustrative of the genre. Her story began: "President Clinton returned today from a sentimental journey to the university where he didn't inhale, didn't get drafted and didn't get a degree."[31] The problem, of course, is that Dowd's imitators pale in comparison. Dowd has edge, but it is an edge forged on insight.

Political coverage has become a world of sound bites, snappy one-liners, and "character" coverage. Today's political coverage is threatened by the cult of celebrity: the celebrity of those deemed newsworthy and, increasingly, the celebrity of those writing the news. And it is a coverage that sows the seeds of its own demise, causing the public that consumes it ultimately to lose respect for the medium that conveys it.

Michael Schudson says journalists, rather than getting hung up on "objectivity," should rely instead on "mature subjectivity"—a reporting that is "firmly grounded in the process of screening tips, assembling and weighing evidence, fitting facts and attempting to disconfirm the resulting story. In the end, these exercises yield a degree of 'moral credibility' about the convergence of facts into a truthful report."[32]

Given the increasingly pronounced tendency for newspapers in particular to reflect a distinctive perspective, Schudson's advice has merit. As a cub reporter at the *Ottawa Citizen*, I worked for a newspaper whose institutional view of the world was small "l" liberal. The *Ottawa Journal*, housed a few hundred yards down Queen Street, reflected a more conservative approach. The subscription lists reflected that fundamental fact. In the early 1980s, the *Journal* folded, as part of a "rationalization" involving the Southam and FP chains. But as competing newspapers folded or merged, the newspaper's editorial biases persisted. Spin doctors play to these biases.

Antifree-trade crusader Maude Barlow knew she would get a more sympathetic hearing at the *Toronto Star* than at the *Globe and Mail*. Conversely, proponents of a renewed federalism built on a "social union" are more likely to get more favorable press at the *Globe*.

When Conrad Black launched the *National Post* in October 1998, the front-page "exclusive" reported on Alberta premier Ralph Klein's predisposition to support the United Alternative. Klein's position was hardly news. The premier had made the same statement to another newspaper months earlier. But the *National Post* believes the various political formations to the right of center should come together under one party banner, so Premier Ralph's news is news, even if it isn't, strictly speaking.

That these institutional biases exist is known to every media-relations consultant in the country and they are a factor in the strategies they devise. It isn't as if the readers are unaware of a newspaper's tendency to have its editorial positions reflected in its news columns.

Gans argues that "the primary purpose of the news derives from the journalists' functions as constructors of nation and society."[33] The challenge for news organizations, therefore, is to provide the citizenry with comprehensive and representative messages, which in turn involves a broadening of the journalistic catchment basin. The Columbia sociologist says: "Currently, journalists select sources and perspectives from among those they know; instead, they must learn to choose from all those known to exist."[34]

Political scientists make repeated reference to democracies' dependency on an informed citizenry, yet citizens are not, in fact, required to pass some civics test or other assessment before being allowed to vote. Declinists argue our political news has less content today than was the case thirty years ago, and that, as a consequence, voters are less well informed.

In recent years, the debate as to why citizens are less well informed despite the proliferation of news and current-affairs products has focused increasingly on television, news that "wiggles."

4

Television's Truth

Television revolutionized the world of political communication. The tube brought candidates for office directly into people's homes, where they could speak "personally" to couch potatoes and political literati alike.

The emergence of the "box" forced a fundamental rethinking of mass-media theory about the impact news coverage had on public opinion and, by extension, on public policy. Television's dominance also confirmed the political apparatchik—the pollster, the spin doctor, and the advertising guru—as the new breed of party bosses. TV also gave rise to a set of political communication practices that transformed government–press relations. The model remained dominant from 1960 until the emergence of Net-based communication in the mid-1990s.

Because television, as a medium, is an educator without peer, television news, in the words of Shanto Iyengar, is "news that matters." Media scholars in recent years have concluded that news coverage is important not because the media tell people what to think, but, more precisely, because the media tell people what to think about. Media coverage dictates the political agenda and determines what problems a political leader must take up and what problems he or she can ignore. The public picks up on the problems the media identify as important. And in the leader-focused world of television, we tend to judge our political leaders based on our assessment of whether the leader solved the problem or not.[1]

Television established unequivocally that there is a science to media relations, and the science is based on the concept of "framing." Frames are principles of selection and salience, a mental shorthand that helps us absorb information and connect it to a previously established view of reality. The best example of a dominant news "frame" is the Cold War, which provided the intellectual and ideological structure for every news story about foreign or defense policy in the Western media after the Second World War. Television news reports are structured around these "frames." The news narrative flows from a precise structure as well.

Television tells its story in either a thematic or an episodic narrative structure. A thematic story speaks to a general phenomenon, such as world economic slowdown. An episodic story focuses on a specific event, such as the closing of the local steel mill. Television news also assigns responsibility for the problem. The responsibility can be causal—in an economic story, a downturn could be blamed on "Asian flu"—or it can focus on a particular person or public policy—high interest rates, for example. Most television news items have both episodic and thematic messages, but one is always dominant—more often that not, the "episodic" structure. Political leaders can find themselves in a tight spot when the news story lays responsibility for solving the problem squarely at the leader's door. This theoretical framework for a television news item is not rocket science, but it is science. A candidate for office ignores the narrative structure at his or her peril, as former prime minister Kim Campbell discovered.

Campbell learned the lesson of television framing the hard way when the 1993 federal election campaign was literally only minutes old. A confident Campbell emerged from Rideau Hall on September 8, 1993, to confirm to the assembled scribes that she had asked the governor general to call a federal election; her message, according to party strategists, was supposed to be one of hope. A briefing note crafted by strategist Nancy Jamieson recommended the prime minister emphasize certain themes in her prepared statement; first and foremost among them was the twinned theme of hope and optimism about the future. The message was particularly important because the economy, especially Canada's jobless rate, was the runaway number-one issue according to public-opinion research. Campbell's prepared text included the words "Canadians want to see real hope restored, not false hopes raised."[2]

In a scrum only minutes later, *Toronto Star* reporter Edison Stewart asked Campbell when Canadians might expect the national unemployment rate to dip below 10 percent. The Mulroney government's last budget in April 1993 had predicted the jobless rate would dip below that particular benchmark within eighteen months. To the dismay of campaign strategists, Campbell reverted to an earlier life as an academic and university lecturer in responding to Stewart's question. "Realistically, all the developed industrialized countries are expecting what I would consider to be an unacceptable level of unemployment for the next two or three or four years," Campbell said. "I would like to see, certainly by the turn of the century, a country where unemployment is way down and we're paying down our national debt, and there is a whole new vision of the future opening up for Canadians."[3]

The exchange, carried live on *CBC Newsworld*, landed at PC campaign headquarters like a scud missile. Jamieson says her instant response was, "Oh my God, she blew it."[4] Campbell, however, didn't see her answer as anything other than factual. As part of her campaign pledge to do politics differently, the Conservative leader made it clear she would not engage in expensive campaign promises or what she considered empty campaign rhetoric. "I could say how many jobs I'd like to create, but I'm sorry, that's old politics. The point is, let's talk realistically about where jobs come from and how we can maximize those jobs across the country." Campbell then headed to her campaign bus, determined to shun "the glib, glad-handing of the past."[5]

The Liberal's Quick Response team couldn't believe their good fortune. Communications director Peter Donolo understood that, in campaign terms, if you're not part of the story before it is written, then you're not part of the story. Within hours of Campbell's campaign launch, Chrétien had a carefully crafted response in time for the evening newscasts. Canada's disturbingly high unemployment rate was the issue of the campaign, and the election call was the episode that put unemployment on the public agenda. Campbell, as the nation's first minister, was positioned in TV news reports as the person with the power to help solve the problem. But in answering Stewart's question the way she did, Campbell, to all intents and purposes, looked into the camera and said: There isn't much I can do in the short term to address the problem that preoccupies you, the voter. Campbell did speak the truth, as unemployment rates through the entire first mandate of Chrétien's government can attest. And in another forum, say, an economic summit of G-7 leaders, her comment would have been endorsed by every participant. Campbell went out of her way to express sympathy, even empathy, for the jobless, but the television news reports were devastating, triggering a series of events that eventually resulted in the complete collapse of the Conservative campaign.

Citizens reward and punish presidents, prime ministers, or party leaders, depending upon the manner in which they, the citizens, attribute responsibility for political issues. These attributions and the political opinions they generate permit citizens to exercise political control, despite the fact that the public may have a low level of factual knowledge of the specifics of an issue.

In Canada, during the 1987–90 round of constitutional talks, news consumers were inundated with public-opinion research reflecting the fact that 60 percent of Canadians were against the Meech Lake Accord. The most chilling number of all, however, was the statistic that suggested fully 60 percent of respondents admitted they knew absolutely nothing about the details of the package.

The simplicity with which television news reduces political issues to a daily episode and then lays the problem directly at the door of a political leader allows viewers to make sense of an otherwise complex and confusing series of world events. For example, the politics of Central America in the early 1980s were particularly complex for North Americans. As Canadian correspondents assigned to the conflict there, we used the "Cold War" frame to help explain the warring factions.

Accessibility is also an issue. Information that individuals can easily retrieve from their memory bank tends to dominate their judgment. Because people rely heavily on the media for political information, patterns of news coverage are critical determinants of accessibility. The CBS public-affairs program *60 Minutes* aired an item in the fall of 1998 linking impotence and smoking. Smokers watching the item likely compared the data to their own experience, and those who had not experienced dysfunction presumably scoffed at the report. But in future if there is an incident of impotence, the frustrated male smoker will most certainly recall the *60 Minutes* item.

Viewers recognize that the ordering of items on a national newscast involves editorial judgment on the part of news organizations, and viewers tend to endorse that judgment. Stories that appear as lead items on a television newscast tend to matter more "because viewers, taking their cues from the networks, confer special significance upon them."[6] According to Iyengar, part of the reason for this weighting by the audience is that lead items appear on screen before the viewers' attention begins to wander. When problems flare up and capture the attention of the media, agenda-setting effects show up almost immediately among those directly affected by the problem. Only when an issue holds the media agenda for a period of time does it register as deeply with those who aren't affected directly. One such example is street crime. A first news report of a mugging is sufficient to trigger it as an issue with someone who has experienced a mugging. It takes longer to become an issue among those without the personal experience of mugging.

Television's "agenda-setting" properties tend to have more influence on those who hold a more independent view than on those with strong partisan leanings. Agenda-setting influence is also greater for those with less formal education, as well as those who are politically lethargic.

Television, particularly the CBC, put "Peppergate" on the national political agenda. News reports suggesting the violent clash between the RCMP and student protesters at University of British Columbia might have been ordered by advisers to the prime minister, or even the prime minister himself, kept Peppergate before the Canadian public for over a year. The intense media scrutiny caused a cabinet resignation, left the RCMP's reputation sullied, and exacted a direct price in terms of Prime Minister Chrétien's job-performance ratings.

There are clear limits to television's power. To state the obvious, television could not sustain a story that was radically at odds with those circulated by other sources of information, such as radio or newspapers.

The most spectacular illustration of the power of the framing theory as it relates to a political leader occurred in the late winter of 1998, when Conservative leader Jean Charest was literally press-ganged into service as leader of Quebec's federalist forces by public opinion. Charest had been a *bleu* his whole life. His father, Red Charest, and his grandfather, Ludovic Charest, had been Union Nationale activists before him.

Elected to Parliament in the Mulroney sweep in 1984 at the politically tender age of twenty-six, the flawlessly bilingual and bicultural Charest served a Commons apprenticeship as Deputy Speaker before being named a federal cabinet minister, one of the youngest in history. A reluctant yet attractive candidate for the party's leadership in 1993, Charest served as deputy prime minister in Kim Campbell's short-lived government. Following the electoral debacle of 1993, it was Charest who stepped forward to pick up the pieces. With his Commons seat-mate Elsie Wayne holding the fort, Charest criss-crossed the country, often traveling on frequent-flyer points donated by party activists, chomping rubber chicken in towns like Kapuskasing, keeping the flame alive. The federal election of 1997 took the party off life support, but twenty MPs elected did not constitute the result Charest was hoping for. He was the leader of an official party, with all that entails in terms of research staff and recognition in the daily Question Period, but the Tories were the fifth party, Preston Manning and the Reformers occupied the official Opposition benches.

A period of personal introspection followed, a period that grew Hamlet-like as Charest contemplated his future. By Christmas 1997 he and his supporters were making it clear in thought, word, and deed that Charest was in for the long haul. Over the winter, Charest and his wife, Michèle Dionne, bought a new home on a fashionable street in the Glebe, and for the first time since he entered politics they decided Ottawa would be home.

Then the Liberals sprang their Supreme Court reference. In the aftermath of the 1995 Quebec referendum, to soften criticism that his leadership on the issue of separation had been less than inspiring, Prime Minister Chrétien promised to refer issues raised by the Parti Québécois referendum rules and the threats of a unilateral declaration of independence to the nation's highest court for a decision as to the legality of the actions contemplated, in terms of both international and Canadian law. The reference was opposed by the Quebec Liberal party, the province's intelligentsia, the pundits, and all partisan actors of other political persuasions, including Charest.

The reference, however, was hugely popular in English Canada, where people were looking to somebody, anybody, to stand up to Premier

Lucien Bouchard and the separatists. Ottawa's decision prompted Charest to support a Bloc Québécois motion reasserting Quebec's right to self-determination, a motion supported by the New Democratic Party as well. Charest's position led to an angry confrontation with Chrétien in the Commons, and widespread castigation on the editorial pages and in opinion pieces across Canada. The moment was captured by Commons television cameras, with Chrétien blasting Charest for having voted with the separatists. Tory supporters groaned. They knew they could expect to see the clip again at the next federal election. That Charest was merely articulating a position that was official party policy, at least since the 1991 policy session in Toronto, was irrelevant. The construct of the news accounts sealed Charest's fate, at least in English Canada. The Supreme Court reference was the "episode" and it was a good thing as far as English Canada was concerned. Charest was opposing it and that was a bad thing. The stories were "fair" and "objective." They also led English-Canadian viewers to one inescapable conclusion: Charest was against them. Suddenly there were the stirrings among the Tory rank and file that maybe it was time to find a leader from somewhere other than Quebec. Unity is, after all, our overarching public-policy issue and the dominant "frame" of our news.

Then, again consistent with Iyengar's theories, a second event occurred that once more fundamentally altered the "frame" around Charest: Quebec Liberal leader Daniel Johnson resigned. A careful reading of the latest entrails from the modern man's oracles—the pollsters—caused Johnson to conclude his leadership coattails were too short to carry himself, his party, and Ottawa's insensitivity to victory in the next provincial election. As a courtesy, Johnson called Charest at home to give him a heads-up, acknowledging the fact that Charest was the most popular federalist in Quebec, and had been for some time. Reportedly polls had shown Charest to be the leader most likely to defeat Bouchard in a provincial election.

Charest, Michèle, and their fourteen-year-old daughter, Amélie, knew Johnson's Sunday-night call would renew the pressure on him to jump to provincial politics, but as the *Star*'s Edison Stewart reported, "they were stunned at the tornado of public-opinion that has likely changed their lives forever."[7] Charest decided to keep to a schedule that called for him to tour Western and Atlantic Canada. The coverage was overwhelming. Charest, in the days of two seats, had to struggle to get the mainstream media to pay any attention to him. His coverage hadn't increased much even as a leader of an official party. But suddenly Charest was front-page news in stories that carried banner headlines in a type size reserved for events of great significance. Editorial writers who days before were denouncing Charest as unfit to even be prime minister reversed themselves so quickly they were breaking out the surgical collars to treat the whiplash. A talk radio host in Western Canada called the television cameras to record the fact that he intended to literally wrap Charest in the Canadian flag.

Charest had every reason in the world not to want to go to Quebec, but the media "frame" meant his decision was preordained. Charest had defined himself in political terms, on the unity issue. In the 1997 federal election he was deemed to have "won" the televised leaders' debate on the strength of an emotional, impassioned intervention on the unity issue. He positioned himself as a more viable national alternative to Reform leader Preston Manning because of the unity issue. The bad news, from the perspective of Charest's personal preference, was that the people of English Canada heard him. They accepted his assertion that Canadian unity was his defining public-policy issue. They believed him when he said he was determined to pass on to his children the same Canada he inherited from his parents. Whatever differences they may have felt on other policy issues, Charest's message to English Canada on unity was received loud and clear.

Once fate, in the form of Daniel Johnson, intervened and Charest was given an opportunity to take the unity battle directly to the perceived enemy—Lucien Bouchard—it was inconceivable to English Canadians that Charest would decline. And his standing as a national leader would have been sharply diminished had he done so.

As Charest wrestled with what was increasingly a no-option decision, his federal party supporters posted concerns about how his lack of familiarity with provincial issues was an important part of the equation. They talked of how difficult it would be for any lifelong opponent of the federal Liberals to have any confidence in either their instincts or their policies regarding Quebec. These concerns certainly resonated in

Quebec, particularly with the French-language media majority. But they fell on deaf ears in English Canada—again because of the structure of news reporting.

In English Canada there is but one Quebec issue, and that is unity. Who controls the kiosk at a Human Resources Development Canada employment office is a matter of no consequence. In English Canada, Quebec's independence movement is the dragon, and Charest fits the bill as Saint George. Having taken maximal political advantage of the Supreme Court reference, at Charest's expense, the Liberals were quick to herald Charest as a possible savior. Their public declarations were designed to ensure opinion in English Canada would be clear as to who the villain of the piece would be if this "tide in the affairs of men," to quote the Bard, was avoided. Whoever coined the truism "You can't have your cake and eat it too" clearly never met a federal Liberal. The Liberals were simply applying the same thought process to unity that they have applied in recent years to everything from free trade to the GST to wage and price controls: maximize the political benefit, then embrace the policy when circumstances suggest a viable alternative.

Charest's decision to take his unity fight to Quebec City was a direct and incontrovertible consequence of media framing. And as *Globe and Mail* columnist Jeffrey Simpson suggested, like the butterfly in chaos theory, it is still working its way through our political ecosystem.

Charest moved quickly to address the "expectations" issue as well, arguing that it was a mistake for people to consider him something of a messiah, that no one person can defeat a movement such as the Parti Québécois. Reason, of course, is on Charest's side. But unfortunately for Sherbrooke's favorite son, the structure of television news reports isn't. Quebec separation was identified as the problem, and Charest was positioned as the *individual* with the ability to solve the problem.

The news reports set Quebec sovereignty as the agenda, prompting news consumers to consider Charest in the context of his abilities to deal with the agenda. For federalists, Charest was advanced as the answer to their dreams.

However, the media "frame" was different in French-speaking Quebec. Among *les Québécois*, unity is an issue, but not the only issue. While federalists believe Canada can prosper as a federation only if a

Liberal government is in power provincially, strong nationalists believe the federation works best when the pro-sovereignty Parti Québécois uses the threat of independence like a knife held to our collective throats. In this frame, Charest is not a savior, but Lucien Bouchard is.

Unfortunately for Charest, by the time Lucien Bouchard called the Quebec election in November 1998, French-language media in that province had settled on a different "frame"—competence. The issue for French-language journalists, and by extension their audiences, was which party leader was best able to govern the province. Not surprisingly, the incumbent Bouchard enjoyed the advantage in this situation, particularly among French-speaking Quebeckers.

Competition for control of the dominant media "frame" around a candidate or an issue is the essence of media relations. Politicians compete with each other, and with journalists, to control the news frame. In the Mulroney government, ministers worked to establish its agenda for change as the dominant frame. The Liberals, led by the Rat Pack, worked to divert media attention to lifestyle issues. In political war rooms, this process is known as coming up with the "ballot question."

As his strategists prepared for a televised leaders' debate on November 2, 1997, Charest was being advised to address the "competence" frame by attacking Bouchard on the health-care issue. A perceived mishandling of a situation with Quebec doctors on the premier's part created an opening for Charest. Bouchard, anticipating the attack, put aside the health-care issue and succeeded in substituting as the "ballot question" the measure of who could best represent Quebec's interests in negotiations with the rest of Canada. Having won the "constitutional" exchange, Bouchard went on to win the election.

The fact that television news is politically objective doesn't mean it is politically neutral. Northwestern University scholar Robert Entman says: "Journalists may follow the rules for objective reporting and yet convey a dominant framing of the news text that prevents most audience members from making a balanced assessment of a situation."[8]

Media frames are "works in progress" according to Iyengar, and therefore are subject to change. Consider the case of Canada's Armed Forces.

In the summer of 1990, Canada was in a funk. The "soft landing" predicted by the wizards in Finance had turned out to be the worst recession since the Great Depression. We were collectively irritated over the introduction of the Goods and Services Tax, a tax many considered not only unjust, but immoral. The Meech Lake constitutional accord, which was to resolve the Canada–Quebec question once and for all, had been scuttled by a self-righteous premier whose signature on a formal document turned out to be meaningless, and by a determined aboriginal legislator in Manitoba armed with an eagle feather, and counselled offstage by some of the best legal advisers in the nation. In the middle of this, Mohawk warriors at the Kanawake reserve outside Montreal rose in armed defiance against civic authorities planning to expropriate an ancestral burial ground for a golf-course extension. Quebec's provincial police force—la Sûreté du Québec—was unable to restore order. The late Quebec premier Robert Bourassa asked Ottawa, as he had during the October Crisis of 1970, to send in the troops.

The image frozen in our collective memory of that confrontation was of a young private standing nose-to-nose with a Mohawk warrior, refusing to be cowed or intimidated by the warrior's threat. But the young soldier personified everything Canadians cherish in their civil society—peace, order, and good government. That Canada's Armed Forces would provide such leadership at a time when the federal government seemed to have lost its moral authority was doubly reassuring.

Three years later, the media portrayal of Canada's Armed Forces was decidedly less flattering. Our peacekeepers in Somalia stood accused of murder. Handheld video cameras recorded the "Stars and Bars" flag of the Confederacy over the cuts of our elite paratroopers. Hazing rituals that were at once racist and repugnant were exposed, and a dedicated military doctor insisted the brass hats at National Defence HQ were spending most of their working hours involved in a coverup. An ensuing commission of inquiry constituted a serious setback for the forces' image. But in the spring of 1997, the Red River flooding in Manitoba afforded Canadians a new look at military resourcefulness at its best. And the ice storm in Quebec and eastern Ontario in January 1998 resulted in news accounts heralding the inventiveness and dedication of the army's Corps of Engineers. Once again, the "frame" around the Armed Forces was changing.

Iyengar's frame theory has a particular application to major government initiatives. The Mulroney government's efforts at deficit reduction are a case in point. When the Conservatives took office in the fall of 1984, the federal budget deficit topped $38 billion a year. Further debt servicing had grown to be the largest single-line item in the budget, larger than spending on all social programs combined. The prime minister and Finance minister Michael Wilson were determined to reduce program spending, reduce the federal deficit, and reduce the federal government's alarming dependency on foreign debt. Each of these fiscal realities created upward pressure on interest rates. Higher interest rates, in turn, compounded the deficit situation by driving up the amount required to service that debt.

Wilson had a compelling story, but it was a story told in a "thematic" structure, which Iyengar describes as placing "public issues in some general or abstract context." This narrative invariably takes the form of a major "takeout" or backgrounder in a weekend edition of a newspaper, or a full-length profile on a television network public-affairs program, such as the CBC's old *Journal* or the *CBC National's Magazine* segment. These pieces, more often than not, follow a "causal responsibility" structure, a structure that attributes responsibility or "blame" for a particular situation on general, societal factors. The deficit-reduction story, as told by the Mulroney government, did in fact succeed in communicating in thematic terms a public-policy problem—too much debt. And while Mulroney and his colleagues worked hard at fingering the Liberals as being responsible for the sorry state of the nation's finances, the electorate has a short attention span for partisan rhetoric. The electorate, after all, held up their end of the bargain: they voted the Grits out of office. The public was more interested in looking to the future.

The prebudget "thematic" storyline was advanced by Wilson and others with measurable success. And the political communication on budget day was equally successful because the setting and circumstances lent themselves to the telling of a broad-brush, master narrative. Wilson's deficit-reduction message was endorsed by any number of third parties, from bank economists to business leaders to leading academics. Anticipated denunciations from organized labor and the Left actually work to the minister's advantage in these situations. It's a variation on the old adage "By their enemies shall you know them." The briefing packages, talking points, speech modules, weekly newspaper columns, and constituency mailers all help caucus members carry the "message" forward. The Finance department, historically, rolls out its budget-day communications strategy with military precision. The media-coverage analysis, in the early days, invariably reports a positive press. The problem arises when the thematic message loses its novelty. After about a week, even the party rank and file have grown tired of repeating the same four "bullets" at cocktail parties and over lunch. And because these policy pronouncements, while sound and maybe even profound, lack the novelty media require, the news coverage shifts to a different footing, a footing that can be particularly troublesome for a government.

Having told the "big picture" story, the media searchlight seeks out the anecdotal. News stories, says Iyengar, move to an "episodic" structure, which he describes as depicting "public issues in terms of concrete instances or specific events"[9]—a base closing or plant closing, a laid-off worker or superannuated public servant. The episodic is particularly appealing to television news because they tend to be rich in visuals. This episodic structure is linked to a "treatment responsibility" construct— in other words, the "episode" is linked directly to the person with the power to either solve the "problem" or not.

The media's preference to highlight an episode and then assign responsibility for the problem to a politician on their news reports is understandable, given the inherent requirement for the different, the unusual, and the bizarre, coupled with a predisposition to identify heroes and villains in any piece.

Public servants facing departmental spending cuts are certainly familiar with media-coverage patterns. Ask the RCMP to consider a round of budget cuts, and the first thing on their list is the fabled Musical Ride, which, as the commissioner is quick to explain, doesn't have anything to do with law enforcement. Similarly, in the early days of the Mulroney government, the Department of National Defence invariably put CFB Summerside at the top of its hit list, knowing the base closing there would have a disproportionately negative impact on the economy of Prince Edward Island.

The Mulroney/Wilson approach to deficit reduction, while sound in a managerial sense, meant the government was particularly vulnerable to these kinds of tactics. The cabinet had decided to impose across-the-board cuts, based on the premise that senior mandarins were best suited to identifying those areas where economies could best be achieved. However, that meant decisions that were particularly sensitive in political terms were being made by individuals who were not politically accountable. The tradition of budget secrecy means ministers of the Crown are consulted about program cuts in their particular ministry, but are not consulted about proposed cuts in other areas. The most controversial element of Wilson's first budget in May 1985 was the proposal to partially deindex certain social-program payments. The change was particularly problematic for senior citizens. Communications minister Marcel Masse did not know about the pension component of the proposal until the cabinet briefing on budget day. Masse was incensed. While he supported the objective of deficit reduction, he wondered why the government would *start* a battle on the deficit on the backs of seniors. Had the issue been considered by the full cabinet, Masse might have been able to convince Wilson to start somewhere else. As it was, the Quebec minister had no choice but to join in the defense.

Not every mandarin is particularly savvy at identifying budget-cut targets. Former CBC president Pierre Juneau's management team thought they were being clever when they listed the closing of the Radio Canada affiliate in Sept-Îles, Quebec—in the prime minister's riding of Manicouagan—as the first victim of cutbacks. The "threat" had the prime minister chuckling for weeks.

But the "human interest" stories that flesh out news accounts of lay-offs, base closures, or less money for social-entitlement programs exact a high price. My personal favorite was a *CTV News* report on the cutbacks to passenger-rail service between Halifax and Cape Breton Island in Nova Scotia. Canada's passenger-rail service had been losing literally billions of dollars a year, primarily on lines to smaller, lightly populated centers away from the St. Lawrence Seaway corridor from Quebec City to Windsor.

The news report in question featured a poignant interview with a fifty-seven-year-old Cape Bretoner who signed up for a final ride to

Halifax before the service was lost forever. As the camera rolled, recording his every reaction to the countryside floating by the window, the Cape Bretoner revealed it was also his *first* ride on the train in his fifty-seven years. It didn't seem to occur either to the man or to the reporter that had he taken the train two or three other times in his life, the service might have been financially viable.

Canadians "of a certain age" have a deep emotional attachment to trains. A mythology has built up around the rails as a unifying force in the new dominion. That mythology has grown in words, through works such as Pierre Berton's *Last Spike* and in songwriter Gordon Lightfoot's "Canadian Railroad Trilogy." The cutbacks to passenger-rail service fit the media's need for a daily "fix" perfectly. The news stories of rail-service cuts exacted a significant political price. A sardonic Mulroney once remarked: "Canadians love their trains; they'll do anything for them, except take one!"

These "episodes" were exploited effectively by Opposition members in the House of Commons. The base closing or layoffs in an MP's riding or region provided a national news "hook" in the made-for-TV forum known as the daily Question Period. The message to newscast viewers was as simple as it was effective: the government is about to make your life miserable and we're here to help.

Flash-forward to February 1994. Liberal Finance minister Paul Martin was about to bring down his first budget. Deficit reduction was still the number-one fiscal priority. The progress recorded by Martin's predecessor, Michael Wilson, had suffered a severe setback as a direct consequence of the 1990 recession, a setback compounded by budget decisions made by a cabinet weary of nine years of saying no. Seizing the opportunity to inflate the deficit number with a series of one-time-only entries, Martin and company posted the deficit for the last year of Tory rule at $42 billion—lower as a percentage of GDP than the $38 billion the Tories inherited in 1984–85 but the highest total, in strict dollar terms, in Canadian history.

Martin had prepared his "thematic" message carefully. With the support of Prime Minister Chrétien, the one-time leadership rival announced significant, across-the-board budget cuts. Crown corporations such as the CBC, who had been praying for a Tory defeat the way farmers pray for rain during a drought, were shocked to discover there would be no exemptions for the people's network in Liberal Ottawa. But where Martin showed particular foresight, in political communication terms, was in concentrating his cuts on block transfer payments to the provinces. Martin's approach to deficit reduction was off-loading, pure and simple. And the impact of that off-loading is being felt in hospital emergency rooms and in classrooms from coast to coast today. But the strategy effectively precluded any "episodic" treatment/responsibility coverage of Martin's budget measures by the media. There were no hospital closures, base closures, or massive layoffs that could be laid directly at the feet of the federal Finance minister. As a consequence, the media were forced to stick to Martin's thematic message: that the nation's sick financial circumstances had to be treated if our economy was ever to be healthy again. The minister was building on endorsements from important "third parties"—from the International Monetary Fund to the *Wall Street Journal*. Martin also had the advantage of a Commons Opposition that, with the exception of a handful of New Democrats, enthusiastically shared his determination to reduce the deficit. Finally, the Finance minister and the Liberal government were the beneficiary of lower interest rates and a robust economy; the first dramatically reduced the cost of debt servicing, and the second resulted in a marked improvement in government-revenue projections.

Martin, assisted by my former colleagues at the Earnscliffe Strategy Group, did a masterful job in communicating a difficult and ambitious public-policy initiative to Canadians. But that exercise in political communication was made infinitely easier by the fact that the minister denied the media the daily "episode" that could have been featured on supper-hour news shows across Canada.

TV news, as mentioned before, prefers an episodic frame, largely for commercial reasons. The principal effect of this dominant episodic frame is what some media scholars have termed the "hegemonic" model of public communication, a model that disseminates information in a manner than ensures existing societal power structures are maintained through "an elaborate code-control process."

The lesson here is that the system survives, even if individual office-holders do not. A media crisis can inflict significant damage on any elected leader's or candidate's political standing. The ability to stave off a media crisis is, therefore, a critical political skill.

The inherent problem, however, is that political leaders soon realize there is no reward for being responsible, for facing tough choices. It is government by risk avoidance, ruled by the doctrine of "plausible deniability."

The battle for control of the dominant media frame is the crux of the work carried out by media-relations and communications consultants, working on behalf of clients in the public or private sector involved in major policy disputes. Typically, a communications consultant crafts the strategic plan, like an architect on a construction project. The media-relations officer puts the plan into operation. The communications consultant can, on occasion, serve as the spin doctor. The media-relations officer, typically, is the designated spokesperson.

Dominant news "frames" apply to individuals as well as to specific policies, governments, or institutions. For example, former prime minister Pierre Trudeau carefully cultivated his celebrity status, donning a public persona as a mask, the better to enchant or enrage the Canadian people. He was, in turn, the philosopher king, the quintessentially bilingual and bicultural Canadian, worldly, urbane. Trudeau could quote Rousseau or John Stuart Mill at length, but at the same time understood the political value in being hip enough to date Barbra Streisand. His scene-stealing pirouettes at gatherings of world leaders obscured policy pirouettes that were even more breathtaking.

The long-time Liberal leader feigned indifference to the national press, yet spent hours developing his skills as a television performer. Such was the aura of Trudeau as celebrity that even after he retired from public life, Christina McCall concluded, "He haunts us still."

The tragic death of his youngest son Michel in an avalanche while back-country skiing in the interior of British Columbia in November 1998 reinforced how deeply Trudeau and his family were imbedded in our collective national consciousness.

Yet Canadians seemed to understand intuitively that the face the former prime minister showed the nation was not always reflective of the complex persona behind the public visage.

Prime Minister Chrétien's dominant frame flows from the "little-guy-from-Shawinigan" public persona he has carefully cultivated for more than thirty years.

Political reporters have long experience with political figures whose *modus operandi* on media relations can be summarized in the quip: "Ask me about a fish and I'll tell you about wheat." In Chrétien's case, his operating premise seems to be: "Ask me anything you want, and I'll tell you I'm just an ordinary guy, a nice guy, but an ordinary guy."

Donolo says the persona "is basically rooted in reality. The prime minister really is an easygoing, decent guy." Chrétien's political opponents routinely underestimate "how remarkably able he is to make non-statements and skate around issues," according to Donolo.[10]

Chrétien, his media adviser says, defies conventional wisdom. In politics, shelf life is supposed to work against you; familiarity does, in fact, breed contempt. In Chrétien's case, the fact that he has been around forever actually works in his favor. "It's like your mother or your uncle," explains Donolo. "If they say something stupid, you can be angry with them over it, but it doesn't change your core view of them based on a lifetime of shared experience. It's the same with Chrétien—you feel as if you've known him forever."[11]

The prime minister, not surprisingly for someone who has been in public life for thirty years, has made many public statements that could fall under the general heading of "stupid" or downright misleading, and he has been called on these declarations by political opponents, the public, and the pundits. The effort to brazen out an argument that his government never promised to eliminate the GST, an argument he made during a nationally televised CBC Town Hall meeting, is a particularly vivid example. Yet these examples did not seem to alter the public's perception of him during his first term of office.

Chrétien uses Mulroney as a foil to reinforce the Liberal leader's image as "Everyman." The Liberals created a whole issue around the Armed Forces Airbus A-320 that they dubbed the "Taj Mahal," positioning the aircraft as a symbol of Mulroney's extravagance in office. Donolo readily concedes that the Liberals use the Mulroney trump card to the former prime minister's intense irritation. "We work that, yeah," Donolo says, "Lifestyles of the Rich and Famous persona. We didn't create it, but we certainly promote it."[12]

These campaigns exact a price, however. Chrétien runs the risk of becoming a captive of his public persona. Donolo admits Chrétien would like to use the specially configured aircraft for his international travels, particularly on the Team Canada trade missions. But the prime minister's adviser states flatly that in so doing Chrétien would run the risk of a fundamental breach of faith with the Canadian electorate.

The prime minister deliberately adopts a low-key approach to even the most serious public-policy issues. The approach works most of the time, but is high risk when a situation degenerates into a crisis, as was the case during the 1995 Quebec referendum campaign.

Throughout the campaign, Chrétien assured Canadians there was nothing to worry about, the federalist cause would prevail. When the Bouchard-led forces came within 0.5 percent of the popular votes cast of carrying the day, critics turned on Chrétien with a vengeance.

Chrétien was dismissed as lightweight, a leader without a plan, a leader who isn't up to the job. Donolo insists this characterization "is not fair." But he concedes it is an inevitable consequence of Chrétien's carefully cultivated image.

Through the fall of 1998, the dominant frame around Chrétien had undergone a fundamental and perhaps career-threatening change. The "little guy from Shawinigan" is, in the opinion of editorial cartoonists, spending too much time on the golf course.

His office's reported involvement in the APEC controversy raises questions of whether Chrétien's assault on a protester at a Flag Day ceremony on Parliament Hill really was out of character.

Suddenly, media reports suggest Chrétien is laying off the cost of a new road to his cottage on the Canadian taxpayer, and ill-considered comments to two *La Presse* reporters on the eve of the 1998 Quebec election gave the Parti Québécois a precampaign boost. The emerging theme of news and commentary about Chrétien is now whether or not he is past his prime and ought to step aside for the good of the party. Comments once cited as part of Chrétien's man-on-the-street charm are now quoted as proof the job of prime minister is beyond him.

The PMO launched a counteroffensive. As is often the case with politicians with major problems, the counteroffensive focused on the media as messenger.

Chrétien's larger problem is that his recent actions are in conflict with a second phenomenon of news reporting, identified by New York journalist and academic Andie Tucher as the "congenial truth."

Congenial Truth

Andie Tucher, former associate editor of the *Columbia Journalism Review*, says congenial truths are a pact between the reporter and the reader, an understanding of reality that is mutually acceptable.[13] A congenial truth develops around a person or an event. The image of Prime Minister Jean Chrétien as "nice guy" is a congenial truth for English-speaking Canadians. Even when he physically assaults a protester at a Flag Day ceremony on Parliament Hill, Chrétien is largely forgiven in English Canada. Because of the nice-guy persona, the predisposition of news consumers is to believe the protester must have done something to incur Chrétien's wrath and therefore deserved the throttling.

French-speaking Quebeckers, however, have a different "truth" about the prime minister that dates back to November 1981, when all first ministers except René Lévesque agreed on a plan to patriate Canada's constitution from Westminster. The all-night negotiating session is known in Quebec as "The Night of Long Knives." Chrétien, then Pierre Trudeau's Justice minister, is perceived as having conspired with his English counterparts against Quebec's interests.

These conflicting "truths" to a significant degree shape the prime minister's dominant news "frame" and his media coverage. And that coverage, in turn, helps explain the radically different perceptions of Chrétien between English-speaking and French-speaking Canadians.

Newspapers that reflect an ideology or core belief can advance the same "facts" to construct radically different "stories" that, in turn, are accepted as "truth" by the readers. The recent controversy over the aggressive RCMP tactics against student protesters is a case in point. Former solicitor general Andy Scott's cabinet career came to an abrupt end because of an in-flight indiscretion as Scott headed home to Fredericton. Unwinding with a friend, lawyer and fellow Liberal Fred Toole, Scott suggested that RCMP staff sergeant Hugh Stewart would be fingered as the fall guy in the Peppergate affair. Unfortunately for Scott, New Democratic Party MP Dick Proctor was sitting in the seat behind Toole. Proctor, a former reporter, took copious notes, then read off his account of Scott's musings in the House of Commons. Scott's and Proctor's versions of events were at variance; and Scott's version suffered from his initial assertion that he couldn't remember who was sitting next to him, or whether the person was male or female. Within hours, Toole was identified. The media showed up at Toole's law offices, cameras rolling, to ask the lawyer to confirm or deny. Toole's response was factual, yet carefully considered. The *Toronto Star*'s front-page headline declared "Seatmate Clears Scott on APEC."[14] The *Toronto Star*, as an institution, is predisposed to believing Liberal cabinet ministers tell the truth; *Star* readers are thus also so predisposed. *Toronto Sun* readers, by contrast, are less likely to accept a Liberal version of events. Significantly, Toole's formal affidavit stating his recollection of the conversation did not support Scott's version and ultimately cost the minister his job.

The congenial truth also can lead reporters to ignore established fact if it is inconsistent with conventional wisdom. Congenial truths can take hold even in circumstances where the truth is not sustained by the facts. In fact, "congenial truth," when combined with theories of dominant media "frames," can create a version of the truth far removed from reality. And when these "truths" are "assembled" in the product we call news, media coverage can create an image of a public person completely at odds with reality. The joust between political reporters and political apparatchiks is a battle for control of this dominant news frame. The frame is the underpinning of any congenial-truth theory.

Jean Chrétien's media managers have successfully maintained the prime minister's image as "le petit gars de Shawinigan" despite the fact that the Liberal leader has been part of Ottawa's governing elite for more than thirty years.

Brian Mulroney, on the other hand, led one of Canada's most activist governments, yet the Conservative government he led is perceived as one of the most scandal-plagued in recent history.

In the opinion of Brian Mulroney's supporters, one Canadian journalist, Stevie Cameron, stands above all others in the creation of a congenial truth they wear, collectively, like a scarlet letter. The "congenial truth" in this case is that Mulroney's supporters, if not the former prime minister himself, were "on the take."

Cameron's books *Ottawa Inside Out* and *On the Take* defined Mulroney's Ottawa for many Canadians, to the intense frustration and anger of Mulroney and his cabinet colleagues. Mulroney's supporters inside and outside government believe they revolutionized Canada by any objective measure of public policy, only to have their work buried in a blizzard of newspaper headlines celebrating the excesses of Tory "arrivistes" and their Gucci ways.

It is not my intention to respond line by line to Cameron's assertions, but rather to site certain specifics as examples of Tucher's congenial truth.

Cameron, and other investigative reporters, made effective use of access-to-information requests to establish a congenial truth that Mulroney and his entourage enjoyed the high life at the world's best hotels at taxpayers' expense. They would report on the rate charged for Mulroney's hotel suite at the Pierre in New York City or the Plaza Athenée in Paris, but the reports do not provide the reader with any context. The Pierre, for example, was also Trudeau's hotel of choice, and Canadian prime ministers have been staying at the Plaza Athenée since the 1950s, in part because the Canadian embassy in Paris is around the corner, on rue Montagne.

These lifestyle stories exact an immediate, and I believe significant, price in terms of public opinion. A Canadian taxpayer punching a clock at a factory in southwestern Ontario or heading out to the icy-cold waters of the North Atlantic in search of ever-depleting fish stocks has difficulty imagining a hotel room that costs more per day than he or she might make in a month.

"People think in narrative. People interpret the world in narrative," Tucher says. It is easy for the journalist, therefore, to fall into the trap of providing a storyline that squares with the readers'/listeners'/viewers' interpretation.

Andie Tucher describes the congenial truth, or "Colt Syndrome," as "the easy triumph of the most inoffensive and orthodox of truths. Too much of the time, in other words, news executives and news consumers collude to drape the vestments of journalism gently over their own chosen version of the way the world ought to be."[15]

Tucher says the collusion is "quiet" rather than conspiratorial, that reporters assemble "facts" as line items, but assemble only enough of them to explain their story in a way that makes sense to the journalist and the reader alike. Over the long haul, Tucher says, the overarching question for journalism is whether "the enthronement of the objective voice will survive the public's growing conviction that true objectivity is not actually possible."

Politicians, having constructed congenial truths about themselves, can use these truths to advance their political agendas. Richard Nixon established himself as a national figure in the United States by his aggressive anticommunist stance during congressional hearings into the "Red Scare" in the late 1940s and early 1950s. His image as being tough on communism allowed him to pursue a detente with China because American public opinion rejected any suggestion that Nixon was soft on communism. "Only Nixon can go to China" became political shorthand to explain why any leader perceived to take a hard line on any issue was in fact the leader best positioned to strike a compromise. In later years, Bill Clinton would use a similar congenial truth about his own "liberalism" to reform America's welfare system.

Former Conservative party leader Joe Clark was ridiculed in the press for asking an Indian peasant about the "totality of [his] acreage." Former prime minister Pierre Trudeau, touring a Bell Canada installation outside Riyadh, Saudi Arabia, once asked a member of the royal household who Saudis talked to on the phone. The crown prince's startled expression suggested he found Trudeau's "badinage" as mindless as did the rest of us who witnessed the exchange. But Trudeau's comment, while reported, made no impression on the public because it was at variance with the image Canadians and the Canadian media had set. The Trudeau of public perception was an intelligent, educated, worldly individual. Social awkwardness was not part of his persona. Clark, in contrast, was incessantly and invariably portrayed in the press as less than Trudeau—less polished, less poised, less comfortable on the world stage. Individual Canadians who actually meet Clark invariably discover he is a thoughtful individual, impeccably tailored, and considerably taller than his nemesis, but the media image was what the majority of Canadians had to rely on.

Former U.S. senator and presidential hopeful Eugene McCarthy once suggested that reporters were like blackbirds: when one flew away from the wire, the others tended to follow. Yet critics are mistaken when they suggest the media are involved in some conspiracy. Pack journalism evolves around congenial truths; conventional wisdom is the expression of the latest congenial truth.

Congenial truths are the stuff of political analysis in national, provincial, or state capitals. The problem for pundits, however, is that congenial truths can be highly localized—inside the Beltway, to use a Washington descriptive. Political reporters advance assertions widely shared in their local precincts, only to discover, to their horror, that their truth isn't shared as widely as they assumed. The phenomenon helps explain why political reporters miss major political stories. Ontario premier Mike Harris's "Common-Sense Revolution" victory in the 1995 Ontario election is but one example.

Political parties are active players in helping the media establish congenial truths. Chrétien can tell Canadians they would never have to worry about him spending any time fishing with the president of the United States. He would mock his predecessor as America's errand boy, and reassure Canadians he would act in Canada's best interest and not at Uncle Sam's beck and call. Yet Chrétien plays golf regularly with Bill Clinton, and during the 1995 Quebec referendum campaign the prime minister instructed his senior advisers to be in regular contact with the U.S. ambassador, James Blanchard, and okayed the sharing of federal government polling data. The Canadian Unity Information Office even hired James Carville, the "Ragin' Cajun," to come up for a day to share his insights on how best to launch a campaign counteroffensive.

Congenial truths are a regular feature in U.S. political reporting as well, according to former White House press secretary Marlin Fitzwater. And these "truths" can have a disproportionate impact on public opinion.

On a luxury bus ferrying a group of former press secretaries to a formal dinner in our honor, Fitzwater regaled us with his version of the now celebrated campaign incident of the supermarket scanner and

President Bush. The former president had been invited by Bob Graham, the head of NCR (once known as National Cash Register) to see a new scanner the company had developed that not only was capable of processing data from the magnetic strips on canned and packaged goods, but also included a built-in scale for produce. Bush was intrigued by the new technology, as anyone who had ever walked through a checkout counter at a supermarket and watched the cashiers swivel from scanner to scale would be. Andrew Rosenthal, a *New York Times* White House correspondent at the time, was covering Bush that day from the comfortable confines of the press filing center, according to Fitzwater. Rosenthal, said Fitzwater, "chose this opportunity to be clever." His story appeared on the front page of the *Times* the next day under the headline: "Bush Encounters the Supermarket, Amazed." Rosenthal's account suggested Bush didn't actually know how the scanner worked. The *New York Times* reporter used that assertion as an illustration of how Bush was out of touch with Americans, and, in particular, with their economic circumstances. "Other newspapers and TV and radio stations picked up the story, all suggesting the president was out of touch," Fitzwater states. "It was one of those stories where the truth never catches up with the lie. No other reporter at the event wrote the story this way."[16]

Fitzwater was particularly irritated at the fact that Rosenthal had filed his story from the comfortable confines of the media center, declining the opportunity to board a press bus to witness Bush's tour of the NCR facility firsthand. The story is set out in detail in Fitzwater's book *Call the Briefing: Reagan and Bush, Sam and Helen—A Decade with Presidents and the Press.*

Reporters, invariably, dismiss beleaguered press secretaries who challenge such reporting as being thin-skinned and overreactive. These same reporters, however, insist on absolute precision of language from any political candidate or his or her spokesperson.

"Congenial truths" also can cause reporters to miss major stories. In *Call the Briefing.* Fitzwater makes the case that the American media missed the Strategic Defense Initiative story, also known as Star Wars, because "the U.S. media always thought Star Wars was a quack idea. They didn't believe it could work, so why would the Soviets?"[17]

The Canadian media missed the biggest story of the "Shamrock Summit" in March 1985 because they were pursuing confirmation of the congenial truth that Brian Mulroney was ready to sell our sovereignty to Uncle Sam.

The Quebec City summit policy focus evolved around proposed negotiations on a comprehensive trade agreement between the two countries. The meetings were barely under way when U.S. Defense Secretary Caspar Weinberger inadvertently pressed a Canadian nationalist "hot button." In an interview with CTV's Washington correspondent Craig Oliver, Weinberger revealed that the United States had requested permission to stage fighter airplanes in Canada's far north. The aircraft, presumably, would be armed with nuclear tactical weapons. For Weinberger and his U.S. counterparts, the discussions were standard operating procedure for NORAD partners. For the Liberal Opposition, particularly Jean Chrétien and Lloyd Axworthy, the request constituted an assault on Canadian sovereignty. Soon after Weinberger's interview went to air, Chrétien was on his feet in the House of Commons. Given the long-standing friendship between Oliver and Chrétien's long-time adviser Eddie Goldenberg, Chrétien's intervention came as no surprise. Craig always did know how to give a story shelf life.

The Weinberger story became the focus of media coverage. Ironically, my colleagues and I—including Bruce Phillips, the newly appointed minister of public affairs at our embassy in Washington—were working desperately to try to get the media to pay attention to the announcement that Canada was prepared to entertain trade talks with the United States.

The Canada–U.S. trade initiative, in public-policy terms, was arguably the most important initiative undertaken in Mulroney's first term. It became the defining issue in the 1988 federal campaign, was credited or condemned as being solely responsible for the success or failure of every business for decades, and in the eyes of many Canadians placed us back in the continentalist path first laid out by Sir Wilfrid Laurier and Mackenzie King. Yet in Quebec City, the trade initiative barely registered on the media-coverage scale.

Mulroney made the pundits' job even easier when he took to the stage during the nationally televised gala to sing a few bars of "When Irish Eyes Are Smiling" with Reagan.

Mulroney and his cabinet colleagues invariably saw the trade initiative as an "economic" story. The media, by contrast, saw trade as a "sovereignty" story. For Mulroney, better ground rules governing trade with the economic colossus to the south meant more exports. More exports meant more jobs. For the media—and the Liberal and NDP Opposition—new trade rules constituted a threat to our cultural identity, and reinforced concerns about Canada's branch-plant mentality. It was no coincidence that support for the trade initiative was strongest in Quebec, where cultural identity is defined in linguistic terms, not economic ones, and in Western Canada.

Brian Mulroney grew up in an isolated paper town on Quebec's North Shore. The *Chicago Tribune* owned the plant. Local folklore holds that a young Mulroney was summoned to the plant manager's home at the age of nine to sing "When Irish Eyes Are Smiling" for the legendary Colonel Robert McCormick. When Mulroney repeated the performance at the "Shamrock Summit" in Quebec City in March 1985 with President Ronald Reagan at his side, wags cited it as proof that Mulroney had been singing for American masters all his life.

Fitzwater quotes a journalism professor who once told him, "There are two kinds of truths: the kind you can prove in court and the kind any fool can plainly see. It has always amazed me how many times the government tries to establish courtly truth, without establishing the kind that any fool can plainly see." Fitzwater says the press works from the other direction. "They quickly adopt the obvious truth without bothering to prove it."[18]

Fitzwater's observation may help explain why political reporters in North America have been caught out of position in a number of important recent elections. Washington reporters accepted the congenial truth that the Monica Lewinsky affair would cost Democratic candidates significant support in the November 1998 midterm Congressional elections. This assumption turned out to be incorrect.

A few weeks later, pundits in Quebec suffered a similar fate. Sharply critical of Liberal leader Jean Charest's performance on the hustings, the pundits predicted that Premier Lucien Bouchard's Parti Québécois government would win in a walk. Charest, in fact, won the popular vote. And Bouchard, portrayed as the most charismatic, if enigmatic, leader of his generation, attracted fewer votes than the party garnered in the 1994 provincial election.

In these cases, the pundits may be victims of their own punditry. Their preoccupation with "horse-race" journalism causes political reports to define campaigns as a game, and to establish "winning" as the agenda. News consumers are then "primed" to view party leaders in the relatively narrow context of their ability to win. Media assessments of the leader's electoral chances, supported by published polls, create a bandwagon effect that makes the predicted result more likely— unless the predicted outcome exceeds the public's desired outcome. Quebeckers were relatively satisfied with Bouchard's government, and therefore were predisposed to re-elect the Parti Québécois. What they weren't prepared to do was give Bouchard "carte blanche" for an early referendum on sovereignty. The instant Quebec's pundits proclaimed that a landslide win for Bouchard was likely, public opinion began to shift. Television's truth, as proclaimed from anchor desks at Radio Canada and TVA, was at variance with the public's true opinion, as Bouchard discovered to his chagrin.

5

Bay Street Blues

The single-column headline on the obituary page of the October 2, 1995, edition of the *New York Times* reported the death of G. Prescott Low, newspaper publisher. Low was the third generation of his family to own and manage the *Patriot Ledger* in Quincy, Massachusetts.

The news story described Low as an advocate for local ownership of newspapers, and the Associated Press account attributed the following quote to Low: "To me, the newspaper was a responsibility, a public trust. I think the whole thing that is wrong with the chain newspapers is that there is no sense of public trust."[1]

Low's musings about the evils of newspaper-chain ownership were given less prominence in that day's paper than obituaries for comedian George Kirby and a British detective named Arthur Benfield. And there is something ironic, even anachronistic, about Low's ruminations.

This is, after all, the era of the megamerger of media and entertainment companies. Disney buys ABC and the editorial cartoonists take a nanosecond to sketch Mickey's Mousketeer ears on Peter Jennings as the definitive word on the future of news. The message is clear: the blurred line between the network's news and entertainment divisions is likely to disappear altogether.

The lightbulb makers at General Electric wonder what to do with NBC, particularly after news-division executives cancel a full hour of prime-time advertising for an exclusive O.J. Simpson interview, only to have O.J. opt for a telephone chat with the *New York Times* instead.

The increased focus on ratings versus content prompts *Newsday* columnist Marvin Kitman to ask if the Westinghouse people aren't working on technology to transfer CBS's signal to your refrigerator door during commercials—the better to boost Dan Rather's sagging numbers.

Rupert Murdoch, at Fox, proved it is possible, at least for a while, to have a successful television network without a news and current-affairs division. Murdoch's ambivalence toward the value of news came as no surprise to readers of the *New York Post* and the *Times* of London—both News Corp. properties, located at opposite ends of the journalistic spectrum.

Here in Canada, Conrad Black turns federal laws restricting foreign ownership of newspapers into a Trojan horse, and adds the Southam empire to his already impressive list of holdings around the world.

And Winnipeg lawyer and entrepreneur Izzy Asper's Global television system becomes *de facto* Canada's second-largest network after a series of mergers and acquisitions.

The jargon of today's news executives is the jargon of Wall Street. The attributed quotes from media moguls in news accounts of the 1990s mergers were replete with references to the "maximizing of synergies," "vertical integration," and "cross-promotion."

And it all started the day Mr. Neuharth went to Wall Street. That's Al Neuharth, former head of the Gannett newspaper chain, former chair of the Freedom Forum, and the person most responsible for this writer's extraordinary sabbatical year at the Freedom Forum Media Studies Center in New York.

Neuharth is a particularly colorful character whose personal motto adorns many a frat-house wall: *Ne illegitimus carborundum*—Don't let the bastards get you down. Neuharth stood conventional wisdom on its head with the bold decision to launch *USA Today*, a newspaper derided by critics as a "McPaper." With the creation of *USA Today*, however, Neuharth seized on the fundamental truth that escaped the media elites along the eastern seaboard for a generation. After probing public interest regarding the concept of a new national newspaper, Neuharth remarked: "The message I was hearing over and over was that newspaper people thought they were putting out better newspapers than newspaper readers thought they were reading."[2] Neuharth's personal credo was that news stories should always give readers enough to substitute fact for rumor. Neuharth advocated a journalism of hope, not despair. A factoid worth noting: 30 percent of *USA Today*'s circulation is in the eighteen to thirty-eight age range, a demographic group that is turning away from established dailies.

Neuharth, as former *Chicago Tribune* editor James Squires report-ed, presented the newspaper business to the Wall Street analysts as a "profit machine," a business that made money whether the economy was booming or sputtering. Neuharth's model featured monopoly newspapers in smaller centers poised on the brink of industrial growth. "Once invited into the tent, the analysts quickly determined that news-papers were prime targets for reengineering, or downsizing. It took no genius to realize that a business being threatened by the first great tech-nological invention—television—might be saved by the second—the computer,"[3] Squires states. Suddenly, newspapers, once a people busi-ness, became a business whose future success was ensured by more efficient machines and fewer people.

Neuharth, says Squires, believes the changes he brought to the news-paper business were inevitable, and that in bringing those changes he showed other newspaper publishers how to ensure their business could survive longer than they might otherwise have done.

Like most journalists of his generation, Squires knew newspapering was a business, but clung to the notion of its being a business with a higher purpose. As Squires put it: "You hadn't taken a job, you had answered a calling."[4] But Neuharth fundamentally changed the rules of the game. "What Al Neuharth and Wall Street have brought most con-sistently and permanently to the management of the press was an over-whelming compulsion for high earnings."[5]

Nevertheless, Squires, like the author a direct beneficiary of Al Neuharth's corporate success, says that Prescott Low had it right: the "dirty little secret" about corporate ownership is that it is incompatible with good journalism.

What differentiates the media companies from widget makers or natural-resource extractors is the impact the media have on society's ability to organize itself.

Ben Bagdikian argues media ownership has a direct consequence for democracy. "Freedom of choice in politics can be sustained only by freedom of choice in the mass media. The two cannot be separated."[6]

Students of government agree the political agenda in Western liberal democracies is set by the news media. A consensus has also emerged that the media themselves set the news agenda, the manipulative efforts of public officeholders and aspirants notwithstanding. Not surprisingly then, media ownership has become a major preoccupation for officeholders and, to a lesser extent, the public itself.

At the weekly gathering of the Freedom Forum fellows at Columbia University School of Journalism during the academic year 1995–96, the "declinists" among us attributed many of the shortcomings of today's journalism to the slavish adherence of media managers to a quarterly-earnings-driven corporate agenda.

The group, whose fellowships had been granted by the charitable foundation Neuharth established, identified four major concerns that were the inevitable consequence of media concentration:

1. reduced editorial budgets to enhance profitability;
2. the potential for corporate conflicts of interest;
3. self-censorship, and a predisposition to fold when confronted with libel actions; and
4. the silencing of voices—particularly voices of dissent.

The declinists argue that problems created by the media's move to the corporate market are multiple and flow from one overarching demand: the need to maximize profit.

Despite the predisposition of individual reporters to see journalism as something akin to a religious vocation, the news business is precisely that—a business. Mark Jurkowitz, former ombudsman at the *Boston Globe*, says while reporters consider journalism a high calling, "we are a consumer product." Referring to the reader, Jurkowitz continues: "They want it easy, they want it understandable, they want it friendly and they want it to be to their liking."[7] The late Robertson Davies, Canadian newspaper editor and literary titan, once said newspapers "like to represent themselves as wonderfully romantic and hitched to world events" when they are, in fact, "really an entertainment and manufacturing business. The news is what you can squeeze in before you have to go to press; it's not what's happening in the world."[8]

The creation of profit has been the foundation of North American journalism—with the notable exception of public broadcasting systems—

ever since entrepreneurs succeeded political parties as operators of the press 150 years ago. For most of this period, media proprietors in the main subscribed to Professor Fred Siebert's "social responsibility" theory of mass media. Journalism was a cross between a profession and a public service. Media voices were expected to make a positive contribution to the common weal. Proprietors were allowed to accumulate wealth, subject to the Progressive Movement's philosophy of "responsible capitalism." This approach lent credence to the notion of the press as a public service and its responsibility to "provide the raw material for public dialogue," in the words of former CBC anchor Knowlton Nash.

When I was a cub reporter at the *Ottawa Citizen* in the mid-1960s, we referred to the parent corporation as "Mother Southam." The publisher was R.W. Southam, known affectionately in the newsroom as "High Pockets" when out of earshot, but always addressed as Mr. Southam in person. The Southams lived in the community, held prominent positions in local charity organizations, and personified the higher calling journalism aspired to represent.

This media construct has been dubbed the "Golden Age" of journalism, lasting roughly a generation, from the late 1950s to the early 1980s. Then market pressures seeped into the newsroom, particularly private television newsrooms.

Two developments accelerated the trend to "market sensitivity" in news coverage. The first was the aforementioned shift in media ownership, from families whose members were pillars of their respective communities to computer-wielding wizards operating on behalf of publicly traded corporate entities with diverse holdings. Media properties were simply a part of the portfolio mix for the shareholders, and the media properties were expected to provide a return on investment comparable to other company holdings. The dominant media culture, built on a dogma of social responsibility, was set aside by a new breed of corporate managers with business-school backgrounds whose eyes were firmly fixed on the bottom line.

Salomon Brothers analyst Larry Barker told the *New York Times* that the power shift in newspapers is now in favor of the business side of the news. "Many [newspapers] have been able to operate with two out of three decisions being made by editors. But we are moving into an era where two out of three decisions are going to have to be made in favor of publishers."[9]

Ken Auletta's *Three Blind Mice: How the Television Networks Lost Their Way* provides a fascinating glimpse into the clash of corporate and news cultures that occurred when General Electric took over the National Broadcasting Corporation (NBC) and Larry Tisch's Loews Corporation assumed control of the Columbia Broadcasting System (CBS), known for years as the Tiffany Network. Referring to Jack Welch, CEO of General Electric, Auletta reports: "A pet peeve of his was the belief, embraced by Larry Grossman and others at the network, that those engaged in television had a unique public trust. Welch saw no difference between the public trust in his aircraft-engines division and that of news."[10] Auletta quotes Welch as saying that "every GE engine attached to a plane, people bet their lives with. That's a public trust that's greater in many ways than a network."[11]

Welch is known as "Neutron Jack," after he trimmed 100,000 people— fully one-quarter of the workforce—from GE's payroll in the early 1980s. In seventeen years at the helm, Welch has increased GE's annual earnings from $1.7 billion a year to $7.3 billion. As a result, GE stock soared 54 percent in a single year.

According to Auletta, the conflict was addressed directly by NBC news-division president Larry Grossman, who asked network president Robert Wright whether GE was running NBC or whether NBC was running NBC. Wright's response was chillingly succinct to traditionalists: "As long as I'm here, NBC has to be sensitive to what GE shareholders think." As Auletta observed, "News had traditionally worshipped another totem—the public trust."[12]

News-division presidents at NBC were expected to be every bit as cost-conscious as the production manager at a General Electric manufacturing plant. These kinds of Wall Street–inspired budget and personnel cuts were described by one analyst as "management by bolo knife."

Even Cap Cities/ABC chief executive officer Tom Murphy—a business leader with an extensive background in television—would admonish his network executives: "If you want to give people what you think they need, go into public broadcasting."[13]

Newspaper editors, equally vulnerable to these cost-cutting pressures, soon discovered the economies of "parachute" journalism over the cost of maintaining a far-flung network of resident foreign correspondents. As an unsuccessful candidate for the position of president of the Canadian Press in early 1996, I was asked whether I considered CP an institution or a business. My muddled response that CP was an institution, but that, like all institutions, it needed a sound business plan to survive and prosper was deemed less than Solomon-like.

Conrad Black's acquisition of the Southam newspaper chain in 1996 and Thomson's *Victoria Times Colonist* and *Nanaimo Daily News* in May 1998 highlighted Canadian concerns about corporate concentration in terms of its impact on editorial quality. Black's companies owned 66 of 105 daily newspapers in Canada, more than 60 percent of the total, as well as 100 other newspapers around the world. Of more concern to his critics was the fact that Black owned all the dailies in Newfoundland, Prince Edward Island, and Saskatchewan, and 14 of 16 dailies in British Columbia. Not surprisingly, *Toronto Star* publisher John Honderich called for an inquiry into the issue of corporate concentration in Canadian papers—a proposal supported by Sun Media Corp. head Paul Godfrey, as well as by New Democratic Party MP Nelson Riis. Honderich's response was quoted in the May 22 edition of the *Star*: "Is that healthy for this country? Is it not important that some of the politicians look at these issues to find out whether there's enough diversity?"

David Radler, Black's partner at Hollinger Inc., dismissed an inquiry as unnecessary and warned that such a probe could result in political interference in the newspaper industry. "Are we in the business going to leave it to the politicians?" Radler asked. *Times Colonist* publisher Peter Baillie insisted the sale to Hollinger by Thomson Inc. was not an issue to readers, reporting the newspaper's switchboard recorded but a single call of protest. Baillie said the newsroom would have received sixty or seventy calls if the crossword puzzle had been inadvertently left out of the paper. Baillie's point wasn't lost on Maude Barlow, head of the Council of Canadians, who had attempted unsuccessfully to get the federal competition bureau to intervene in Black's acquisition. Barlow told the *Star*, "I don't understand why people are so concerned about the banks and not so concerned about a sector that's more important to democracy."[14]

Radler argues corporate ownership by Hollinger does not, in fact, lead to a dictated editorial line. "I don't know of one instance where we walked into a newspaper to change opinions," he told the *Star*.[15] Honderich, in turn, acknowledges that Black does not dictate editorial policies, but suggests instead that the editors of Black's papers know what he likes and know what he expects. "There is potential in that situation to have a homogeneity of views,"[16] the *Star* publisher said. *Star* watchers might be bemused at Honderich's observations, given the sensitivity the *Star*'s middle managers have historically shown to *Star* causes and crusades. And the ability to "manage up" has moved more than one aspiring editor up the corporate ladder at One Yonge Street, as well as at Mother Southam's—a fact not lost on Black.

Emerging from Southam Inc.'s annual meeting in late May 1998, Black accused his competition of using their newspapers to promote the idea of a royal commission, denouncing their "self-righteous hysteria." Black also said he does not intend to add to his Canadian dailies any time soon.

The council joined the Newspaper Guild and the Communications, Energy, and Paperworkers Union to form a lobby group to fight the Hollinger takeover in April 1997. Known as the Campaign for Press and Broadcast Freedom, the lobby group commissioned a content analysis of Hollinger newspapers. Some 3,000 items from a representative group of Hollinger newspapers were analyzed in three distinct time frames: from July 1 to November 30, 1991, when Hollinger's stake in Southam was negligible; July 1 to November 30, 1995, when Hollinger held a minority of shares; and July 1 to November 30, 1996, once the takeover had been effected.

The study concludes: "For the most part, there is little diversity in the Hollinger press."[17] Coverage, in the main, focuses on business and parliamentary affairs. "Coverage of labor, women's issues, and native affairs was virtually non-existent."[18] Certain of the newspapers, such as the Montreal *Gazette*, seemed to have improved in terms of the quality and diversity of items featured on their front pages. Other papers, such as the *Calgary Herald* and the *Cambridge Reporter*, declined significantly in the opinion of analysts. And the *Windsor Star*, published in a city whose major industry is the Chrysler plant, seemed to lose interest in labor news.

The study itself, however, is flawed. For example, the report makes no reference to changes in the senior management at any of the papers. As a reporter for seventeen years, I am firmly of the opinion that the editors—people in corner offices—do make a difference in the quality of the editorial product. But the Barlow group's report concludes: "As newspaper holdings become more and more concentrated, the large chains such as Hollinger can be expected to starve the smaller dailies for profit to finance one or two flagship papers. This allows Hollinger to point to newspapers such as the *Ottawa Citizen* or the *Vancouver Sun* as examples of its commitment to journalism. The truth, however, is that the quality and diversity of news most Canadians receive suffers. Ultimately, our democracy suffers too."[19]

Barlow's group commissioned a second study, of the *Regina Leader Post*, acquired by Hollinger from Armadale Co. Ltd., owned by the legendary Sifton family. Conducted by Jim McKenzie, associate professor at the University of Regina's School of Journalism and Communications, the study "shows Hollinger has put profit ahead of substance, seriously eroding the quality of news that readers in southern Saskatchewan receive."[20] McKenzie states that the Armadale Co. Ltd. "was producing a newspaper that was mediocre to begin with, but that has declined further under Hollinger's stewardship."[21] McKenzie accuses Hollinger of turning the *Leader Post* into a cash cow. McKenzie's report includes the story of how eighty-nine *Leader Post* employees—fully one-quarter of the newspaper's staff—were fired within days of the Hollinger takeover in a particularly brutal manner. "All *Leader Post* employees were ordered to report to two large rooms at the Regina Exhibition Centre on Saturday, March 1," the report states. "The people assigned to three rooms were told they were the lucky ones. They still had jobs. Those in the fourth room (quickly dubbed the death room) were told they were finished, effective immediately."[22] According to the report, the employees deemed surplus weren't allowed back into the *Leader Post* building to clean out their desks.

The detailed content analysis concluded there was "no sign at all that Conrad Black was using the *Leader Post* to put forward his political ideas."[23] The Left has been preoccupied to the point of paranoia that Black might order his editors to the right-of-centre line from the front page, through the funnies, and, most important, on the editorial pages.

The study noted the *Leader Post*'s "news role" is higher under Hollinger, but local news coverage has been reduced. Hollinger also uses significantly more wire copy and photos at the expense of locally created editorial content. McKenzie observes that the reporting of local news is more expensive than taking material off the wire, and concludes that "in the case of the *Leader Post*, big chain ownership has not improved the quality of journalism the news readers receive, but has, in fact, had the opposite effect. As newspaper ownership becomes increasingly concentrated in fewer and fewer hands, the conclusion reached here may only be a portent of things to come."[24]

Not surprisingly, McKenzie celebrates the survival of competition in the form of the twice-weekly *Free Press*—founded by former *Leader Post* and *Kingston Whig Standard* publisher Bill Peterson. According to McKenzie, the competition forced Hollinger to reinvest, however modestly, in the *Leader Post* newsroom.

Black, however, can point to a significant new investment in the Montreal *Gazette* and the *Ottawa Citizen*, in terms of both physical plant and editorial staff. The *Citizen*, for example, was nominated for nine National Newspaper Awards in 1998, well above the paper's average.

The *National Post* is far more indicative of Black's determination to turn the world of Canadian print journalism on its ear. The *Post* blends traditional layered headlines from the 1950s with decidedly new-media-inspired columns. And the paper has assembled a stable of columnists and reporters that is arguably the strongest in the country. Exceptional storytellers such as Roy MacGregor routinely cross over from sports to politics. Christie Blatchford provides specialized coverage of criminal proceedings of societal importance. Even Allen Abel was lured back to print from Holy Mother Corp., which, for his long-time admirers, is reason enough to start a newspaper.

The *Post*'s journalism is sometimes more quirky and personal than is the case at the good old *Globe and Mail*; it also has its predictable causes—such as the Preston Manning–inspired United Alternative political movement.

In one bold move, Black created a national alternative to the *Globe and Mail*, provided a new forum for some of Canadian journalism's best storytellers, and raised salaries in every major newsroom in the country. Pre-*Post*, journalists interested in working at the *Globe and Mail* were expected to pay a salary premium for the privilege. And while Ken Thomson is a fine fellow, it was always a mystery to me why any journalist would want to subsidize a family whose holdings are measured in the billions. Yet the *Globe* employees were happy to do just that in exchange for the prestige of working there.

What is significant about these media corporate maneuvers is that Canada's newspaper companies have clearly decided bigger is better. Even community newspapers—the last refuge of the mom-and-pop shop—are now dominated by people like the other Black—David.

The Honderich/Godfrey alliance opposing corporate concentration was short-lived. In August 1998, Sun Media Corp. swapped a number of media properties with Southam Inc., relinquishing control of the *Financial Post* in exchange for the *Hamilton Spectator*, the *Kitchener-Waterloo Record*, the *Guelph Mercury*, and the *Cambridge Reporter*.

The *Financial Post* was folded into Black's national newspaper. The *National Post* was launched with a major advertising and promotional campaign October 27, 1998. The *National Post* was printed on *Sun* presses.

Before the chattering classes could develop much "buzz" around the *Post*, Honderich sent another shock wave through the journalistic community when he and his colleagues on executive row at the *Toronto Star* launched a hostile-takeover bid for the *Sun* newspapers.

The hostile-takeover attempt was itself the subject of extensive media coverage, coverage that didn't reflect particularly well on the media moguls. Godfrey and company basically accused *Star* executives of lying—fighting words at One Yonge. The *Star* responded in fulsome detail in its own news pages to set the record straight. Godfrey's search for a white knight led him to Montreal and Quebecor's Pierre-Karl Péladeau. Two years earlier, when Péladeau's late father, Pierre Péladeau, bid for the *Sun* group, his advances were spurned with near rabid denunciations of Péladeau's separatist leanings. In mergers, as is life, everything is relative. They still don't like separatists much at the *Sun*. They just like people from the *Star* a whole lot less. Once again the "s" word—synergies—dominated the boardroom chatter.

There is intense speculation as to how the Canadian newspaper market in general, and the Toronto newspaper market in particular, will fare in the post-*National Post* era. Toronto, with four dailies, even if two declare themselves to be national, is the most competitive newspaper market in North America. *Globe* editor William Thorsell foresees a protracted newspaper war, but predicts "at the end of the day, everyone will be left standing."[25]

Canadian television networks, like their larger counterparts in the United States, are also busy merging and acquiring—looking for economies of scale. Baton Broadcasting takes over CTV; Izzy Asper's Global system becomes a network without ever declaring itself to be one, the better to avoid the CRTC-imposed Canadian-content program-spending requirements.

Baton Broadcasting executives, having taken control of CTV with the help of public markets, are then forced to appease market analysts by "downsizing" the number of reporters, producers, writers, and news bureaux at *CTV News*.

The cuts are dictated in the glass towers on King Street or Bay Street. They are translated at network headquarters, and articulated to line managers in terms of arithmetic formulae—set percentages for each department or division. The price—in terms of career carnage and editorial content—is exacted on the newsroom floor.

Even public broadcasters, such as the Canadian Broadcasting Corporation, get swept up in the turbulence of restructuring and budget cutbacks—cutbacks that ultimately are reflected in the content of news and current-affairs programming.

Any journalist working in Canada throughout the 1970s and 1980s was familiar with the press club bar's advocacy of CBC's wanton profligacy. Unfortunately for the CBC, however, the stories were factual, not apocryphal, though the Holy Mother Corp. did serve the public interest best when it gave a voice to the Canadian people.

This move to the megamerger by media companies isn't without risk, because of the difficulty in assembling the large audiences advertisers want.

Fragmentation of television's audience began in the early 1970s with the introduction of cable systems. Bruce Springsteen's world of 57 channels with nothing on quickly gave way to the 500-channel universe. This fragmentation accelerated with the development of digital signals and the Internet, which transformed the worlds of media and entertainment. A front-section story in the January 11, 1996, edition of the *New York Times* featured a photo of the twenty-three most important figures in the world of media and entertainment. They had gathered at a retreat in Sun Valley, Idaho, hosted by Hubert Allen of Allen and Company. The photos of Kate Graham, John Malone, Robert Wright, Edgar Bronfman, Jr., and Barry Diller appeared under a caption that read: "From Gurus to Sitting Ducks: Media executives lose their edge."[26]

Ev Dennis, our mentor at Freedom Forum Media Studies Center, put it as follows: "When there were only three pipelines, it made sense to be in the pipeline business. Now it makes sense to be in the oil business.[27] What Dennis was saying is that, when media products were created in an analogue form, the money was in distribution. In the digital world of the new media, the money will be in content—which is problematic if, like traditional television networks, you have invested your money in distribution systems.

A corporate profile of these megamedia companies reveals the extent of the cross-ownership web of control. Time Warner Inc., for example, is involved in motion-picture and videotape production, periodicals and a weekly newsmagazine, books, records, audiotapes and disks, cable and other pay-TV services, amusement parks, and various and sundry patents. Time Warner's brand names include HBO, *Time, Sports Illustrated*, Book-of-the-Month-Club, Little, Brown, and all of Turner Broadcasting.

These cross-ownership patterns cause concerns in news departments about self-censorship. Auletta reports that once GE acquired NBC, "What troubled people at NBC and elsewhere was the danger of self-censorship from a powerful conglomerate with major interest in defence and nuclear power plants."[28] How likely is it that NBC would broadcast a major newsmagazine item on power-plant safety?

James Squires puts the conflict potential this way: "The news director who spends NBC's resources investigating GE won't be news director very long."[29]

Analyst Marc Gunther says the recent mergers will force reporters to cover their parent companies and their various subsidiaries. "The result, some believe, will be that many more reporters will be forced to engage in a kind of journalistic incest when covering their corporate parents and siblings."[30] Adds Jeff Chester of the Washington-based Center for Media Education, "You cannot trust news organizations to cover themselves."[31] *Toronto Star* publisher John Honderich's call for a royal commission on newspaper ownership was covered extensively in his own newspaper, but rated nary a mention in the Southam-owned *Vancouver Sun*.

In an engagingly cheeky advertisement placed in the November 19, 1998, edition of the *New York Review of Books, Mother Jones* declared, "Anyone can buy our magazine, unless you are a predatory multinational news conglomerate." The text declared: "It's always bothered you that the same people selling you the six o'clock news could also be selling you television sets or washing machines." *Mother Jones* positions itself as "one of the last remaining independent magazines on earth" and trumpets "our unique brand of hell-raising, investigative journalism."[32]

Olivia Ward, of the *Toronto Star*'s European bureau, highlighted the self-censorship problem posed by megamergers. Australian-born media mogul Rupert Murdoch found himself immersed in an international scandal in early 1998 when word filtered out that the book-publishing company he owns—HarperCollins—had dumped a book by Chris Patten, the last British governor of Hong Kong. HarperCollins initially tried to peddle a media line that they had rejected the book because it was "boring." Patten immediately countered with a lawsuit, which resulted in an apology from HarperCollins. Rumors persist that Murdoch ordered the book dropped for his own personal business reasons. In addition to owning HarperCollins and the *Times* of London, Murdoch also owns the satellite broadcaster BSkyB. Murdoch negotiated for four years to have his Star pay-TV channel carried on a Chinese cable system. My Freedom Forum colleague Orville Schell chronicled Murdoch's earlier decision to drop BBC World News Service from Star pay-TV offerings to the mainland because of Chinese concerns over news coverage of human-rights violations in the People's Republic of China. The Patten book debacle is seen by critics as a second example of Murdoch putting his multibillion-dollar business interest ahead of the free expression of ideas. Clearly, Murdoch was not prepared to publish a book that might embarrass the Chinese, and there was a risk that Patten's book would embarrass the Chinese. Timothy Garton Ash, the widely read East European expert, described the decision to dump Patten's book as "a classic piece of appeasement out of commercial self-interest," in an article carried in the *Weekly Observer*. "This is one example of why it is so difficult to achieve a common Western stance against regimes that violate human rights."[33] The *Star* reported that HarperCollins novelist Doris Lessing called the scandal "too shocking for words." Stuart Profit, HarperCollins's editor-in-chief, resigned and filed suit for constructive dismissal.

The media conglomerate with diverse business interests creates other potentially serious issues of conflict of interest. Rupert Murdoch's Sky Broadcasting paid $1.65 billion for Manchester United, Britain's richest and most successful soccer team. Analysts stated that Murdoch had overpaid by as much as $500 million, yet hailed the move as successful in the context of the growing convergence of television and sports.

Murdoch, who also owns part of CTV's Sportsnet, also owns the Los Angeles Dodgers, and has options on minority stakes in the Lakers and the Kings, as well as in New York's Rangers and Knicks. His Fox Network holds broadcasting rights to National Football League games, major-league baseball, and the National Hockey League.

Walt Disney's corporate heirs own ABC, ESPN—America's dominant sports channel—as well as the Anaheim Angels and the Mighty Ducks. The name of Disney's hockey team was telegraphed some years earlier in a film the studio released starring Emilio Estevez which featured a kids' hockey team called the Mighty Ducks.

This "vertical integration" of news and entertainment, as the stock analysts describe it, raises the issue of conflict of interest to an art form. Just how critical is a Fox Network sports reporter going to be about the Dodgers? Who will help Fox decide what teams should be featured in baseball's game of the week? How would ABC plan to cover antitrust hearings involving professional sports franchises?

Yet Murdoch and Disney are simply following a trail originally blazed by Atlanta entrepreneur Ted Turner, founder of CNN, the world's first all-news channel. Turner used TBS—his Atlanta-based superstation—to help make the Braves America's team. His basketball team, the Hawks, also benefits from TBS exposure. And Turner plans to bring NHL hockey to the city Sherman reduced to ashes during the Civil War. Having supplied his network with a lot of relatively inexpensive programming, Turner will be free to pursue other interests, such as run for the White House in the year 2000.

Turner, of course, may have to confront another media baron on the hustings. *Forbes Magazine* owner Malcolm Forbes, Jr.—also known as Steve—has been seeking the Republican nomination through much of the 1990s and isn't likely to stop any time soon.

This situation begs the question: How do news organizations cover presidential campaigns when their principals are the candidates?

Journalism in the "vertically integrated" era of global corporation may have to set aside objectivity in favor of a journalism of full disclosure. In the early 1990s, for example, Southam Inc. owned the public-opinion research firm the Angus Reid Group. Reid's Ottawa office was a direct competitor of my old firm, the Earnscliffe Strategy Group.

Through the Charlottetown round of constitutional negotiations, the federal government retained the services of Bruce Anderson, my friend and a business partner in Earnscliffe, to provide research analysis on the unity file. Before joining the company, Bruce had been president of Decima Research and had extensive experience as a supplier to the government on a broad range of public-policy issues.

In the aftermath of the subsequent referendum in October 1992, we were in receipt of a faxed missive from *Ottawa Citizen* reporters Chris Cobb and Mark Kennedy, setting out a series of questions asking how Earnscliffe was awarded these contracts, citing my close relationship with the prime minister of the day, Earnscliffe's collective involvement with the ill-fated "Yes" Committee, and the fact that Bruce's wife, Nancy Jamieson—quite simply one of Canada's premier public-policy strategists—was advising Senator Lowell Murray, the keeper of the unity file.

The fax included the usual investigative reporter's threat: you have until Friday to respond because we are going to print on Saturday. We invited the *Citizen* scribes to our Sparks Street office and provided detailed answers to their questions. What followed was a mini-feeding frenzy, a dozen front-page stories hinting at all manner of conflict and collusion on our part, the frenzy fed by our competition, civil servants from Supply and Services currying favor with the Liberals, and even folks we once considered friends.

For the record, I have no quarrel with the *Citizen*'s right to probe the awarding of government contracts. Public funds were involved and, therefore, the contracts should be subjected to rigorous examination by the press. What did frustrate me was the *Citizen*'s steadfast refusal to acknowledge its own *prima facie* conflict of interest. Imagine any other circumstance where the employees of a corporation arrive in the offices of a privately held company and demand proprietary information relating to government contracts without acknowledging the conflict. Kennedy and Cobb, and subsequently Jim Travers, then the paper's editor-in-chief, and Sharon Burnside, the managing editor, insisted there was a clear division of church and state between the *Citizen*'s editorial operations and Reid's polling company despite the fact that *Citizen* publisher, Russ Mills, sat on Reid's board of directors. As a former reporter myself, I understand Travers's reluctance to see any conflict, but I knew the conflict would be readily apparent to anyone in any other business.

About halfway through the saga, Travers acknowledged my point, and the *Citizen* began inserting a boilerplate paragraph with subsequent stories. Naturally, my colleagues and I were suspicious of assertions from Reid's employees that they had nothing to do with the story. As Reid himself said to me on the set at CTV the night of the 1993 federal election, the polling business in Ottawa is like Palermo, Sicily, in the old days of the Mafia. Every day we take our *luparas* down from the mantel over the fireplace and blast away at each other.

A 1995 dispute between the CBS network's flagship public-affairs program *60 Minutes* and the giant tobacco company Brown &

Williamson underscores another inherent problem in publicly traded companies controlling major media outlets. A *60 Minutes* story featuring a "whistle-blower" source once employed by the tobacco company alleged the company spiked their products. The tobacco company filed a massive lawsuit alleging "tortious interference."

Host Mike Wallace led the chorus of voices denouncing CBS for caving in. However, the CBS decision is reflective of the increased business pressure on news executives. General counsel in any media corporation in the United States today is not likely to be a First Amendment scholar, but is more likely to be a corporate counsel. And corporate lawyers are quick to set the amount of financial risk they are prepared to let the company take. Directors and senior managers, with fiduciary responsibilities ascribed by law, ignore the advice of corporate counsel at their legal peril.

The Brown & Williamson action against *60 Minutes* afforded working reporters with a whole new definition of libel chill. The tobacco company had attacked on a new front, based on an issue of business practice largely unfamiliar to reporters instead of the usual issues around free speech. Publicly traded news organizations, facing quarterly statements themselves, might be less aggressive in their search for the truth when the object of their attention is another large corporation with deep pockets.

My personal suspicion is that news organizations tend to compensate for such craven behavior toward corporate giants by being even more aggressive in their reporting of political and community leaders. Brown & Williamson may have the financial wherewithal to fight a protracted legal battle—particularly with "home-court" advantage in a state like Kentucky—but an individual in politics, even a successful individual, is less likely to be able to finance such a challenge. Reporters—in particular, investigative reporters—are concerned to the point of preoccupation with libel chill. But the fact is that, in most circumstances, it is the news organization and not the subject of the news story that is the proverbial 800-pound gorilla.

Few newspapers express their mission statement as succinctly as the *Daily Herald*, an Illinois newspaper founded by the Paddock family in 1872. The paper's masthead declares: "Our aim: To fear God, tell the truth, and make money."[34]

The problem with this preoccupation with the bottom line is that invariably the public interest is subordinated to the short-term interest of investors. And the investors aren't restricted to the suspender-snapping, hair-gel-coiffed denizens of Bay Street; the investors include every segment of our society, from religious orders to teachers through their pension funds.

Traditionally, the internal separation between the business and editorial sides of news organizations was as sharp as the idealized division between church and state, Squires says. But when newspapers decided to compete with television by seeking advertisers on the quality rather than quantity of the readers, the wall between editorial and advertising came tumbling down. "For the first time, American journalism has become truly a news business built on a successful three-way relationship between news content, advertising sales and target audience."[35]

At the 1997 American Magazine Conference in Phoenix, Arizona, delegates wrestled with how to put the readers first while satisfying the needs and demands of advertisers. In 1963, Henry Luce, the founder, editor, and publisher of Time Inc., stated: "The one thing that is unusual about Time Inc. is that we set up a management which is required to produce a profit and yet has no control over our essential product, the editorial content of our magazine."[36] The 1997 rule, as set out by Henry Muller, editorial director of Time Inc., reflects a decided shift in the balance of power. "What a lot of people in this building now understand is that editors who communicate with their publishing counterparts here are in fact in a stronger position to influence outcomes than editors who wall themselves in. The church that talks to the state, and works with the state, is a stronger church."[37]

Thomas Florio, president of *The New Yorker* magazine, contends the old analogy of church and state is hopelessly outdated, and that a more timely and relevant metaphor is that of an ecosystem. "If advertisers are allowed to influence material it is like dumping toxic waste into the environment; but if writers and editors are going to publish things that are constantly going to offend the clients who make it possible to publish the magazine, they will not have the environment that allows them to publish the magazine."[38]

To pick up on Florio's analogy, the key to any ecosystem is balance. Major retailers such as Winn-Dixie or Wal-Mart now ask magazines what they plan to feature on their covers, out of respect for "community values." But at what point does this defense of community values constitute editorial interference? And with the emergence of "big box retail," how big a price—in terms of newsstand sales—are magazines prepared to pay to maintain editorial integrity? What happens when the marketers ask editors for a helping hand on advertorials? If a writer is doing a feature on a new development in the automotive industry, is there any harm in calling an advertiser for comment rather than a dealer who takes space in another publication?

The short answer is yes. A person's inability as a "source" for a news story cannot be determined by the individual's history as an adviser.

There is no shortage of experts prepared to tout the "declinist" line and lay all blame for decline in editorial standards at the feet of the money managers. "Essentially this business imperative to match up the editor's content with the advertiser's desired audience profile would be the battering ram that broke through the most revered and important press tradition—the wall between the editorial, which constituted the soul of the press, and the revenue-generating side that was always its heart," observes James Squires. "All CEOs of publicly traded corporations eventually learn what Neuharth did when he first took Gannett's stock to the public market. Investors are only interested in good news. And it must be delivered year after year."[39]

Observers make much of the fact that the growth in newspaper circulation in North America has failed to keep pace with population growth. Yet in Los Angeles, the *Los Angeles Times*, under Otis Chandler, simply stopped delivering the paper into certain areas that had limited appeal for advertisers. Before Conrad Black's takeover, the *Ottawa Citizen* was said to be pruning its circulation lists. As Squires observed: "The camel's nose had gotten into our tent when newspapers decided that in order to compete with television, they had to sell the quality of the audience just as television was doing."[40]

My Freedom Forum associate Leo Bogart says that, while it is unlikely that the habit of reading a newspaper daily will regain the near-universal status it enjoyed in the 1960s, "the notion that they [newspapers] are bound to go the way of the dinosaur does not sustain serious inspection."[41]

Newspaper publishers, like magazine publishers before them, are look-ing for higher penetration in the top 35 percent of the socioeconomic market. "The old journalist-proprietors nourished and cherished jour-nalism as society's most valuable forum for the expression of opinion—and did not have to answer to Wall Street analysts demanding 35 percent profit margins," Squires states. Journalistic excellence, he believes, is only possible when a newspaper's owners are willing to put high-quality report-ing and editing ahead of profits. The new media owners and managers, however, prefer to tailor editorial content to the demands of advertisers."[42]

Squires, who admits he himself succumbed to the lure of the "golden handcuffs" of the Gannett newspaper organization, has concluded that "the marriage of corporations and journalism is an unnatural, unhappy union."[43] Like the newspaper proprietors of old, newspaper workers considered themselves special. Squires believes they have now "come slowly and painfully to the realization that they are not."[44]

Squires's argument that quality journalism cannot exist in a news-paper, magazine, or television network targeting a certain audience doesn't stand up. In fact, some of the most successful media companies attract advertisers precisely because their editorial product is superior. The *New York Times* doesn't pretend to be Everyman's newspaper. The paper's editorial voice is relentlessly educated and middle class. The advertising in its pages reflects that fact. The *Globe and Mail*'s news stories bear little resemblance to the articles in the *Toronto Sun*. And the *Globe* doesn't get many stereo ads as a consequence. The fact is, General Motors is buying space in both papers, pitching Chevy Cavaliers in the *Toronto Sun* and Oldsmobiles in the *Globe and Mail*.

The paradigm shift away from news coverage of issues of impor-tance to news coverage of issues that are titillating, controversial, and/or entertaining has convinced Squires and the declinists in our group at the Freedom Forum "that what the news media do for a living today is no longer journalism at all."[45]

In a speech at the University of South Dakota, former CBS anchor Walter Cronkite summarized the problem succinctly: "With television's competition for people's attention, and hence for the advertising dollar, many more newspapers have tried to compete by becoming more enter-taining and reducing their news coverage to barely more information than television itself provides. We are filling the airwaves with more words and pictures and grinding out newspapers in record numbers, and yet to the average news consumer we are imparting less information of importance. We are producing a population of political, economic and scientific ignoramuses at a point in time when a lot more knowledge rather than less is needed for the survival of democracy."[46]

The root cause of this down-market trend is the determination to "entertain." News managers today, as Freedom Forum colleague Michael Janeway observed, are largely reactive, preoccupied with what to do about the flight of the audience.

Professor Jerome Barron, notes that "the main interest of media owners and controllers is to maximize profit, not discussion."[47] An institution that was once dedicated to educating the public now seeks only to entertain consumers. Squires sees the irony inherent in the fact that this decline of journalistic values is occurring even as emerging technologies create the potential to deliver the best journalism ever.

"For all its imperfections, the press, traditionally, has been a people-oriented, privately owned, spirited, politically involved enterprise concerned with the preservation of democracy," he argues. "Under the new order, it is no longer an institution dedicated to the public interest but rather a business run solely in the interest of the highest possible level of profitability."[48]

The headlines around the *Star* takeover bid for the *Sun* newspapers tend to trumpet the declarations of Torstar CEO David Galloway and Sun Media Corp. president Paul Godfrey. *Sun* staffers rail away in their columns at the prospect of being taken over by their arch-enemies at the *Star*. There is much barroom barracking about how the journalistic cultures at the respective news organizations are incompatible. But the fact remains that the decision will be made by pension-fund managers in Toronto and Montreal who couldn't tell you a single thing about *Sun* founder Peter Worthington's career.

New York Times managing editor Eugene Roberts, during a wide-ranging discussion at the Freedom Forum Media Studies Center in early 1995, picked up on Squires's theme: "Newspapers have come to think they have to please stock analysts, which I think is a screwy, wacky game."[49] Roberts says newspapers may be the most cyclical business in our economy. Newspapers are quick to feel any downturn in the economy through reduced retail, real-estate, and help-wanted advertising; but newspapers may also be the quickest to benefit from any economic growth. "The market is being led to believe that by good management you can put on extra profits," Roberts said. "Based on my experience at big city newspapers, that's not true."[50] Corporate managers invariably seek to improve profit margins by slashing newsroom budgets, "and that's fatal. News gathering by its very nature is efficient."[51] Roberts argued that only those news organizations who invest in news gathering will prosper in the future.

Roberts is a much-revered figure among declinists. Yet what is most appealing to neo-Pollyannists is his assertion that the future prosperity of news organizations is predicated on their editorial products. Roberts, in effect, is saying to the next generation of editors, make your business case based on a market for editorial quality. It may not be a mass market, but it can be a profitable market.

Neiman Foundation curator Bill Kovach says the Times Mirror Corporation in the United States killed *Newsday* strictly to keep stock analysts happy. Corporate values, Kovach says, come first, and the values of the press second. Citing the creation of the New Century Network, an audience of 200 of the country's largest and most important daily newspapers designed to create a unified system nationwide for ad placements, Kovach wonders how long it will be "before unified national advertisers influence unified national editorial space?"[52]

As another commentator, Alicia C. Shepard, has concluded, the great newspaper families, with their "sense of noblesse oblige," are gone.[53]

Stuart Garner, president and CEO of Thomson's Stanford, Connecticut–based newspaper division, refers to himself as the *Globe and Mail*'s "banker." And Garner likes editors who are market-driven. Thorsell, arguably Canada's most erudite newspaper editor, speaks openly of what the focus groups are telling the people whose names appear on the *Globe* masthead.

Garner believes writing in newspapers can be authoritative without being boring, and argues the only worthwhile yardstick of good journalism is growing circulation. In a speech to the fiftieth World Newspaper Congress meeting in Australia in 1997, Garner said: "It makes me

angry to see complacency in lots of newspaper departments, and particularly among editors and journalists sitting in Ivory Towers believing
they are on God's work and above all this marketing stuff."[54]

While James Fallows insists that newspaper reporters fear they are
working in a sunset industry, balance sheets for 1997 suggest the sunset in question is the proverbial "red sky at night, sailor's delight."

Torstar reported record profits for 1997, and the picture was every
bit as rosy at Hollinger International Inc. and its subsidiary Southam
Inc. Of particular significance to financial analysis, Hollinger's
EBITDA—a "street" term for "earnings before interest, taxes, depreciation, and amortization"—was up a staggering 61 percent, to $402.3
million from $250 million a year earlier.

Hollinger's chair and chief executive officer announced almost
simultaneously a $63-million investment in new high-speed Goss presses
and a new production plant for the Montreal *Gazette*. He had earlier
committed $180 million for new presses and plants for the *Vancouver
Sun* and the *Vancouver Province*.

With the *National Post*, Conrad Black, clearly, is betting the newspaper business has a better future than Fallows suggests.

Another trend of significance in the context of news as business was
the emergence of a new style of journalistic culture on local television
news, a culture that was spawned by the market itself, a culture John
McManus dubbed "market-driven journalism." On advice from a small
cadre of "TV doctors," local stations discovered in the late 1960s that
there was serious money to be made in local news. Operating on the
premise that local news programs were not competing in a news market but rather in a public-attention market, these consultants argued the
endgame was to attract the largest possible audience at the lowest possible cost. The challenge, as John McManus defined it, was "to offer the
least expensive mix of content that protects the interests of the sponsors
and investors while garnering the largest audience advertisers will pay
to reach."[55]

University of California professor Daniel Hallin summarized the
inherent conflict succinctly: "Television news is both journalism and
a business, a key political institution as well as a seller of detergent
and breakfast cereal."[56] The difficulty, of course, is that the logic of

maximizing financial return often conflicts with the logic of serious news reporting.

Fred Siebert would have journalism contribute to the democratic process through public empowerment, an empowerment based on information. McManus, however, says the market logic that is the foundation of local television news suggests stories should advance, or at least minimize, the harm to the interests of advertisers and investors. Having conducted an extensive study of local news operations in four distinct U.S. television markets, McManus concluded: "When market logic and journalistic logic conflicted at the first stage of news production, market logic won most of the time."[57]

Even a casual viewer of local television newscasts on Canada's private networks can see that McManus's findings would have been consistent had Toronto, Vancouver, or Winnipeg been part of his study group. The approach may be different at the public broadcaster, but in the era of cutbacks there is increased pressure on the CBC to get out of the local television-news business entirely.

The economics of television favor breadth of appeal over depth; as a consequence, market-driven journalism will sacrifice enlightenment for audience assembly most of the time. As one news director told McManus, "There is no use in preaching to an empty church."[58]

Broadcast executives have decided television is inherently an action medium rather than an information medium. Therefore, television journalism disseminates the visually appealing in as entertaining a manner as possible, so much so that Bill Moyers felt obliged to resign from CBS to protest the encroachment of entertainment values into the news division, an encroachment Moyers claims was not only encouraged, but exalted. Says Moyers: "The line between entertainment and news was steadily blurred."[59]

While on fellowship at Harvard in 1995, I was able to experience the makeover of the Channel 7 newscast in Boston and concluded it was illustrative of market-driven journalism. The core thematic, to use University of Calgary professor Barry Cooper's terminology, is structured around a storyline that highlights deviance and then reports on how that deviance is overcome. Newscasts typically open with a spectacular local crime, fire, or accident. Pacing is important. Theme music conveys a sense of urgency; reports are short and snappy, and given an up-to-the-minute look through the use of satellite technology, ENG equipment. Anchors throw to reporters "live on location" even when the location is another corner of the newsroom. Pundits and panelists on political broadcasts are familiar with the style. On the old *Journal*—the CBC's flagship public-affairs program—technical wizardry created the illusion that participants were being beamed in via satellite from the dark side of the moon when, in fact, they might have been seated in chairs inches apart. To protect the illusion, guests are instructed to speak directly to camera and avoid eye contact with the person seated next to them.

The newscast is divided into local, national, and international news, but each segment is a variation on the theme. Whereas the national segment might once have been built around reporters in Washington or Ottawa, today's version features coverage of the O.J. Simpson trial, flooding along the California coast, or visuals from the latest tornado touchdown somewhere in the Midwest or the flooding in Manitoba. The international-news segment might include a terrorist attack, a plane crash, or the latest travails of the British royals.

Health-care snippets, Hollywood gossip, sports highlights, and seemingly endless weather reports with "happy talk" transitions round out the offering. A final critical component of local television news is the lead-in program. The "audience-flow theory" suggests a strong lead-in program can create an audience that can be held throughout the newscast. *Cheers* reruns are good. *Oprah Winfrey* may be even better.

In Toronto, the CTV affiliate CFTO has perfected the format, introduced a few wrinkles of its own, and enjoys a dominant position in the local market. For years, national and international news was covered by Tom Clark, who prepared a daily summary of short, snappy items to put the events of the day into some sort of context, with live inserts from *Sunday Edition* host Mike Duffy.

Defenders of local TV news, and by extension market-driven journalism, argue that it is the most democratic of news forms, that it is most responsive to a majority, or at least a plurality, of viewers. These defenders say they are not in the business of the journalistic equivalent of medicine, dispensing information that is good for people whether they want it or not. They further argue that local television news integrates communities, that precisely because it is interesting, it attracts the interest of those who would otherwise be uninformed.

However, former Shorenstein Center fellow Judith Lichtenberg counters that "it is disingenuous for the press to claim it simply gives people the information they want, when their desire for it is partly a function of press coverage."[60]

Market-driven journalism is highly susceptible to the manipulative practices of candidates for high elected office because of its dependency on inexpensive yet arresting visuals. Furthermore, because the media's appetite for news exceeds any candidate's ability to supply it, political coverage becomes an unrelenting search for the aberration, the unusual, the unexpected. Journalist Walter Lippmann was writing about the media's predisposition to make mountains out of molehills and molehills out of mountains well before television was invented and market pressures prevailed. However, Lippmann also stated: "You cannot govern society by episodes, incidents or interruptions."[61]

This search for the unusual or the untoward has led to declining standards of political coverage, according to Sabato, and the rise of a journalistic style known as "gotcha" journalism.

In the post-Watergate era, reporters are perceived as being far more interested in finding sleaze and achieving fame and fortune than in serving "as an honest broker of information between citizens and government."[62]

Titillation and trivialization take precedence over enlightenment. Gary Hart's relationships are front-page news; the trillion-dollar savings-and-loan scandal goes unreported for years, despite the best efforts of a congressman to get the media to pay attention. In the 1992 presidential campaign, details of Bill Clinton's trip to Moscow while a Rhodes scholar at Oxford received more coverage than did the economy.

Ironically, the same public that consumes tabloid journalism loses respect for the media outlets that convey it. How many times have you heard friends refer to a headline in the *National Enquirer*, only to add quickly that they never read such trash but simply happened to see the headline while in line at the checkout counter at their local grocery store?

Obviously not all political journalism is the equivalent of "junk food," as Fordham University's Ev Dennis so aptly put it. Specialty channels such as C-SPAN in the United States and C-PAC in Canada provide gavel-to-gavel coverage from the floor of Congress and the House of Commons. Every media outlet can cite award-winning journalistic enterprises worthy of the lofty ideals of the Progressive Movement. But as Kathleen Hall Jamieson's research suggests, the programs with the shortest sound bites, the programs most sensitive to the dictates of market-driven journalism, have the highest audiences. Researchers have concluded that the programs with the largest audience have the most impact in terms of political attitudes.

Former White House correspondent Ellen Hume argues that the emergence of market-driven journalism signals the end of an era. "It represents no less than the erosion of a central professional ethic that has been in place, with varying degrees of effectiveness, for more than 30 years." Hume goes on to say that "historians may well look back on the last three decades as the golden age of non-commercialized news."[63]

Hume's observation can be compared to the nostalgia of hockey fans who remember the old six-team National Hockey League. Yet the old six-team league was damn near indentured service; and I have met few veterans from the "Thomson School of Journalism" who weren't a lot happier once they hit dailies in Toronto, or Vancouver, or Montreal.

Technological advances bring the best news and analysis—from *The Economist* to the *Wall Street Journal*—into our homes with the click of a computer key. We can read the *Washington Post* on-line, surf through the sampling of newspapers from European capitals, and tap into electronic newsletters reporting on the latest developments in sub-Saharan Africa.

In the digital age, news consumers are no longer captives of local media and third-class mail. Because of technology, journalism's better days lie ahead. It is up to newsroom managers to make the Bay Street analysts believers in a business case for better news.

The overwhelming consensus of media scholars is that there is less substance in our political journalism today than was the case even two decades ago. But does media coverage of politics or public policy matter? The short answer is an emphatic yes.

6

Stalking the Leader

On November 20, 1995, M. Brian Mulroney, Canada's eighteenth prime minister, took the unprecedented step of suing the government he'd led for nine years for defamatory libel, seeking $50 million in damages.

Mulroney's legal action was a direct response to an equally unprecedented act. Weeks earlier, Canada's federal government had declared in writing to a foreign power that the former Progressive-Conservative party leader had engaged in a "criminal conspiracy" against his own people. The government communiqué to Swiss authorities stated Mulroney had received $5 million in illegal kickbacks in connection with the largest commercial passenger jet purchase in Canadian history.

A subsequent leak of this confidential letter to Swiss authorities, with its damning assertions of malfeasance on Mulroney's part, made global headlines out of rumors that had hung on like a low-grade fever in Canadian political circles since 1988. It was then that Air Canada—then a Crown corporation—purchased thirty-four A-320 passenger jets from the European consortium Airbus Industries for $1.8 billion to replace an aging fleet of Boeing 727s. The story first broke in the November 19 edition of the Toronto-based *Financial Post*. Investigative reporter Philip Mathias had obtained an English-language translation of the Canadian government's document, and the subsequent headline read: "Justice Seeks Evidence on Mulroney, Moores"—Moores being Frank Moores, a former premier of Newfoundland, a prominent Conservative, and the founding partner of Government Consultants International, a once-dominant Ottawa-based lobbying firm.

"Matchers" of the *Post* story were instantly relayed around the world. The headline in the November 20 edition of the *International Herald Tribune* was illustrative of the tenor and tone of the coverage, declaring: "Canada Suspects Mulroney Got Airbus Kickbacks." The *Toronto Star* was even more direct: "Mulroney Got $5 Million: Ottawa Says."

The original storyline of the "Airbus affair"—an allegation of collusion between shady lobbyists and unprincipled politicians—quickly gave way to a far more complex story that goes to the nexus of press, politics, public-opinion, and public policy in Western liberal democracies.

The Airbus affair is most certainly a story of political intrigue, both domestic and international, a story of big business and billion-dollar deals that net million-dollar commissions for individuals who appear to be operating at the edges, at best.

Stories of corruption and influence peddling are rampant in the airline industry, as Southam News correspondent Carolyn Abraham reported. Canada's de Havilland Aircraft reportedly paid six-figure bribes to Bahamian middlemen to save a $64-million deal with Bahamas Air. The Israelis allegedly bribed an unidentified South American republic with 10 percent kickbacks to secure a major military hardware deal. The problem is considered so widespread that the United States has made cleaning up the industry a priority of its foreign policy.

It is one of the ironies of the Airbus story that Mulroney's government eliminated the tax deductions for such bribes in 1991.

The Airbus saga also exposes the dark side of political reporting practices, the editorial excesses that occur when rumor is taken as fact, and gossip as evidence, and when partisan political considerations take precedence over our system of responsible government. Airbus revealed how investigative reporting, if not held to the highest journalistic standards, can constitute an unprecedented assault on an individual's rights. Airbus is illustrative of Postman's hypothesis described earlier, that in today's world of "news assembly," reporters can apply the professional conventions and rules of their craft and yet produce an editorial product that is the journalistic equivalent of Potemkin's village—artificial, surreal, and largely unconnected to the truth. The story is illustrative of esteemed *Washington Post* editor Ben Bradlee's "kerosene journalism"[1]—where today the best journalism is led by the nose by the worst journalism.

Airbus is the story of a former prime minister who came to the chilling conclusion that he was being stalked—literally and figuratively—by an elite squad of Mounties and certain media collaborators.

At the heart of the Airbus affair is Martin Brian Mulroney's complex relationship with the Canadian people and their interlocutors of the fourth estate. The media put the Airbus affair squarely on Canada's political agenda. And as Northwestern University professor Robert Entman notes, a negative news slant begets negative public opinion.

News accounts of Mulroney's travails invariably refer to him as one of the most unpopular prime ministers in Canadian history. The political party he led for ten years was reduced to rubble in the 1993 federal election. The story of how this came to pass is interesting. Mulroney, after all, won one of the largest majorities in Canadian electoral history. He succeeded in forming back-to-back majority governments—a political achievement that eluded his constitutional nemesis, Pierre Elliott Trudeau. Indeed, Mulroney was the first Conservative prime minister since Sir John A. Macdonald to win back-to-back majorities—a century later.

Unpopular public policies—from the Goods and Services Tax, to constitutional reform initiatives, to deficit reduction—contributed to Mulroney's unpopularity, but the highly personalized nature of the attacks suggest a deeper, more visceral explanation.

As Mulroney's former press secretary and director of communications, I must admit that there is a certain degree of self-interest involved in finding a rational explanation for this set of events. As a long-time political reporter who made the transition from hack to flack and still fosters a lingering interest in returning to journalism, I found part of the answer in a book written by a student of Japanese culture, former *Time* correspondent Frank Gibney. In his 1960 work *The Operators*, Gibney suggests that an interesting dramatic danger results from modern society's emphasis on being "smooth"—an expert role player, shaman, diplomat, tactician. "A loss of public confidence sometimes occurs in which a leader, by his very smoothness, comes to be defined as a 'smart operator' or a 'fast worker'."[2] Mulroney's public persona certainly fits Gibney's profile: an individual who "knows how to play the game," is skilled at manipulating (supporters would say managing) people, never makes a false move, and never shows his full hand, even in showdowns. Gibney says public respect for this prowess is mixed with mistrust. "People somehow think he is slick, oily, too smart for his own good. A vicious cycle sets in which his very skill works against him and once loss of confidence begins, he may be unable to reassure people of his genuineness."[3]

Mulroney's friends and acquaintances, his cabinet colleagues and caucus members, have long bemoaned the fact that the former prime minister's public image did not square with the private person. What they, and perhaps he, overlook is the fact that his cultivation of a public image as one of life's "winners" was integral to his electoral success.

In his 1964 work, *Symbolic Leaders: Public Dramas and Public Men*, Orrin E. Klapp builds on Gibney's premise by examining the phenomenon of the symbolic leader, an individual who functions primarily through meaning or image. Celebrity is a component part of the symbolic leader, who takes his or her cues from the audience itself. Klapp likens this process to tennis and the choreography of volley and return; the symbolic leader cannot project a totally different image from the one he or she has been developing in concert with the audience. A leader's image "may be worse than the one he thinks he is entitled to; he feels resentment and puzzlement at the unkindness of critics, the fickleness of public-opinion and the disloyalty of fair weather friends."[4] The symbolic leader can be aware of the fact that he or she has a bad image, "but usually does not know exactly what is wrong with it, how he [or she] got it, or what to do about it. Image problems make it easier for people to make snide remarks about a leader and for the rest of us to listen."[5] Klapp says, "The more convincing his argument, the nobler the deed, the more ingratiating the manner, the more clever seemed the scoundrel underneath. So the logic of suspicion goes."[6]

Gibney's and Klapp's observations could be direct quotes from conversations I have had with Mulroney over the years and seem to have particular application in the Airbus context. Even after the Chrétien government sued for peace, there was a body of public opinion that believed Mulroney had outsmarted the Mounties.

In Mulroney's case, the downward spiral may have begun hours after an event that had the potential to be the crowning achievement of his political career. On June 10, 1990, in the refurbished railway station that served as the government conference center, Mulroney emerged from a week-long negotiation session with his fellow first ministers with an amended constitutional package that had the potential to end thirty years of wrangling and return Quebec—at least symbolically—to the constitutional fold. The negotiations, afforded maximum coverage by Canada's television networks, tested Mulroney's celebrated skills as a negotiator and political deal-maker. Had the deal stood, Mulroney would have succeeded where Trudeau had failed. On the dominant Canadian news "frame" of our time—national unity—Mulroney would have demonstrably left the nation more unified than it was when he assumed office in September 1984. But the next day, Mulroney, was acting as his own spin doctor in a telephone conversation with William Thorsell. Thorsell mentioned the *Globe* was about to launch a new edition and pressed Mulroney for an "exclusive" interview for the *Globe*'s Ottawa bureau. Mulroney reluctantly agreed because the revered Meech Lake pact still had to be ratified by Parliament and the provincial legislatures.

The *Globe* dispatched its "A" Team, columnist Jeffrey Simpson, bureau chief Graham Fraser, and constitution-beat writer Susan Delacourt. Fraser and Delacourt tended to be on opposite sides of the Meech equation, but the *Globe* benefited from their ongoing ability to bring their different perspectives to the paper's news coverage. The interview, Mulroney felt, went well. But when Monday's edition of the *Globe* hit the street, the proverbial fecal material hit the spinning blades. In the course of the interview, Mulroney spoke of his approach to the negotiations, referred to a deadline for ratification set out in the constitution, and, saying he simply worked back from the deadline date, used the term "roll the dice" in a colloquial manner to explain his strategy. Revealed in the *Globe*'s reporting, the strategy smacked of pressure tactics and manipulation, at least in the eyes of some observers. Newfoundland premier Clyde Wells, looking for a way to walk away from the deal without wearing responsibility for the failure, pounced. The rest, as they say, is history. "When charm is interpreted as 'guile', an actor is damned if he does and damned if he doesn't," states Gibney.[7] The collapse of the Meech Lake Accord, coinciding as it did with the worst recession since the Great Depression, set Mulroney's political stock into free fall.

Ironically, while Gibney's work suggests Mulroney's fall from political grace may have been preordained, it also reveals a comeback strategy. Gibney states that there is an ongoing basic dramatic advantage for anyone cast in the role of giant-killer, and that a *personal* encounter, however small, is better than an abstract policy issue, however large. The Airbus affair created exactly that circumstance for Mulroney, and the former prime minister knew how to work the opportunity to its best advantage.

Mulroney launched his prime-ministerial campaign as the proverbial outsider, pitted initially against then leader Joe Clark and the establishment of the Progressive-Conservative party. Having dethroned Clark, Mulroney then positioned himself as the challenger to the entrenched power of the Liberal party of Canada. His speeches to French-speaking audiences were punctuated with references to "la grosse machine libérale"—the Big Liberal Machine. Not coincidentally, his personal appeal with the public was at its highest level when he was challenging these powerful kinds of interests.

The Airbus affair recast Mulroney's image. While even his most ardent supporters do not anticipate a return in public favor to the heady heights of 1984, there is no denying the fact that the April 1996 court appearance earned Mulroney his most positive press since he left office.

Journalism as an institution embodies the values of the Progressive Movement of the early twentieth century, values shaped by the muckraking journalists of that era. Two of these "enduring values"—altruistic democracy and responsible capitalism—directly apply in Mulroney's case. The Canadian media questioned whether Mulroney's government followed a course of action based on the public interest and the tradition of public service. Further, they questioned whether Mulroney's friends and supporters were exploiting the system on his behalf.

The prevailing journalistic winds through the later years of the Mulroney government swirled around accusations of greed, corruption, and abuse of power. The result was a predisposition to believe the worst about anyone closely associated with the former prime minister—

perfect conditions for the "scandal" the headline writers would dub the Airbus affair.

Mulroney's Call

On November 2, 1995, Mulroney received a telephone call from long-time friend and adviser Fred Doucet, who informed him that German-Canadian businessman Karl-Heinz Schreiber was trying to reach him on an important matter. Mulroney, in Toronto on business at the time, placed an initial call from his room at the Royal York to a number in Switzerland, but there was no answer. Returning to his Montreal home, Mulroney decided to place another call to Schreiber before sitting down with his family for dinner. With the difference in time zones, any further efforts would likely have to wait until the next day.

Schreiber had been introduced to Mulroney some fifteen years earlier. During Mulroney's time in office, Schreiber had pushed the Canadian government to support the establishment of a heavy-armored-vehicle manufacturing facility on Cape Breton Island in Nova Scotia, an area of high and chronic unemployment. The project, advanced by German arms manufacturer Thyssen AG, was dependent on government funding through existing regional-development programs. However, because of the estimated $100 million cost to Canadian taxpayers, Mulroney and his cabinet decided not to proceed.

Schreiber kept in casual contact with Mulroney despite the Thyssen ruling. On the night of November 2, the German-Canadian industrialist answered Mulroney's predinner call and told Mulroney that, as the holder of a particular Swiss bank account, he'd been served a document by Swiss authorities which included separate documentation prepared by the Government of Canada. The text was in German, and Schreiber informed Mulroney: "There are things in here that involve you." In reconstructing the conversation, Mulroney said he responded: "What are you talking about?" Schreiber proceeded to translate the document into English. As Mulroney subsequently testified in a Montreal courtroom, "With each passing adjective, my horror and disbelief grew. I was thunderstruck and said, 'What in the name of God are you talking about?'"[8]

The document in question was prepared at the behest of the Royal Canadian Mounted Police by the federal Justice department and forwarded to Swiss authorities. The Mounties were asking the Swiss to freeze certain accounts and make their contents available to police investigation. The letter cited three specific procurement, or development-grant-related, issues: the Air Canada purchase of Airbus planes, the Canadian Coast Guard's purchase of German-made helicopters, and the proposed Thyssen heavy-armored-vehicle plant in Cape Breton.

A translated version of the letter states unequivocally: "This investigation is of serious concern to the Government of Canada, as it involves criminal activity on the part of a former prime minister."[9] The translated letter further states: "The above three cases demonstrate an ongoing scheme by Mr. Mulroney, Mr. Moores and Mr. Schreiber to defraud the Canadian government of millions of dollars of public funds from the time Mulroney took office in September of 1984 until he resigned in June of 1993."[10]

The Mounties were stating, as a matter of fact, that the three men were engaged in a kickback scheme. The police stated that former premier Frank Moores and Schreiber had opened a special Swiss account for Mulroney under the code name "Devon" and that $5 million had been deposited there as Mulroney's share. Note the lack of any qualifier in the language employed by the Justice department on behalf of the federal law-enforcement agency. The word "alleged" does not appear anywhere in the text.

Mulroney's immediate priority on hearing Schreiber's news was to secure an English translation of the RCMP letter. Schreiber agreed to have his legal advisers forward a draft. Mulroney then retained Roger Tassé, a distinguished Ottawa lawyer and former deputy solicitor general and deputy attorney general for Canada. Tassé was instructed to contact the Canadian government and offer full cooperation, including access to all of Mulroney's bank accounts and income tax returns in exchange for "a new request that is more respectful of basic rules of fairness and decency."[11]

Senior Justice department officials wrote to Tassé, telling him not to worry, Mulroney's name would be held "in the strictest confidence." Mulroney's lawyer subsequently determined that the letter went to at least thirty people, including every member of the board of directors of the Swiss bank, and a number of Canadian diplomats.

In all conversations with Tassé, Canadian officials insisted that they were only dealing with allegations and that the information provided the Swiss in the Canadian request had to be read in that context. However, they steadfastly refused to give Mulroney a copy of the letter sent to the Swiss. Mulroney's representative repeatedly argued that the language used in the letter suggested a conclusive statement of fact, not an allegation.

The former prime minister was well aware of the damage to his reputation that would result from the letter being made public. By November 10, 1995, there were strong indications the letter was indeed being leaked to a number of media organizations.

Harvey Yarosky, described as the best criminal lawyer in Quebec, had also been retained by Mulroney. Yarosky told *Presumed Guilty* author William Kaplan, "Our fear was not what was going to happen with the investigation. We knew that was a canard. Our fear was on the publicity and what would happen when the letter became public, as we knew it would."[12]

The weekly public-affairs program *Zen Vor Zen*, carried on Switzerland's DRS Network, first reported the Canadian government had asked the Swiss for legal assistance and stated the probes of the accounts were designed to uncover payments to Canadian politicians. The television story, aired November 11, triggered an Agence France Presse wire story, carried in Montreal's *La Presse*. By this time Mulroney knew it was important to expand his circle of advisers to include a media-relations expert. Luc Lavoie, his trusted former deputy chief of staff in the PMO, was his choice.

The Strategist

Lavoie, now a senior executive with National Public Relations, first became aware a big story was brewing on November 11, 1995, when he received a call from the former prime minister's law partner, Yves Fortier. Fortier, who served as Canada's ambassador to the United Nations, was beginning to assemble a legal team and asked Lavoie to stand by.

The November 12 editions of *La Presse* featured a page-one story from Agence France Presse claiming an unidentified Canadian politician had received kickbacks as a result of Air Canada's purchase of the A-320 aircraft from Airbus. The next day, Lavoie received a call from Mulroney, asking his former deputy chief of staff to come to Montreal. Mulroney, says Lavoie, "had an air of anguish" about him. By then the Canadian Press had refiled the AFP story, and as Lavoie recalls, "it was on page one everywhere."[13] On arrival, Mulroney asked Lavoie if he had seen the piece in *La Presse* and Mulroney confirmed he was the politician they were talking about.

Lavoie says he asked Mulroney only once if there was any substance to the AFP report, and Mulroney assured him that the charges were completely without foundation. "I chose to believe him," Lavoie would say later. "I never spoke to him about it again."[14] Lavoie's trust and confidence in Mulroney was critical, especially in light of his emergence as spokesperson on the file. As Lavoie would later say, "We were protected by the truth."[15] Luc Beauregard, Lavoie's boss at National, shared his confidence and encouraged Lavoie to "go for it." Lavoie's new role would put him in direct conflict with the federal Liberals. Given the fact that Her Majesty is by far the largest procurer of public-relations services in the Ottawa area, National's commitment took some courage.

Mulroney sent Lavoie to meet former judge Fred Kaufman for a detailed briefing on the legal aspects of the case. Lavoie, in turn, immediately began working on a media-strategy paper, a paper he would present for Mulroney's consideration on November 15.

By November 14, following conversations with RCMP Staff Sergeant Fraser Fiegenwald, the Mulroney team was convinced it was inevitable the former prime minister's name would be leaked. On November 15, Mulroney received a fax from a journalist at *Der Spiegel*, the German newsmagazine. The fax included explicit information about the contents of Canada's letter to the Swiss, including specifics related to the Devon account. Lavoie called the German reporter directly in an attempt to determine whether the German journalist actually had a copy of the RCMP letter. Because of time-zone differences, Lavoie asked for a day to respond to the story. Within hours, Stevie Cameron called his Ottawa office to ask if he was working on the case. "That made it pretty clear that there was a pipeline,"[16] Lavoie says. Later, Mulroney received a fax from *Maclean's*. Lavoie says the *Maclean's* and *Der Spiegel* faxes were essentially the same. "It looked as if they had been written together."[17]

The faxes from *Der Spiegel* and *Maclean's* suggested these news-magazines were either in possession of copies of the document or were aware of its contents in all of its detail. The *Maclean's* fax is particularly revealing: "We have information that your name is on a request sent to Swiss authorities on October 3. We also know that Mr. Roger Tassé is representing you in this matter. And that he met with officials of the Department of Justice and the RCMP to ask for a copy of the document sent to the Swiss government. As you are also aware, there is a discussion that the account number 34117, code name Devon, was set up for you by Mr. Moores at the Swiss bank. The significance of the code name appears to be that your first house in Westmount was on Devon, near Upper Belmont. Is this your account, or an account which is available to you or anyone connected to you?" The fax concluded: "Our deadline for preparation of this article is Friday, November 17. Thank you very much for your attention to this matter. Please comment."[18]

The *Maclean's* fax confirmed to Mulroney that Canadian authorities were indeed leaking information about the letter to the Swiss and other developments in the case directly to reporters, and that consequently the story could break any hour.

The next day, Friday, November 17, Staff Sergeant Fiegenwald, the lead investigator for the RCMP, formally advised Mulroney's lawyers: "I believe that the request has adequately communicated our position to the Swiss. And there is no misunderstanding and therefore no basis for amending the request."[19] Fiegenwald, after stonewalling for more than a year, would later trigger the collapse of the federal government's legal defense when he admitted he had, in fact, discussed the government's letter to the Swiss with a Canadian journalist.

Mulroney's lawyers joined Lavoie, the former prime minister, and his wife for a meeting at Mulroney's Westmount home. "Up to then, the strategy had been to try and get the letter changed," Lavoie said, refer-ring to attempts by Roger Tassé to get Canada to at least insert the words "alleged" into the official communiqué to Swiss authorities.[20]

With the receipt of the fax from *Der Spiegel*, Lavoie recommended a shift in strategy. The former television correspondent used the example of an oil fire to illustrate his point. To put out an oil fire, you need an explosion—nitroglycerine—to use Lavoie's term. Lavoie said Mulroney needed the equivalent of a big bang. "We had to take the lead. We had to go heavy and very, very fast,"[21] Lavoie says. The lawyers, not surprisingly, were cautious about Lavoie's recommended approach. But Mulroney was immediately in favor of the approach.

After receiving the *Maclean's* fax, Mulroney and his advisers began to prepare their counteroffensive. The expectation was that either *Der Spiegel* or *Maclean's* would break the story. Both were on the same news cycle—a Sunday-evening news release trumpeting the stories that would be on newsstands Monday.

The Scoop

As it turned out, Mulroney didn't have to wait through the weekend for the story to break. The *Financial Post* had the scoop in its Saturday edition. Philip Mathias's balanced report included a strongly worded denial by a Mulroney adviser of any wrongdoing on the part of the former prime minister. Mulroney knew he had to "get ahead of the story." His legal team convened a full news conference at a Montreal hotel that Saturday afternoon, inspired by Mark Twain's observation that "a lie can travel half-way around the world while the truth is putting on its shoes."[22]

There was no shortage of media speculation about who had actually leaked the letter. *Globe and Mail* columnist Jeffrey Simpson said the consensus in official Ottawa, including the parliamentary press gallery, was that Mulroney's friends had leaked the letter to Mathias; after all, what are friends for? Mulroney insists the first he heard of the *Post*'s story was when Senator Marjory LeBreton telephoned him shortly before 11:00 p.m. on the Friday before to say she had been contacted by CTV Ottawa bureau chief Craig Oliver and asked for a comment on the *Post* scoop. Oliver knew the *Post* piece would include a specific reference to Mulroney and the payment of $5 million. Oliver was also trying to contact Lavoie. Mulroney, following the call from LeBreton, instructed Lavoie to contact Oliver.

Lavoie, Mulroney said, then dispatched an associate from his firm's Toronto office to the King Street headquarters of the *Post* to pick up a paper as soon as the presses started to roll. A faxed version of the *Post* story was sent to Mulroney's Westmount home at approximately 2:00 a.m.

Mulroney knew from experience the imperative of answering any serious charge in the first available news cycle. "If this had happened on a working day, we would not have had a news conference," Mulroney said in a later interview. "We would have just gone down to the courthouse and filed our action. But we couldn't let the weekend go by. If we had, the government's version would have stood up through the entire weekend."[23]

As a former parliamentary press gallery reporter and senior adviser to the prime minister, Lavoie is an experienced Ottawa hand, wily in the ways of his former press colleagues and singularly adept at managing the complex relationships that are Quebec politics. Yet even Lavoie was taken aback at the force of the media feeding frenzy around Airbus.

In the first days after Mulroney's legal team held their Saturday news conference to announce Luc's "big bang"—a $50-million lawsuit against the government—Lavoie conducted seventy detailed interviews with journalists.

As spokesperson, Lavoie kept hitting three key messages:
1. Mr. Mulroney never received any payment or kickback of any kind.
2. Mr. Mulroney does not have, and never did have, a bank account in Switzerland.
3. Mr. Mulroney is entitled to the presumption of innocence.

The premium of a timely response is particularly acute in the age of computer-assisted reporting. Mulroney's lawyers used the news conference to announce their intention to launch a $50-million libel suit against the Canadian government and the RCMP. In a written statement released to reporters, Mulroney declared: "The false and reckless allegations made by the Department of Justice have the effect not only of damaging my reputation and hurting my family, but also of besmirching and distorting the good name of Canada."[24]

Boston Globe correspondent Colin Nickerson noted Mulroney appeared "to be using the judicial system in an aggressive public-relations campaign to clear his name."[25] The strategy is known as "litigation public relations." Purists argue attempts to influence public opinion *before* a trial jeopardize the notion of fairness that is a cornerstone of our legal system. Through his political career, Mulroney had come to appreciate that a court of law and the court of public opinion, while not one and the same, have to be managed with equal skill. Mulroney's preemptive strike was roundly criticized by certain media commentators. *Winnipeg Free Press* editorial writer John Dafoe wrote: "Now, in one grand, arrogant gesture, Brian Mulroney has reminded Canadians of why he deserves to be remembered as one of Canada's most disliked and least trusted prime ministers."[26] Dafoe denounced Mulroney's action as "an unexpected attack on the independence of the RCMP and the Canadian people. This pathetic attempt to intimidate the federal government and the RCMP serves only to convince Canadians that, at best, Mr. Mulroney believes the RCMP should not treat him like any other suspect, or at worst, he is a man with a lot to hide."[27] Dafoe's flawed reasoning ignores the core truth that under Canadian law, everyone—including former prime ministers—is entitled to the presumption of innocence. The editorial is illustrative of how journalism's self-declared mission to "afflict the comfortable and comfort the afflicted" can lead the pack to set aside the most fundamental principles of democracy if the quarry is someone they collectively dislike.

There was some discussion among Canadian journalists about whether Mulroney would have been able to launch his suit had he been a citizen of the United States. Jurisprudence in the United States is unequivocal. In cases as varied as *Sullivan v. The New York Times*, *David Price v. Viking Penguin Inc.* and *Larry Buendorf v. National Public Radio*, U.S. courts have consistently ruled in favor of free speech. In the *Sullivan* case, the Supreme Court concluded "that even vilifying falsehoods relating to official conduct are protected unless made with actual malice or reckless disregard for the facts."[28] An appellate court ruling in the *Buendorf* case is instructive: "Plainly, many deserving plaintiffs, including some intentionally subjected to injury, will be unable to surmount the barrier of the *New York Times* test. This court wholeheartedly echoes the Supreme Court's conclusion that the First Amendment requires that we protect some falsehood in order to protect speech that matters."[29]

Canada's constitution does not include a First Amendment, although the Charter of Rights and Freedoms does enshrine "freedom of thought, belief, opinion, and expression, including freedom of the press and other media of communication." Canadian jurisprudence does not include a *Sullivan*-style precedent; however, the Crown and its agencies, including the police, do enjoy a qualified privilege. Mulroney's case, if it had gone to court, would have evolved around the issue of whether the federal government showed "reckless disregard" for his rights. As Toronto media lawyer Stuart Robertson said of the RCMP, "Any privilege that they had in doing their jobs and carrying out their inquiry they could lose if they acted with malice. But so long as they are just carrying out their jobs, they are protected."[30]

The controversy swirling around Mulroney and the Mounties dominated the Canadian news agenda through late November and early December 1995. A report prepared for Mulroney by Doris Juergens, director of research at National Public Relations, and obtained by the *Globe and Mail* from Quebec Supreme Court records, underscores the fact.

From November 1995 to June 1996, a total of 2,352 reports on the Airbus affair were carried by various media outlets. The NPR analysis concluded that only 1 percent of these stories could be considered favorable to Mulroney. Fully two-thirds—67 percent—were unfavorable and another 32 percent were described as neutral. The study includes major dailies, magazines, and TV and radio stations in both English and French. The survey tracked only those stories that included a specific mention of Mulroney. Selected foreign-print media and news wires were also included.

Even more troubling, from Mulroney's perspective, was the fact that news accounts contained what Juergens described as 2,481 "negative associations" for the former prime minister. The number of reports that associated Mulroney with kickbacks, commissions, or illegal or improper payments totaled 1,559. The Justice department, specifically Justice's letter to the Swiss, was extensively quoted in the press, both domestic and international, and is the principal source of negative associations. Justice, the RCMP, and the Canadian government were included in 79 percent of the news reports.

Significantly, the study revealed that proportionately fewer editorials and columns were negative compared with news reports. These opinion pieces tended to be more critical of the RCMP and the Justice department's conduct of the affair. The study concludes that news of the Justice department's letter made headlines around the world—particularly in the first week—and undoubtedly reached a significant audience of world opinion leaders.

Some months later, in preparation for the trial itself, the federal government hired York University political scientist Frederick J. Fletcher to rebut Juergens's study. Fletcher described the methodology as "uncertain" and insisted two of the words Juergens categorized as negative—"suspect" and "commission"—did not "have an obvious negative connotation."[31]

The claim that the word "suspect," used as either noun or adjective, does not have an obvious negative connotation is itself suspect.

The Feeding Frenzy

Mathias's "scoop" unleashed what author Larry Sabato dubbed the "feeding frenzy" phase of the saga. A professor at the University of Virginia, Sabato likens a media feeding frenzy to an attack by sharks. Feeding frenzies are fed by "wiggle disclosures"—the daily revelations of competing media organizations that give the story "legs." In the Airbus affair, the wiggle-disclosure phase lasted weeks. Investigative reporters traveled to Europe to track down mystery "sources" who may or may not have provided the Mounties with accusations against Mulroney. The CBC's *the fifth estate* aired an interview with Giorgio Pelossi, a former business associate of Schreiber's, who said he was with Frank Moores when the former Newfoundland premier opened two Swiss accounts. Pelossi said he was told one of the accounts was for Mulroney.

On November 28, Lavoie was visited by a crew from *the fifth estate*, including two of the principals involved in the program on Frank Moores, which aired in March 1995, Trish Wood and Harvey Cashore. "They said they had something very meaningful that would be on the show that night,"[32] Lavoie said. There was some discussion of whether there was any value in meeting *the fifth estate* crew; certain of Mulroney's legal advisers were opposed to any interview. Jacques Jeansonne, another member of Mulroney's legal team, supported Lavoie's argument that it is always better to tell your side of the story. "It's PR 101,"[33] Lavoie said.

Prior to the interview, the media strategist watched the tape of an earlier *the fifth estate* report four or five times and noticed the crew was partial to practicing some old tricks of the television trade, such as flashing something the interviewee has never seen before in his or her face while the camera is running. Lavoie ushered the crew into his office and told them he would answer their questions on one condition: they were not to flash anything in his face. "My instinct was good," Lavoie said later. "When I put my condition to them, they asked to go outside and talk."[34]

When Woods and Cashore returned, they agreed to show Lavoie what they had in exchange for a commitment he would do an on-camera interview. Lavoie says *the fifth estate* interviewed him "for an hour and a half for what turned out to be a minute and ten seconds of airtime."[35]

The reporters showed Lavoie a business card with the handwritten initials "B.M." on it, as well as the number of a bank account. Lavoie professed Mulroney's innocence, and, as the camera zoomed in for a close-up, Woods asked him how he knew this to be true. "Thank God I know television," Lavoie said. "When they zoomed in for the close-up, my eyes did not blink at all. I just said, 'Mr. Mulroney told me.' I had a look of enormous determination and credibility."[36] Lavoie believes that, in a strange way, the interview was a turning point of sorts. The surprise or ambush techniques pioneered by Mike Wallace and his colleagues at *60 Minutes* are a standard in current-affairs program interviews. These techniques can make even the innocent appear uncomfortable or evasive if they are less than TV-savvy in their response. Lavoie's background as a television reporter served him and his client well. Subsequent requests to *the fifth estate*'s executive producer, David Studer, for an interview to discuss Lavoie's account were declined.

From Mulroney's perspective, the most important wiggle disclosure occurred December 16, when the *Toronto Sun's* Bob Fife revealed that the infamous "Devon" account had indeed been set up by Frank Moores, and the fact that the account had never held more than $500—a far cry from the $5 million the Mounties claimed. Fife later revealed the initials B.M. on the Devon account stood for "Beth Moores"—Frank's wife—and not for "Brian Mulroney," as the Mounties claimed. Mrs. Moores subsequently confirmed that she had signing authority on the account.

Days earlier, the *Toronto Star* uncovered information that suggested the U.S. State Department, the U.S. economic intelligence committee, and the Boeing Aircraft Company had actively been claiming high-level kickbacks had occurred on the Airbus deal as far back as 1988. Former U.S. ambassador Tom Niles made direct representations to that effect to then Finance minister Michael Wilson and Mulroney's chief of staff Derek Burney. Boeing executives were particularly vocal, according to former Transport minister John Crosbie, who was the minister responsible for Air Canada at the time.

FBI liaison officers at the U.S. embassy in Ottawa admitted to reporters that they had been feeding information to the Mounties regarding the Air Canada purchase and expressed dismay when the RCMP investigation didn't seem to be going anywhere. One FBI source told the *Toronto Star*, however, that he was "flabbergasted when Mulroney's name came up. Back in 1988, the reports Mulroney was getting [on the investigation] from the RCMP certainly named Frank Moores as being involved, but it was another Canadian politician who kept cropping up."[37] Boeing's chief of security, a former FBI agent, also pushed the RCMP to investigate the kickback rumors.

Despite the repeated interventions of Ambassador Niles, the direct involvement of the FBI liaison officer in Ottawa, and the reported intervention of former secretary of state and White House chief of staff Jim Baker, there is no evidence the issue surfaced with the White House press office.

Contacted at his Alexandria, Virginia, home, Marlin Fitzwater, spokesperson for presidents Ronald Reagan and George Bush, said he had "absolutely no recollection" of any mention of the Boeing/Airbus controversy at the White House. Fitzwater, busy building a new home on the Maryland shore of Chesapeake Bay at the time, confirmed he had been contacted by a Canadian reporter in January 1996 about the Airbus story, but Fitzwater told the reporter, as he told me, he had no recollection of the issue ever being raised with him.[38]

As each "wiggle disclosure" would break in the Canadian media, Mulroney would work the phones, sharing his recollections with advisers and confidants. Mulroney confirmed that Niles did in fact approach his chief of staff with the American allegations. The timing was particularly sensitive in the context of Canada–U.S. relations, since negotiations for the Canada–U.S. free-trade agreement had just been completed and Mulroney was fighting a general election that had settled on the free-trade agreement as the defining issue. "Derek [Burney] told Niles: 'If you have any evidence, bring it right in,'" Mulroney revealed. "Nothing was ever produced by the U.S. side."[39]

Mulroney also confirmed that John Crosbie had asked the Mounties to conduct an investigation into the Air Canada purchase because of rumors swirling around Ottawa. An RCMP superintendent subsequently confirmed that the 1989 investigation "didn't develop into anything substantial at all."[40]

Lavoie says "third-party endorsations" were an integral part of the media strategy at this stage of the investigation. Journalists were looking to Mulroney's friends and former associates in cabinet for signs of support or distancing. Quebec premier Lucien Bouchard was particularly helpful, in Lavoie's view. Though relations between the two were severely strained as a result of the collapsed Meech Lake constitutional initiative, Bouchard and Mulroney have a deep friendship that goes back to university days. "Even English journalists who hate him [Bouchard] know him to be a man of integrity," Lavoie said. Former ministers such as John Crosbie and Pat Carney were quick to rally to Mulroney's defense. Others, says Lavoie, "were cowards."[41]

Once Mathias and Fife broke the stories about the Devon bank account, Lavoie says the story began to "swing around very dramatically." The RCMP began to exert pressure with a series of leaks on issues unrelated to Airbus, such as a dispute over concessions at Pearson Airport involving the Bitove Corporation.

Through the early months of the Airbus affair Lavoie believes the federal government was basically operating without a media strategy. But even when the federal response began to show signs of some organization, Lavoie says the Mulroney team enjoyed certain advantages.

First, Lavoie says, the federal side was "a political animal," embracing the Privy Council Office, the Justice department, the Prime Minister's Office, the solicitor general's department, and the RCMP. "In our case, you had a tightly knit group with a highly cooperative client who was deeply demoralized and deeply hurt by what had happened to him," Lavoie says. "We could make a decision literally in five minutes."[42]

The second advantage was the extensive media monitoring system that NPR put in place, a system that was so efficient, so tight, that Mulroney's team was always in a position to know what was being said about the case and, therefore, always in a position to respond. Lavoie says the system "was very costly to the client, as Canadians have since seen." He is referring, of course, to Judge Alan Gold's decision to order Ottawa to cover Mulroney's public-relations expenses, costs that totaled nearly $600,000. (Lavoie and NPR would subsequently be subjected to intense media scrutiny over their bills to Lucien Bouchard's Parti Québécois government for a joint Quebec–Newfoundland announcement of a major hydroelectric project at Churchill Falls.)

Lavoie, who was working up to twenty hours a day at that point, was able to use material gathered through this monitoring process as briefing material with other journalists.

The *Globe and Mail* Sidebar

In early December the "wiggle disclosures" led reporters to an unexpected storyline, triggered by off-the-record conversations between a minister in the Liberal government and two veteran political reporters.

Justice minister Allan Rock, whose department had drafted the letter to the Swiss, insisted he had no prior knowledge of the RCMP investigation into Mulroney, that the very first time he had heard of the investigation was when he was contacted at his Toronto home on November 4 by Mulroney's lawyer Roger Tassé. Some time later, Rock said he had, in fact, contacted the RCMP about rumors of Tory wrongdoing shortly after taking office in November 1993. Rock said he had passed on rumors of certain Tories with Swiss bank accounts, but insisted he didn't urge any particular course of action on the Mounties. Rock also said the rumors he passed on weren't about the Airbus purchase. What set the parliamentary press gallery buzzing was Rock's revelation that his sources for these rumors were two reporters—subsequently identified as the *Globe and Mail*'s Susan Delacourt and *Maclean's* writer Mary Janigan. Rock's revelation triggered reports of cooperation, if not collaboration, between the RCMP and key media figures.

In a story on the front page of the December 11, 1995, edition of the *Globe and Mail*, Paul Koring reported that Allan Rock had alerted the RCMP to allegations about Progressive Conservatives and Swiss bank accounts within days of being elected to Parliament in November 1993. "At least some of Mr. Rock's information was apparently gleaned from conversations with journalists," Koring wrote.[43]

Delacourt says the swirl of controversy she weathered during the Airbus affair caused her to question the caliber of political reporting in the nation's capital, where she had worked as a member of the *Globe*'s Ottawa bureau for years. "It also taught me that the world is gray," Delacourt says.[44]

"What I was shocked to find was the quality of the journalism," Delacourt said over lunch, her disapproval underscored by every gesture. "Bob Fife [of the *Toronto Sun*] wrote every one of his stories without ever speaking to me."[45] Fife vehemently denies her assertion. Delacourt recalled a telephone conversation with a fact-checker from *Saturday Night* magazine, whose "facts" were so wrong, "so completely off the wall," she was utterly taken aback.

Colleague Paul Koring's decision to treat Delacourt as a "source" rather than a colleague also caught her by surprise.

A political science graduate, Delacourt says her approach to political reporting is less adversarial than that of other political reporters. "I see myself as part of the institution," she says. "I'm not here to knock it down." Delacourt cultivates her sources, convinced "you can't understand the politician if you don't understand the person."[46] Her editor-in-chief, William Thorsell, is a target of newsroom sniping because of his relationship with Mulroney. Delacourt's view is that "nobody serious or sensible has a problem with the fact he is friends with Brian Mulroney."[47]

Delacourt's account of the conversation with Rock begins with an acknowledgment that she is unclear as to how the conversation regarding corruption and the Tories got started. But the *Globe* writer has a very clear recollection that it was Rock who asked if he could seek Delacourt's advice on a sensitive issue. Rock then told Delacourt another journalist had told him that Mulroney had spirited money out of the country. Delacourt told Rock she had heard Stevie Cameron was working on a book about corruption in the Mulroney years.

Rock told Delacourt that, as Canada's attorney general, he felt he had to do something with the information he'd received, but insisted neither he nor Jean Chrétien was interested in running some "scorched earth" campaign against Mulroney.

In fact, the information Rock was referring to was given him by another journalist, reportedly Mary Janigan. Janigan, a personal friend of long standing, is declining all comment on the Airbus affair on advice from legal counsel.

Delacourt says some six months after their conversation she asked Rock what he had done with the information. Rock told her he had passed it on to Deputy Prime Minister and Solicitor General Herb Gray. The *Globe* reporter would say later of Rock, "He is a boy scout, a complete boy scout."[48] But the night of the conversation, Delacourt says she remembers going home and thinking, "Holy fuck," but not giving it any more thought.

Some two years later, the *Globe* national editor Sylvia Stead was in Ottawa. Delacourt "did the feminist thing" by organizing a dinner so that Stead could meet leading figures in the Chrétien government. Rock and his wife, Debbie, were invited. When, a few days before the dinner party, Delacourt heard a newsflash about Mulroney and allegations of corruption, she assumed the story was related to her conversation with Rock. Delacourt called Rock at his home, but says she got Debbie on the phone and instead asked her if the story had anything to do with her conversation with Rock. Delacourt says Debbie insisted that her husband didn't know anything about Airbus.

Delacourt's dinner party for Stead was well attended by cabinet glitterati, including current Newfoundland premier Brian Tobin and Sergio Marchi. Rock didn't attend; his wife did. At one point, Delacourt overheard Debbie say that Rock didn't know anything about the police investigation. Later, in the kitchen, Delacourt told Debbie she shouldn't be making such statements, that Rock did in fact know about a police investigation. Rock's wife insisted her husband didn't know anything about an Airbus investigation. Stead, a superior editor and journalist, overheard Delacourt and asked about the conversation. The *Globe* staffers didn't see the story at the time. "All of a sudden, a week later, it was the story Koring wanted to do,"[49] Delacourt says. What ensued, says Delacourt, was a "professional dispute. Everyone exercised their profession in the way they thought they should."[50] Koring, she says, was just doing his job as he saw it. Stead and then managing editor Colin MacKenzie were also responding to pressures that were professional in nature. Delacourt says she and Koring are still friends. But the experience, she says, left her bitter about Ottawa. "It is a sick place," she says flatly.[51]

Delacourt says she is fairly certain she and Rock will never speak again.

The *Globe* reporter had to contend with highly personal attacks, including a rumor that she'd had an affair with Rock, a rumor triggered innocently by a friend but spread through the village that is official Ottawa by Mulroney's media adviser Luc Lavoie. Lavoie believed the source who told him the story, and later apologized to Delacourt with a bottle of champagne at a restaurant. As Lavoie went to open the champagne, Delacourt recalls, he said he needed a knife. Delacourt says she turned her side, pointed to a spot in her back, and said: "That would be here."[52]

This "wiggle disclosure" period was the hardest on Mulroney, who felt as if the country had reverted to the days of the Star Chamber— abolished by Henry VII some 500 years ago. The former prime minister felt accused of serious crimes in the eyes of the world by unidentified sources without having had an opportunity to confront his accusers, answer the charges, or defend his good name. "It is the weirdest, most unbelievable thing I've ever heard of and I'm in the middle of it," Mulroney said during one conversation. "This thing comes down to two fairly simple questions: Is there a Swiss bank account in my name and does it, or did it ever, have $5 million in it?"[53]

Mulroney was particularly vexed that no one in the RCMP ever interrogated him on the allegation. It wasn't as if the RCMP didn't know where to find him. As a former prime minister, Mulroney is still afforded a minimal, and occasional, security service by the force's VIP security detail.

While in New York on board business for Archer–Daniel–Midland in early December 1995, Mulroney took advantage of a crisp, clear December day to walk off some nervous energy on Park Avenue and to talk about his situation. "This is the action of a fascist state. I can't believe this is happening in Canada."[54]

He knew his court case would be "long, hard, and expensive." Estimates of the legal costs of his defense exceeded $1 million. Mulroney was worried at this stage that the federal government would engage him in a war of legal attrition by filing a mountain of legal motions and appealing every judicial decision every step of the way. "The resources of one man, even a successful one, pale in comparison to the collective resources of the Canadian taxpayer," Mulroney said. "All my savings, to the extent I had any, are gone."[55]

The government's charges hung like a dark cloud over Mulroney. "It is a soul-destroying thing they are putting me through," he said as he made the turn toward the Waldorf-Astoria Hotel. "My enemies would be delighted if they knew how downcast I really am."[56]

Mulroney, in the early days of December, identified three journalists as "key" to the Airbus travails—nemesis Stevie Cameron, *the fifth estate* co-host Trish Wood, and *the fifth estate* producer Harvey Cashore.

As the story rolled out through early December, Mulroney believed he was being treated fairly by the French-language press, and that the coverage on the CTV network was "fair" and "balanced." He did, however, feel the CBC's *The National* was unrelentingly negative at that point and, if successful in his libel suit, intended to use tapes of the CBC reportage to establish the damage done to his reputation both in Canada and abroad.

Mulroney's analysis of police documents led him to conclude CBC employees had acted as RCMP informants, an issue he intended to instruct counsel to pursue at trial. Two days later, in another telephone conversation, Mulroney was still irritated at the CBC's coverage. "The only constant is the malice of *The National*," Mulroney said. "It is an ongoing, nightly thing."[57]

Mulroney took some solace at this time from news reports through mid-December that quoted former Air Canada executives to the effect that there had been no political meddling in the decision to purchase the Airbus jets, particularly because the Mounties' conspiracy theory was predicated on their assertion of political influence.

Through the Christmas season of 1995, Mulroney regrouped with his family and prepared for the court appearance he expected in the New Year.

The Court of Law versus the Court of Public Opinion

Mulroney's decision to press his legal case struck certain of his critics as a high-risk strategy. Lawyers for the federal Justice department and the RCMP made it clear they intended to put Mulroney through the wringer during the legal process known as "examination for discovery." A routine pretrial procedure, examination for discovery allows the defendant to grill the plaintiff about assertions made in the lawsuit. Examination for discovery is usually conducted in the privacy of a lawyer's office, but the Montreal *Gazette* took the issue of public access to the courts, claiming the discovery procedure is an essential part of the open court system and therefore should be held in public. The courts agreed.

Lawyers for the various federal parties signaled their intent to question Mulroney about his client list, his sources of revenue, tax returns, bank accounts, and all manner of personal financial information, once they got him in open court. Mulroney's team, anticipating the federal strategy, ensured his lawsuit did not claim any loss of income as a result of the alleged libel. Mulroney intended to argue any discussion of his revenue stream was therefore irrelevant to the case at hand.

Understanding the latitude afforded by the examination process, Mulroney played directly to the public through their intermediaries in the fourth estate. Mulroney denounced his travails as "straight out of Kafka," and said the federal government's action "reeks of fascism" and then declared his determination "to fight for my honor and my reputation."[58]

The *Toronto Star*, among others, denounced Mulroney's statement as characteristic of his penchant for hyperbole. But the former prime minister's utterances dominated headlines, radio news bulletins, and evening newscasts from coast to coast, and in both official languages. Mulroney understood that, having been accused by the Canadian government of pocketing $5 million, his denial would have to be framed in language that was stronger than the government's in order to have any effect. He knew his aggression would offend some editorialists, but he was gambling it would serve as a clarion call for others.

Earlier, the former prime minister had received calls from friends volunteering to set up a fund to help meet the costs of his legal defense. Mulroney was touched, but believed it important that he meet all costs associated with his case, even if he had to sell his house to do it. He cited the unwavering support of American Barrick chairman Peter Munk, the risk Munk was taking in keeping him on his board, given the fact Barrick is a publicly traded company.

New York provided a refuge of sorts for the former Tory leader through this period. "Here in New York, people know [about Airbus]," Mulroney said, "but they don't get fed a steady diet of details." Mulroney arranged one night for my wife, Bonnie, and me to join him and Mila at a performance of *Smokey Joe's Café*—a celebration of the musical genius of Leiber and Stoller. The performance was splendid. Mulroney appreciated the respite and said later, "I knew it would be fun and lively and I wouldn't have to think."[59] During intermission, a woman in the audience and a waiter both approached Mulroney and asked for his autograph. Their support and enthusiasm helped bolster Mulroney's spirits tremendously.

Each day, in concert with adviser Luc Lavoie, Mulroney tried to keep on top of storylines that various news organizations were pursuing. One day he was excited that *Le Soleil* columnist Michel Vastel was probing the angle that the Airbus attack against Mulroney was part of a willful political plot to discredit him. On another occasion, he was buoyed by reports that Radio Canada correspondent Norman Lester was on a similar trail.

News organizations, caught up in a competitive environment, began to wonder whether the RCMP was cooperating with the CBC at this point. Indeed, one scenario floating in conversation suggested the RCMP might agree it was being pressured by media queries to pursue an investigation of Mulroney. The "spin" on this scenario suggested aggressive journalists were accusing the RCMP of a coverup and the only effective way for the Mounties to refute the allegation was to press on with a probe.

The *Maclean's* December 4, 1995, issue provided two particularly interesting wall posters for Mulroney's team in a story that appeared under the headline "The RCMP Under Fire." A worried, unidentified senior Liberal organizer in Toronto expressed concern that the Mounties might have overstepped their boundaries and that the Prime Minister's Office might be left holding the bag. The story makes a specific reference to a PMO official who privately expressed delight at Mulroney's woes to *Maclean's*. The story also reported grumbling from front-line RCMP officers about the difficulty in investigating political targets "which must be vetted not only by the forces brass but by Solicitor General Herb Gray, the minister responsible."

On Friday, December 15, Mulroney was abuzz with news that Frank Moores "is ready to drop a bomb."[60] Once again, the media were in the middle of this latest development. Mulroney had heard reports Moores had contacted journalists, including Bob Fife of the *Toronto Sun*. Fife was reportedly in possession of a prepared statement from Moores, photocopies of bank statements from the Swiss accounts, and an interview with Moores's wife, Beth.

Beth Moores told Fife the Devon account was opened February 3, 1986, and $500 was deposited. The code name Devon was used for telephone-access purposes, she said, and the account was intended primarily for her use. It was closed in 1990 with a balance of $317.

"All hell is going to break loose,"[61] Mulroney said with some satisfaction.

For several days, the former prime minister had been urging Moores, through intermediaries such as Craig Dobbin, to release details of the Devon account to the press. Moores, reportedly, needed to settle certain issues with Revenue Canada before going public.

Mulroney's second-floor den in his Montreal home served as his command post. The den is elegant, masculine, and comfortable. A partner's desk is a particular focal point, and there's a window view of the city of Westmount and across the St. Lawrence River. The room is cluttered with family photos, and there is a portrait of his daughter, Caroline. A huge soapstone carving of a walrus with ivory tusks sits perched on a side table; contents of the wall-to-wall bookcases reflect Mulroney's life-long interest in history—Lenin and Bourassa, Churchill and Eamon De Valera. A bust of John Fitzgerald Kennedy occupies pride of place. Over the fireplace, an arresting portrayal of Notre-Dame-de-la-Garde, Quebec, by Lorne Bouchard portrays a stark winter scene of Mulroney's native North Shore. There is escapism as well, from Tom Clancy to Tom Wolfe, as well as the Blackford Oakes novels of William F. Buckley, Jr. Under a portrait of his wife, Mila, Mulroney's ear was semipermanently attached to his speed-dial phone.

"I have discovered the beauties of a fireplace because I have spent the past six weeks by and large in this room," Mulroney said in an interview. Reflecting on events, Mulroney moved from anger to melancholy, with the Chrétien government the focus of his anger. "It is like a death in the family," Mulroney said in one conversation. "On this one, I had lost my country. The preposterous idea that this could happen isn't so preposterous when it happens to you."[62]

Mulroney was sharply critical of the country's civil libertarians, noting not a single letter to the editor had appeared from that particular constituency. He reflected on the silence from individuals and associations he had personally intervened to help—from Joyce Milgaard to the Japanese Canadians. He duly noted the fact that former Tory leaders Joe Clark and Kim Campbell had made no attempt to contact him and neither had he heard a word from Jean Chrétien, John Turner, or Pierre Trudeau. "The idea that politics is a lot of camaraderie and friendship is bullshit,"[63] Mulroney said bluntly.

Mulroney drew his strength from a small group of friends, his in-laws, his eighty-five-year-old mother, Irene; his children, and, most importantly, the "absolutely indomitable spirit" of his wife, Mila.

Mulroney's law partner and former Canadian ambassador to the United Nations Yves Fortier encouraged the former prime minister to take heart. "Fortier said, if you look at this clinically, the body of evidence for three weeks has been moving steadily your way,"[64] Mulroney recalled.

Mulroney is known as an avid user of the telephone, but in the early weeks of the Airbus crisis an avocation became an addiction. The loquacious Mulroney says his home phone bill topped $25,000 in the first six weeks of his Airbus battle. He also had taken "copious notes" since the first call from Karl-Heinz Schreiber. "It's the only way I've kept my sanity in this thing,"[65] Mulroney said.

When the evening *CTV National News* led with a report of a "major development in the Airbus affair" and anchor Lloyd Robertson's assertion that "it could help clear former prime minister Brian Mulroney," it was a particularly satisfying night for Mulroney. The network news item was based on a *Financial Post* report by Mathias, who seemed to have settled a personal score with CBC reporter Neil MacDonald by tipping CTV to his report's contents. Five weeks to the night from Mathias's original story, details of the Devon account were finally in the public domain.

Mulroney was like an expectant father wondering if the wire services—particularly international wire services—would pick up the story. He was pleased with the play and the detail of Mathias's story, although he had anticipated that more space would have been devoted to the yarn. The *Toronto Sun*'s headlines were even more pleasing: "Ex-PM Smeared: Moores" and "Mulroney Clean … So am I, Moores." Mulroney also was seized of a *Sun* column by Michael Harris that suggested the Airbus affair would be Allan Rock's Bay of Pigs.

A few days later, Mulroney was invited to dinner with a dozen leading Republicans at the Alibi Club. The guest list included a former president, George Bush; a would-be president, Bob Dole; and the then House Speaker Newt Gingrich. Mulroney brought along a copy of the *Financial Post* to bring the group up to speed. Mulroney's travails inspired group discussion about media coverage and its significance to one's political agenda. Mulroney told the group that, in his opinion, the Ottawa gallery had succeeded in promulgating a caricature of the Tory leader "that is false and misleading." "But they got it out … over the past nine and a half years. I told Newt that the liberal media would do the same to him."[66] It was doubtful even Mulroney could appreciate just how prescient his admonition to Gingrich would be.

Mulroney had long believed people in public life have to accept the slings and arrows of media commentary and coverage, however difficult. Even with the publication of Stevie Cameron's *On the Take*, Mulroney believed it would be untoward for a former prime minister to launch legal action against a journalist. The Airbus affair, however, caused him to change his mind. "If I had it to do all over again, I'd be in the courts,"[67] Mulroney said. The former Tory leader said he thought the government's political agenda would carry the day—in terms of coverage—and he thought Canadians "would see the wisdom of it." Mulroney now believes that, in his case, it will be years before Canadians can get past the personal to reflect on the policy.

As he headed into the new year of 1996, Mulroney was convinced the Airbus affair was "100 percent political." Allan Rock, prime-ministerial adviser Eddie Goldenberg, chief of staff Jean Pelletier, and Solicitor General Herb Gray "are all involved somehow. We also know the CBC is involved big time."[68]

A call from former Ontario premier Bob Rae over the New Year bucked Mulroney's spirits, as did his legal team's determination that the federal government's allegedly secret document went to at least thirty people, from bank directors to diplomats.

Mulroney's priority, at this stage, was to get his case in front of the court as quickly as possible. He was aware of Ottawa's defense of qualified privilege, but believed his legal team's argument that Ottawa forfeits its qualified privilege because of malice. "These people are playing Ping-Pong with my life," Mulroney said. "It is pretty nightmarish stuff, but the more I find out about it, the better I feel."[69] Counsel for the federal government, at this stage, were salivating at the prospect of getting Mulroney on the witness stand and under oath. "They want to get into my finances and everything; my guys are telling them to buzz off. Whether I made $60,000 or $6 million last year is irrelevant."[70] The former prime minister also thought the cockiness of federal counsel anticipating a courtroom showdown was misplaced. "Getting someone in a courtroom is a double-edged sword,"[71] Mulroney warned.

Through the early months of 1996, a series of back-channel discussions occurred between Mulroney's Ottawa counsel Roger Tassé and representatives of the federal government to see if there was basis for an out-of-court settlement. Mulroney summarized the federal position as follows: "They say, 'We are entitled to libel you as a doctrine of privilege.' And they are pretty cocky about it." Mulroney, however, was encouraged by Ottawa's willingness to explore a settlement. "If they [the RCMP] had any evidence of wrongdoing by me, they wouldn't be talking to us at all,"[72] he said.

During this period, *Ottawa Citizen* columnist Greg Weston found out firsthand how hard a phenomenon of news reporting identified by journalist and academic Andie Tucher as a "congenial truth" can be to overcome. Tucher describes a congenial truth as an agreement between reporters and their readers about what constitutes truth or reality. And in the early weeks of the Airbus affair, the congenial truth about Mulroney was that he had received a $5-million payoff.

Weston had earlier run afoul of *Citizen* editors when he wrote a column giving some context to a controversy over living accommodations for former Mulroney speechwriter L. Ian MacDonald, who had been named minister counselor for public affairs at the Canadian embassy in Washington. Weston had been chastised in a note from then editor Jim Travers, who suggested he was a "shill for your Tory friends." Travers put Weston on notice that "this will never happen again."[73]

At one point, much of the journalistic attention on Airbus was focused on how the *Financial Post* had obtained a copy of the RCMP letter to the Swiss. Journalists were probing whether the leak had originated from the Mulroney camp. Weston worked the phones for a few days and put a column together that suggested four other possible explanations for how the letter had found its way into Mathias's hands. The column had been completely rewritten by *Citizen* editors, without any notice to Weston. "There was no call to me; there was no attempt to call me; I was here all evening," Weston said in a telephone interview from his home. "The column just appeared in the paper totally rewritten."[74] Newspaper tradition dictates that columns are either published or spiked, but are never rewritten.

Weston called *Citizen* editorial-page editor Peter Calamai, who had recently become Weston's editor. Calamai, Weston says, dismissed his column as "just more Tory bullshit" and added, "I don't trust your sources."[75]

Weston decided to speak to another *Citizen* editor, who explained in no uncertain terms that, as far as the *Citizen* was concerned, if a story wasn't going to help send Mulroney to jail, then the *Citizen* wasn't interested in seeing it in print. "Whatever happened to following the facts?"[76] Weston said later.

The former columnist still considers Travers and Calamai friends and says, "I have the utmost respect for both of them." But he did and does resent the notion that somehow he was shilling for his Tory friends. "The limit of my tolerance on this issue is being called a liar," Weston said. Looking back on the incident, he says, "I thought, come on guys, you're bigger than that."[77]

Calamai says he has no recollection of the exchange. But the perception that Mulroney had finally been caught wasn't restricted to the *Citizen* newsroom.

Bob Fife, now with the *National Post*, says this instinctive reaction was typical of Ottawa reporters when the Airbus story first broke—namely, "We finally got the guy." Fife had been one of Mulroney's toughest critics. In all fairness, however, he is just as aggressive in his coverage of the Chrétien government. Like many other journalists in Ottawa, Fife heard rumors that there had been payoffs on the Airbus purchase. According to Fife, the rumors were being circulated "by the lobbyist for Boeing," but, like other journalists, Fife had been unable to either confirm or deny the watering-hole gossip.

Once Mathias broke the story of the RCMP letter to the Swiss, Fife aggressively pursued his own inquiries. "I quickly realized there was no foundation to it, that it was a House of Cards,"[78] Fife said of the investigation.

Fife described a conversation with former Speaker of the Senate Guy Charbonneau. Charbonneau told Fife he had offered to set up a trust fund of between $4 million and $5 million for Mulroney when the former Iron Ore Company president first entered public life. Similar trust funds had been set up for party leaders in the past, including Lester B.

Pearson. Charbonneau told Fife Mulroney turned him down flat. Mulroney told his old friend he did not want to be beholden to anybody. Charbonneau, in his conversation with Fife, raised a question the *Sun* columnist had been asking himself for some time: Why would Mulroney turn down access to a perfectly legal source of outside income and then succumb to the lure of an illicit payoff?

Fife says Mulroney's policy agenda, from free trade to the GST, ensures that he will be remembered by historians down the road. Mulroney may have had image problems while in office, stemming from his predisposition to blarney, Fife says, "but these are not big issues." Fife couldn't understand why Mulroney would jeopardize his place in history by being part of any kickback scheme.

Fife began to talk to a number of central figures in the story, including Pelossi. "I began to realize the man was a liar," Fife says. As he probed Pelossi's past, Fife also concluded Pelossi was "a crook." Fife says "the more you looked at the story, the more it simply wasn't adding up." The Airbus story "was coming from an embezzler and being promoted by people who hate him [Mulroney] with a passion."[79]

He recalls telephoning Pelossi to inform him the Swiss account in question did not hold the millions Pelossi claimed. Pelossi's first response was to say the money must be somewhere else. Then he told Fife, "The RCMP can't just be relying on me?" Fife said at this point he had caught Pelossi in too many lies, big and small. Pelossi, he says, had no credibility as far as Fife was concerned, although other news organizations continued to file stories based on his claims. Fife's approach to the Airbus story was fundamentally different from the approach of the journalistic pack. "I wasn't pursuing this to get Brian Mulroney; I was pursuing this to get the story, and that's the difference,"[80] he says.

Fife became convinced Mulroney was being framed, and that troubled him deeply because, as he said in a telephone conversation, "it could happen to you or to me."[81] Mulroney, he said, is a man of means with extensive contacts. If *he* could be framed in such a manner, what did that portend for the rest of the population?

Fife arguably broke the most important story of the Airbus affair when he reported the Swiss account was actually held by Beth Moores. Fife believes he was able to break the bank-account story precisely because he was filing copy that was running counter to that of the press pack.

While other journalists were racing around Europe, looking for breaks in the Airbus case, Fife was breaking pivotal stories "just using the phone." He says it was clear to him that Staff Sergeant Fraser Fiegenwald was working closely with Cameron and *the fifth estate*. Fiegenwald was also trying to co-opt other members of the parliamentary press gallery. Fife always thought it strange a case of this magnitude was assigned to a staff sergeant.

As the story unfolded, senior Liberals began to insist the government had nothing to do with the RCMP investigation. "The closer it got to the PMO, the more nervous they got,"[82] Fife says. At one point, Chrétien's senior adviser Eddie Goldenberg approached Fife at the airport to tell the *Sun* columnist he had nothing to do with instigating the police investigation.

Fife is convinced Rock is responsible for the investigation, having passed on information he received from Delacourt and other journalists. Delacourt insists Fife wrote stories about her without ever speaking to her, a claim Fife emphatically says "is an absolute fucking lie."[83] Fife says he approached Delacourt in the lobby outside the Commons about rumors that she was the source for Rock's information. Fife says Delacourt told him to be very careful. "She was frightened,"[84] he says. Ten minutes later, when he got back to his office, Fife says he received a call from the *Globe*'s then managing editor, Colin MacKenzie, who answered all his questions on the issue.

Fife's reporting has always been aggressive; his writing has a decided edge to it. "Our job is to be hard-hitting, to expose stuff," he says. But Fife believes he is even-handed in his approach, bringing the same edge to his writing about the governing Liberals as he did to his coverage of the Conservatives. He feels that he "is one of the exceptions in the gallery." Fife says he is "appalled" at the lack of rigor in the press scrutiny of the current government.

Fife says the Mulroney story cannot be told without a reference to the poisonous atmosphere that existed in the parliamentary press gallery, where, he says, there was "almost hatred of the guy." This hatred permeated throughout the country as a direct result of Mulroney's media coverage, a coverage Fife says he helped shape. "I feel responsible. I certainly helped create it."[85] Fife says reporters during the Mulroney years could basically get away with anything when it came to attacking the former prime minister. The more negative the piece, the more likely it was to find itself on the front page.

In the years since then, Fife likens the atmosphere in Ottawa to a pogrom. "We were persecuting this guy based on the fact that we didn't like him. That is really dangerous in a democracy."[86]

Journalists are paid skeptics. They should be rigorous in their examination of political, business, and social leaders, especially where the public interest or the expenditure of public funds is involved. But journalists aren't supposed to be cynics. They aren't supposed to roll over on fundamental principles to appease the pack. Journalists are presumed to be able to exercise independence of thought. And reporters capable of independent thought shouldn't be intimidated by their peers. Perhaps because of my training as a reporter, I am not troubled by aggressive reporting, although I readily admit to being uncomfortable and anxious when I was the subject of that reporting. What is troubling is the ease with which journalists allegedly committed to objectivity and fairness will set both principles aside to give the public what it wants to hear, having created the appetite for trash talk in the first place.

The Courthouse Studio

Mulroney's appearance at Montreal's Palais de Justice on April 15, 1996, was a major Canadian media event. The television mobile units were double-parked out front, their antennae stretched up into snow-flurried skies. The examination for discovery was scheduled for one of the courthouse's smaller courtrooms. One member of the public registered a quiet complaint with a courthouse security guard, wondering why he couldn't take a seat in the media-spill-over room next door where there were empty spaces. The man even offered to leave if other journalists showed up. The guard wasn't having any of it. The guard later said the session should have been scheduled for one of the larger chambers on the fifth floor, where there would have been plenty of room for everyone.

No cameras were allowed inside the courtroom; so the crews were arranged at the front door when Mulroney arrived in the family Jeep, his wife, Mila, at the wheel. The camera operators raced past their competitors, focused, shot frames, then raced to their next position—Mulroney smiling for the cameras all the way. The accurate, if slightly inelegant, term used by camera crews to describe this type of scene is a "cluster fuck," everyone scrambling leapfrog-style to get their shots and cutaways. Global TV cameraman Phil Nolan said later, "It was just like a campaign."

There was an ill-fated attempt to settle the matter before the examination for discovery process in April, but the federal offer was, in Lavoie's words, "insulting."

As friends, cabinet colleagues, and former staffers looked on—people like Brian Gallery, Gilles Loiselle, Paul Thérien, and Fred Doucet—Mulroney effectively turned the courthouse into a television studio, with himself center-stage. With Lavoie working the reporters, Mulroney began dropping the verbal images and charges he knew would make headlines around the world. Referring to the November 2 telephone conversation with Karl-Heinz Schreiber, Mulroney said: "That's when I heard for the first time the horror of what had been inflicted upon me."[87]

Federal counsel Claude-Armand Sheppard sat across from Mulroney. Sheppard has matured from his days as a legal firebrand. In a measured, nonconfrontational way, Sheppard sought to establish the nature of Mulroney's relationship with Schreiber, as journalistic heavyweights such as Global TV's John Burke and CBC's Neil MacDonald looked on. Mulroney explained his government was interested in Schreiber's proposal to create jobs on Cape Breton Island, and later to do the same in the east end of Montreal. He added that the Department of National Defence had decided to accept a proposal from another company (General Motors—based in London, Ontario).

Mulroney even had a bit of a bombshell to drop in the midst of the exchange, when he informed the assembly that former Trudeau cabinet minister Marc Lalonde now represented Schreiber's interest.

As to the specifics of the Airbus case, Mulroney said then Transport minister John Crosbie had asked the RCMP to investigate allegations of kickbacks in 1988. "There were rumors flying around then—generally acknowledged to be generated by a losing company, Boeing," Mulroney said. "Boeing was pressing, and all of the Americans were pressing, to get us to buy Boeing,"[88] Mulroney said, before reiterating his assertion that Boeing was the source of the rumors of wrongdoing.

Over the lunch break, Mulroney and his team felt good about the morning session. His attack on the Chrétien government for its "fascist" tactics was the consensus pick for the headline of the day.

The legal team already had a first cut of the transcript of the morning's proceedings, which was reviewed in detail. Mulroney had taken a swipe at certain of Sheppard's colleagues, who at one point were openly derisive of certain of his answers. The former prime minister made a specific reference to the "smugness and smirks of the young lawyers opposite."

Reflecting on the implications of the appearance, Mulroney said: "The minute I set foot in the courthouse this morning, war was declared."[89]

As Mulroney prepared to return to the courtroom, Ralph Benmergui's noon-hour program was devoted to the Airbus story. His special guest was Stevie Cameron. Benmergui rolled tape of Mulroney's exchange with John Turner in the 1984 televised leaders' debate over patronage—highlighted by Mulroney's now famous "You had an option, sir" rejoinder. The parallel was drawn to Mulroney's patronage practices. The structure so offended one Canadian journalist covering the story that he suggested the CBC "should be co-defendants in this case."[90]

A *Washington Post* reporter was busy filing by phone—and, as Mulroney's team has predicted, the "reeks of fascism" quote featured prominently in his report. The *Post* reporter, evoking Mulroney's "roll the dice" quote from Meech Lake, said the former prime minister was rolling the dice once again.

As he left the courtroom at the Palais de Justice, Claude-Armand Sheppard stepped into an elevator and told a journalist: "I was a little surprised by his choice of epithets, but Mr. Mulroney is Mr. Mulroney. That's why he was elected prime minister." Sheppard dismissed media probes about an out-of-court settlement as "wishful thinking." As the elevator descended, Sheppard repeated his observation that he was "very, very surprised at his [Mulroney's] attack on the political system. You're dealing with an angry person," Sheppard said. As he took his leave of the reporter, the Montreal lawyer ended the conversation by saying, "Anyway, you got a lot of speeches ... which are often self-defeating."[91]

The news coverage following Mulroney's appearance pleased the former prime minister. In Mulroney's view, CBC reporter Neil MacDonald had "hit it pretty hard," while Global's John Burke "says there is nothing left in this case."

Libel expert Julian Porter, appearing on *CBC Newsworld*'s "The Lead," hosted by Allison Smith, predicted Mulroney would win "the largest damage suit in Canadian history."

A news-analysis column carried in the Montreal *Gazette* reflected the press-box perspective. Written by William Marsden, the article suggested Mulroney had hit a home run.

The Airbus story was a top-of-mind concern across Canada during this period. Hugh Segal was on a cross-country promotional tour in support of his best-seller *No Surrender*. As he made the rounds of radio and call-in shows from Vancouver to Halifax, Segal confirmed "the Airbus question is the first question asked."[92]

Sheppard, as he had predicted in news accounts carried in the *Gazette*, filed a series of questions, ranging from social clubs Mulroney was a member of to his income in 1995. Mulroney was adamant in his response to probes about his personal finances: "I had offered to give them everything before" (including tax returns, bank accounts, etc.), Mulroney said, "but now the damage has been done. Piss on them."[93]

Mulroney believed the Chrétien government had made a strategic error in allowing the examination for discovery to proceed. "The government has crossed its own Rubicon," he said.

The CBC's Neil MacDonald says the examination of discovery process was the turning point for many of the reporters covering the Airbus story. The dominant news frame around Mulroney had changed. Media perception of the former prime minister shifted from alleged perpetrator to victim. Sheppard, similarly, had been transformed into a figure out of the Spanish Inquisition. "There was an awful lot of reporters that went into that discovery sort of wanting, I think, Mulroney to be guilty," MacDonald said in an interview. "You could hear it in the hall-ways—you know, 'Oh boy, oh boy, oh boy.' And you could almost feel the moment during discovery when the whole pack turned and Sheppard —representing the federal government—became the bad boy. And you know, it was almost a snap decision to go from Mulroney the bad guy, who everybody hates, to Mulroney the victim, who we're all going to stand up for."[94]

MacDonald says the journalists' aggressive behavior with Sheppard by the end of the second day of the discovery process signaled the sea change in the press-pack mentality. The discovery process also afforded Mulroney the opportunity to state, for the record, his conviction that the government had been leaking material to journalists.

Mulroney told the proceedings he had received a fax which made it clear a newsmagazine had been informed of a private meeting between Roger Tassé and Justice department officials. "The RCMP clearly had leaked to *Maclean's* magazine that Roger Tassé had been to see them on my behalf," Mulroney said. Sheppard jumped in, telling Mulroney "that you assume, you don't know as a fact the RC …" Mulroney's lawyer Gerald Tremblay intervened, telling Sheppard, "Don't interrupt the witness." Mulroney then said, "Let me withdraw that. We will ask the RCMP at a given time. You can be certain of this. Roger Tassé did not phone Stevie Cameron and say that he had just been to see the RCMP. It is perhaps more likely that the other thing occurred."[95]

The exchange was pivotal for MacDonald and other reporters. MacDonald subsequently got a transcript of the exchange and went to the court reporter for a copy of the voice tape of the discovery. The exchange, he says, "was the first time that it had been made clear that somebody within government was leaking stuff to reporters, which of course is the reason the whole thing caved—because of the expectation of absolute privacy."[96]

Mulroney's performance in general, and his references to Kafka in particular, stunned the government, MacDonald said, including Prime Minister Chrétien. "It was a nice turn. I mean, he's the master of a good turn of phrase. Plus, what a lot of people forgot was that that's a lawyer in discovery."[97]

A Media-Inspired Miscalculation

Mulroney believes the federal government's decision to haul him into court for the examination for discovery was "the greatest strategic blunder in the history of Montreal courtrooms." The flaw in Sheppard's approach, said Mulroney, was that "he doesn't know what I know." Mulroney noted: "They thought I was going to go into a box and answer his [Sheppard's] questions."[98] Mulroney instead took full advantage of the media crush to ensure instant and widespread dissemination of statements and charges that would take dead aim at his opponents in government. Accustomed to sparring in the House of Commons with Trudeau and Turner, the former prime minister was confident he could handle the queries of Sheppard, whom he described as a "bothersome gnat."

On one level, Mulroney almost regretted the fact that his case did not go to trial. "We had an explosion a day," Mulroney said of his legal strategy. "We had lots of dynamite."[99]

During a telephone conversation from Florida on January 13, 1998, after the Chrétien government had folded its cards hours before the case was to go to trial, the former Tory leader was delighted with the turn of events. "I feel thirty years younger and thirty pounds lighter,"[100] Mulroney said. One of the first people to call Mulroney with congratulations was U.S. senator Teddy Kennedy, saying "You fought city hall and you won."

Mulroney noted some of his most outspoken media critics had actually weighed in on his side during the Airbus dispute, people such as former *Sun* columnist and former CBC *Crossfire* host Claire Hoy. "I've got to pack it in," a relieved Mulroney chuckled. "Even Claire Hoy is supporting me."[101]

Lavoie is particularly critical, however, of the CBC television network's coverage of the Airbus affair, describing it as "scandalous." He says through the early weeks of the Airbus affair, *The National* would introduce each item with the self-congratulatory reference "as first reported on the CBC's flagship public-affairs program *the fifth estate*."[102] Lavoie says he knew the story was turning in Mulroney's favor the minute the CBC news department stopped patting itself on the back. "That's when I knew it was starting to go our way,"[103] Lavoie says. Through the affair, Lavoie came to appreciate the professionalism of certain reporters assigned to the Airbus story. Despite his characterization of the CBC's early coverage, he considers CBC television reporter Neil MacDonald "a very good journalist" and has the highest regard for Bob Fife's work. The *Globe*'s Paul Koring, who played a pivotal role in the Airbus saga, was always accurate in everything he wrote.

The international media, however, required a different approach than did Canadian reporters. For the international press, Mulroney was lumped in with other disgraced leaders, such as Andreotti, Bhutto, and Collor. French and German reporters had a particular interest because of the Airbus connection.

One interesting observation: Lavoie says Canada's French-language press did not assign reporters to bird-dog the story on a daily basis.

Lavoie says the day Mulroney walked into the Palais de Justice in Montreal and turned the courtroom into a studio was the day the government's case died. A review of newspaper headlines in November, compared with headlines emanating from Mulroney's court appearance, reflected a sea change, Lavoie says. "It was like two different worlds."[104]

In May 1996, Ottawa tried to get the case delayed for a year. The federal government mounted a major public-relations offensive, Lavoie says, hiring media consultant Barry McLaughlin to provide training for individuals such as lawyer Jean Potvin. Journalists were warned when the federal "offer" was on its way, called an hour ahead of time, and told to expect a fax. The reporters received their faxes a full hour before Mulroney's lawyers received theirs.

It is important to note that, in stories such as that of the Airbus affair, with reporters talking to both sides virtually every hour on the hour, a significant information exchange occurs, which helps journalists craft their stories, but also helps each side of the dispute determine what the other side is up to.

On occasion, Lavoie would use a reporter to ensure certain information got back to the other side. Montreal *Gazette* reporter Rod MacDonnell is a case in point. MacDonnell was described by Lavoie as "so essentially, fundamentally anti-Mulroney," yet Lavoie made a point of taking every one of MacDonnell's calls. But, Lavoie says, "we used him about three times for our own purposes by leaking stuff to him."[105] MacDonnell was the vehicle of choice when Lavoie wanted word circulating that Mulroney's lawyers intended to subpoena Chrétien's senior adviser Eddie Goldenberg and his communications director Peter Donolo to probe the extent of PMO involvement in the Airbus affair.

A second bid to settle out of court collapsed in June 1996. Lavoie continued to believe that the matter would never get to court. "I know politics too well," Lavoie says. "We would have stolen the media agenda from them for three months. The front pages would have been about the trial. They would have looked like fools and a bunch of mean-spirited bastards."[106]

On January 4, 1997, a last attempt by the federal government to stall the case was tossed out by a Federal Court judge. Lavoie headed to Montreal the next day, hauling his boxes of material, prepared to testify. The phone rang in the livery car ferrying him to Montreal. Former *Toronto Star* Ottawa editor David Vienneau was on the line. The federal government had leaked the fact that an out-of-court settlement had been reached. The "spin" war the Airbus affair became wasn't over after all. Lavoie says Vienneau told him the Mulroney side had been forced to agree that the police investigation would continue, and the federal government would pay "some" of Mulroney's costs. "In other words, we were portrayed as giving in,"[107] Lavoie says. Minutes later the phone in the car rang again. This time, Montreal *Gazette* reporter Rod MacDonnell was on the line. He had the same spin.

On arrival at Mulroney's residence, Lavoie was adamant a counteroffensive be launched. Lead lawyer Gerald Tremblay was reluctant; he had given his word he and his colleagues wouldn't say anything about the settlement until 10:00 a.m. on the Monday. Lavoie knew the battle to control the headline would be lost by then. He sought refuge in precision of language. Tremblay agreed Mulroney's side would make no comment to the media. Lavoie, with the logic of a Jesuit, decided he wasn't "commenting" by delivering factual information. Thanks to his efforts, the headlines the next morning suggested a complete collapse on the part of the federal government.

With his colleagues at NPR, he put the wheels in motion for a full-fledged media offensive following the court proceeding. Lavoie believes the skirmish explains why Allan Rock was so mean-spirited in his announcement that morning. William Kaplan states Rock's statement was rewritten by the Prime Minister's Office.

Had the libel case gone to trial, a number of journalists would have been subpoenaed. Mulroney's legal team had established that journalists in Canada enjoy no special privilege when it comes to protecting sources, but the strategy was to treat the journalists as if they had such rights. Mathias would have been asked simply to confirm his award-winning "scoop" was not the result of a leak from the Mulroney camp. Similarly, Weston, Janigan, and Delacourt would have been asked to confirm statements in previously published reports attributed to them.

Stevie Cameron would have received different treatment. "For this one, we would have respected nothing," Lavoie says. "We intended to treat her as if she wasn't a journalist, but a gossip, a pamphleteer, a shame to the profession."[108]

With hindsight, Lavoie says one of the keys to Mulroney's cause was the decision by the Quebec Superior Court to have the case heard in its entirety by a single judge. The decision reduced the scope of a problem that is inherent in any strategy of legal redress—the time delay in our legal system.

Had Ottawa been allowed to pursue a delay strategy through a myriad of motions and appeals, Mulroney "would still be thinking about his examination-for-discovery appearance," Lavoie says. "By then, his reputation would have been totally destroyed."[109]

The Airbus story, says Lavoie, was a political battle. The courts and the legal system were weapons in the arsenal. The lesson of Airbus is that the court of public opinion is inextricably linked to any proceeding in a court of law involving a public person. And as much as it is counterintuitive to our view of judges, Lavoie makes the point that judges, like everyone else, read newspapers.

Judge Alan Gold, after awarding Mulroney $1.4 million to cover legal costs, set an interesting precedent in ordering the federal government to pay $587,721 in fees to National Public Relations. In his decision, which was binding on the government, Gold ruled: "I have no doubt that if the claimant [Mulroney] had not received the services rendered by National ... he would have been at a great disadvantage in the prosecution of his suit and unable to meet the defendants' case on many of the issues."[110]

Gold ordered the financial settlement be paid out of the RCMP contingency fund, arguing the "intent and purpose" of the out-of-court settlement "was to right the grievous wrong the claimant had suffered through no fault of his own."[111]

As Gold is one of Canada's most respected jurists in issues of arbitration, his decision has potentially far-reaching implications for our judicial system. Gold, in effect, has endorsed the idea that the accused must defend themselves as aggressively before the court of public opinion as they do before the court of law. Further, because of the protracted nature of legal proceedings, defendants may find themselves convicted in the court of public opinion before their case is ever called in a court of law.

Legal counsel, invariably, is reluctant to engage in any public dialogue outside the courtroom, for fear that an ill-considered comment might compromise their case. But for people with a public profile, the legal issues must be considered in tandem with public opinion, particularly in libel cases.

As Michael Fitz-James wrote in the November 18, 1997, edition of the *Financial Post*, "Even though Gold's ruling isn't technically a court judgment, some prominent lawyers think it's opened the door to bigger damage claims for libel plaintiffs. Not only can they claim injury to reputation, but they can also add the public-relations expenses of defending that reputation."[112] Fitz-James said the case could be made that a libel victim with a public profile may have a duty to hire a public-relations firm in an attempt to afford some measure of protection for a reputation under attack.

The Canadian media, particularly the CBC public-affairs program *the fifth estate*, did much to keep the Airbus investigation alive. And in the end, the media played a pivotal role in forcing Ottawa to settle with Mulroney before his historic libel action could be heard in an open court.

Presumed Guilty author William Kaplan makes the extraordinary charge that *Elm Street* editor Stevie Cameron had a third-party contact, federal counsel Harvey Strosberg, with information that Fraser Fiegenwald had been leaking information to reporters. Cameron reportedly did not want to run the risk of being held in contempt of court for failing to disclose a source.

Strosberg had intended to turn the libel trial into a public-relations war, ironic given Gerald Tremblay and Jacques Jeansonne's determination to turn the Montreal courthouse into an abattoir.[113]

The trial, ostensibly, was about the federal government, Brian Mulroney, and unsubstantiated allegations of kickbacks to Canadian politicians, but certain media practices would most certainly have been on trial as well.

Former Mulroney cabinet minister Michael Wilson, appearing on the same CBC public-affairs panel as Stevie Cameron, denounced a journalism "by innuendo and half-truth as it leads us to certain conclusions." Wilson said he hopes journalists would draw certain lessons from the Airbus affair "that will cause them to back off some of this half-truth nonsense and deal with the truth."[114]

Others, many journalists included, were disappointed when Ottawa's offer to settle precluded a full airing of how Airbus came to pass, but certain conclusions present themselves.

Rumors were morphed into "facts" as a direct consequence of exchanges of information between unnamed journalists and the RCMP. A senior parliamentary correspondent tells Mulroney's media adviser the Liberals had been touting the Airbus story for days even as Chrétien and his advisers insist the first they heard of it was when the *Financial Post* landed on their doorsteps that fateful Saturday morning.

The Montreal *Gazette* saw no conflict of interest in assigning reporters who doubled as researchers for Cameron's *On the Take* to cover the trial.

And the former prime minister argues that the entire Airbus affair was a massive diversion on the part of the Liberals, orchestrated by senior adviser Eddie Goldenberg, to deflect attention from Chrétien's flawed performance in the 1995 Quebec referendum. The government, meanwhile, clings to its defense of "plausible deniability."

Lawyer/author William Kaplan chides Mulroney for a strategy that was part law, part politics, and focusing too much on the politics.

Mulroney's supporters counter with the observation that Airbus was never a matter of law; it was always a matter of politics, the press, and the public.

The Airbus affair was a spectacular confluence of recent reporting trends, and a politician's understanding of media management. The story had all the elements of scandal: power, money, and people in high places. There were investigative reporters with suspect sources, off-shore bank accounts, and a lone-ranger cop. The whiff of a Canadian Watergate was in the air—finally. And like Watergate, at a certain point the story was taken over by society's institutions. While journalists credit Carl Bernstein and Bob Woodward for bringing down Richard Nixon, students of government tend to credit the congressional committee chaired by Sam Ervin. Quebec's court system, the Federal Court, and the House of Commons provided the real backdrop for the Airbus affair.

Airbus had its dueling legal teams—but, of equal importance in this case, dueling teams of media advisers as well. Even the investigators were involved in strategic leaks to key journalists.

Airbus, in the end, was made possible because of a congenial truth about the former prime minister. The Airbus story changed because the congenial truth could not be sustained in a court of law. As prime minister, Brian Mulroney became a decidedly unpopular figure when his media "frame" positioned him as the ultimate political power in the land. Mulroney's public persona changed again when the media frame positioned him as the underdog—albeit a rich and successful one—standing alone against the federal government and its many agents.

The Airbus affair is a textbook example of how the commodity we call news can create a reality that is at variance with the truth. Airbus reveals how reporters, and the investigators themselves, are at the mercy of sources who may have highly personal agendas. Airbus also proves that a media-savvy public figure, with advice from experts, can fight back, using the same techniques as the accusers: rhetorical excess, leaks, wiggle disclosures, third-party endorsations, and, most important, the institutions of government around which the mainstream media are organized.

Even Mulroney's most vocal critics acknowledge the former prime minister's skill in mounting a media-focused counteroffensive on the

Airbus affair. And Mulroney's advisers, in turn, acknowledge that the federal government's version of the story took on more strategic focus when the Justice department sought outside media-relations advice.

Ironically, both sides were approaching the libel trial itself as an exercise in media relations as much as an exercise in law. Both sides express some regret that the final clash did not occur, ironically because of a "media" issue—an ill-advised leak to a journalist known to be antagonistic to the former prime minister.

Mulroney, and his media-relations adviser, Luc Lavoie, may have changed the course of legal history forever with the core assumption/assertion that what happens in the court of public opinion is at least as important as what happens in the court of law. Legal counsel, who typically advise clients facing charges to say nothing, may now have to reconsider their advice, and clients who are on the receiving end of such advice may want to reconsider the legal counsel acting on their behalf who don't acknowledge this.

Airbus, which had the potential to bury Mulroney, in the end afforded the former Tory leader his first real opportunity to start the process of refurbishing his reputation. The impact on the broader public was less pronounced than among opinion leaders because Airbus was mostly a print story.

Mulroney, Lavoie, and his legal team achieved a significant victory in this particular media-relations war. We will never see its like again. The Airbus affair provided a glimpse of the digital-media spin war of the future. While media-relations advisers on both sides of the Airbus affair had to craft strategies for the "Bigfoots" in network television, daily newspapers, newsmagazines, and radio, they also, for the first time, had to monitor Internet chatrooms and news Web sites.

The Airbus affair may have signaled the end of a media era, pointing to a future world of digital bits instead of sound bites. Like the survivors of the trenches of the First World War who looked up one day and saw a tank, veterans of the spin war around Airbus know that emerging media technologies will render the television-oriented media strategies of the past thirty years obsolete.

With the emergence of television, before cable and specialty channels accelerated the process of audience fragmentation, political communicators could reach large segments of the population by getting their "message" out through a relatively small number of news organizations. In the early days of the Reagan administration, for example, White House spokesperson Larry Speakes could reach 90 percent of the American population in a single briefing session. Speakes could sit down with a dozen correspondents—one from each of ABC, NBC, CBS; *Time, Newsweek, U.S. News and World Report*, and the wire services; the *Washington Post, New York Times, Wall Street Journal, Los Angeles Times, Chicago Tribune*, and maybe a major regional newspaper—and get his spin out on any story. Here in Canada, a press secretary's task was complicated somewhat by the requirement to communicate in two official languages. But the same "reach" could be achieved with parliamentary correspondents from CBC, CTV, Global, Radio Canada, TVA, Quatre Saisons, the *Globe and Mail, Canadian Press, Maclean's, Le Devoir, La Presse*, Southam News, Sun Media, and a columnist or two.

The explosion of media outlets has made that process infinitely more complicated. Political communicators now have to consider the total media environment, with messages that hold their editorial integrity despite the medium used for distribution.

The spin wars of the future will be joined, first, on the Net. Positions will be advanced, arguments presented, and information processed by decision makers seated in front of desktop terminals, or slouched in the corner of an airport lounge, laptop at the ready. Net-based communication will seep through the public consciousness, like water through soil, from multiple sources. And in terms of public opinion formation, the outcome of the next generation of spin wars may well be determined before the "news" is even carried in the mainstream media.

7

Cyberspace

Netscape Communications, a software company that hadn't yet turned a dime of profit, went public over the summer of 1995 after fifteen months of operation. The August stock offering of the Web's most popular browser triggered a buying spree on Wall Street. Netscape's stock price soared, and the company ended up with a book value of half the net worth of the oft-bartered, much-battered CBS Network. By November 1998, Netscape was acquired by America Online in a deal valued in excess of $4.2 billion. This scenario could be possible only in today's digital world. For the past three years, magazine covers have been touting a gold rush in cyberspace. Newsmagazines declared that the Internet would change everything we know about mass communication, and consequently everybody wants a piece of the action.

The invocation of the gold-rush analogy is particularly forceful for me. When I was being raised in a gold-mining town in the bush of Northern Ontario, our local lore evolved around a pair of prospectors named Benny Hollinger and Sandy MacIntyre who found deposits in the early days of this century that in today's dollar would have a value in the tens of billions. Hollinger's name, after seventy years of corporate maneuvering, now adorns the letterhead of one of the world's largest media empires, an evolution that is entirely appropriate. Gold, once found in hills or underground, is now found in digital bits.

An eyewitness to Hollinger's original strike offered a colorful account of the prospector, who, after pulling off the moss from a quartz outcropping, suddenly let out a roar. The quartz looked as if someone had dripped a candle along it, but instead of wax it was gold.

The part of the story that always intrigues me the most, however, is Hollinger's later observation that heel prints were clearly visible in the ground near the quartz outcropping, suggesting an earlier prospector had literally tramped all over the area of Hollinger's historic find. So it will be in the gold rush of cyberspace.

Fortunes will be made and missed in the months leading to the turn of the millennium and beyond. The infectious excitement of watching a new medium take shape before our eyes will be tempered to some extent by the uncertainty of the marketplace's impact on these emerging technologies.

As someone who never did figure out how to set margins on the old Royal manual typewriters bolted to the sheet-metal desks of the newsroom of my youth, I am singularly ill-suited for the role of prognosticator as to which companies or line of products will be the winners and losers of the next technology wave. We know from the recent past—for example, Sony's Beta system versus VHS—that superior technology may or may not become the people's choice. What is clear, however, is that these technologies will unleash this century's societal revolution, a revolution that will be every bit as profound in political, social, and economic terms as the Industrial Revolution of the late nineteenth century. The social migration from farm to factory will now be settled in cyberspace. In fact, cyberspace isn't about space any more; like the western frontier, its openness is being transformed and organized.

New York Magazine, in a special report on the Big Apple as Cyber City, asserts the new intellectual capital of cyberspace has shifted to Manhattan, and the medium these Silicon Alley gurus are fashioning will have significant implications for the future of journalism, and journalism's role in society. And because of journalism's place as the world's central nervous system, any fundamental change to the media's traditional role as the fourth estate will have direct consequences for the way we organize ourselves politically.

Two diametrically opposed constructs are being advanced in the debate on the future of journalism as shaped by emerging media. The first revolves around the megamergers of media and entertainment companies and the threat to free speech posed by such concentration. As *Newsday* television columnist Marvin Kitman stated at a Freedom

Forum Media Studies Center seminar: "It seemed like a game of Pacman with one entity swallowing the other entity."[1] Kitman says Time Warner should simply be called "Octopus Inc." and wonders why the antitrust questions raised by these mergers are not being addressed in a meaningful way in Washington.

Kitman's rhetorical question suggests a logical response. When major media companies are doing the merging, who is going to cover congressional voices raised in dissent? And how many U.S. legislators are prepared to do battle with a media mogul? Here in Canada, the recent couplings and uncouplings of Canadian newspaper groups have been greeted with a deafening silence from federal law-makers in Ottawa.

Those preoccupied with ownership concentration issues question the value of a technological explosion if in the end four or fewer global entities control all access to the new technologies. Kitman also argues this centralization of the information media threatens the very future of democracy. John Malone, Ray Smith, and Ted Turner emerge as the new "robber barons" in this narrative, the Information Age's answer to Andrew Carnegie and John D. Rockefeller.

Newsmagazines chart the fragmentation of the network television audience. News stories chronicle how the big four networks in the United States—ABC, NBC, CBS, and Fox—as well as the upstart United Paramount Network and Warner Brothers, are losing audience share to cable channels. But the exodus is somewhat misleading. A young male viewer may have abandoned ABC's prime-time offering on a Tuesday night in favor of a game on ESPN, but he is still a Disney customer, because Disney owns both networks.

The content concerns about corporate concentration is less George Orwell's "Big Brother," as set out in his novel *1984*, than Aldous Huxley's more benign trust in *Brave New World*, an endless cycle of self-promotion.

Consider the control possibilities inherent in Rupert Murdoch's multimedia empire. In 1995, Murdoch's book-publishing company offered the newly elected Speaker of the House of Representatives Newt Gingrich a multimillion-dollar advance for his "story." The book was then reviewed in magazines and newspapers Murdoch's conglomerate owns. Former FCC commissioner Nick Johnson picked up the trail at this point. "It [the conglomerate] runs ads for the book in its publications. Then it puts the author on talk shows or its own television network's morning news shows. It then hires a screenwriter to write a screenplay which is produced as a feature film in a movie studio that it owns, which movie is then run in its movie theatres before it is put on videotapes distributed through video rental stores which it also happens to own. All of which media excitement it continues to promote with features in its own *People*-type magazine. The idea is to hype your own product on your own product. And it's called synergy, which they say is a positive thing."[2]

In November 1997, Sarah, the Duchess of York, hosted her first television special for the ABC network in the United States. The special also aired on CTV in Canada. Entitled *Adventures with the Duchess*, the one-hour special featured the Duchess rock-climbing in Colorado with a world-class climber who has been blind since the age of twelve; scuba diving with Jean-Michel Cousteau, feeding sharks fifty feet below the Caribbean's surface; and on a cattle drive in Wyoming. In the days leading up to the special, ABC booked the Duchess for interviews on a number of network programs, including *Good Morning America* and *Regis and Kathie Lee*. And while the interviews covered a range of topics, including the tragic death of Diana, the Princess of Wales, the dominant storyline through all the interviews was the special.

A similar pattern unfolds five nights a week on the immensely popular *Entertainment Tonight*. And there is always a spot in the chair next to Dave Letterman or Jay Leno for someone whose movie has just opened, or whose record has just been released, or whose book has just been launched.

The preoccupation with corporate concentration appears generational. It seems to be a particular concern of journalists from the mainstream media "of a certain age" who date back to the days of multi-newspaper towns, each publishing several editions a day in head-to-head competition.

It is also, for us neo-Pollyannas, largely irrelevant.

Newsweek technology columnist Steven Levy has been arguing for years that the "propeller heads" have already stolen the revolution, or at least the electronic future. Levy's proposition is enthusiastically endorsed by John Perry Barlow, co-founder of the Electronic Frontier Foundation. The Internet, says Barlow, is the iceberg that will sink the Titanic of the megamedia companies. The present merger mania, he says, is tantamount to rearranging the deck chairs on the ill-fated ship that couldn't sink until it did.

Levy says old media power is based on monopoly, on controlling distribution. "But the Net is built to smash monopolies." Says Levy: "If the World Wide Web shatters the current paradigm of distribution, the channel capabilities of cable systems and even networks will be severely devalued. Anyone will be able to set up a new channel or storefront on the virtual highway, for free, asking permission of no one and accepting income directly over the wire."[3]

The "how" of it all remains something of a mystery to the technology challenged such as myself, but the pre-Christmas newspapers providing parents with this year's guide to electro-toys list software for preschoolers along with robotics invention systems that allow kids to build, and then program, an actual robotic device. The stuffed toys interact with a computer, a television, and the Internet. Small wonder Tufts University professor W. Russell Neuman says, "Take it as a given that, within five years, networked computers in the workplace and the home will compete on an equal footing with the existing news media as a routine source of news for over half the public in the industrialized world."[4]

Neuman, who with colleagues Marion Just and Ann Crigler published an important study that established the medium of television as an educator without peer, offered this warning in the April 1996 issue of the *Columbia Journalism Review*. "All journalists, even the most technophobic, need to understand how digital communications systems are challenging both the business models and the journalistic conventions we've inherited from other ages of technological innovation."[5]

Journalism, as we know it, is as much an artifact of the Industrial Revolution as a tin can. The inverted pyramid writing style still used in newspapers today was dictated by the emergence of telegraphy, a balky system of mass communication in its early days. Wires went down, and stories got cut off before they were moved onto the wire in their entirety. The answer to the problem was to develop a special narrative that treated each paragraph as a stand-alone proposition, and not dependent on the next, which might or might not follow. Radio news required "actuality"—voiceclips from newsmakers. Television needed the newsmakers on film, and more recently, on tape. The anchor desk is a relic of the fixed-camera era of the old-style studio. Today, with satellites, cell phones, and portable edit suites, the news anchor stands in front of the lighthouse at Peggy's Cove to report on the tragic crash of Swiss Air Flight 111.

The next generation of desktop machines will be capable of showing improved-quality digital movies. More significantly, they will also be able to create them. Former Beatle George Harrison created a movie company called HandMade Films. The title proved prophetic. The Hollywood extravaganza will continue to be afforded pride of place on the streets of Toronto, increasingly major studios' "location" of choice. But film students at "Rye High" will be able to give expression to their creativity on shoestring budgets.

In the digital world, traditional divisions between media and entertainment will disappear, as chroniclers of society's momentous events choose the narrative form that works best for their message.

The wired world has particular importance for a group emerging as a societal concern in North America—the high-school dropout. Says Powell: "Any teenage drop-out who can master high-powered video games at the corner arcade can master multimedia CD-ROMs and virtual reality data displays."[6]

Technologist Jaron Lanier says the media landscape of the future will be dominated by two groups: "the gorillas and the guerrillas," the megamedia companies, and the small, nimble innovative firms.[7] A similar shakedown occurred in the world of retail. Suburban "big box" stores offered everything from clothes to condiments under a single roof. For the more discerning, there was a proliferation of smaller specialty shops. The folks stuck in the middle—Eaton's, for example—couldn't compete on price at one end, or on quality at the other. So it will be in the new world of media.

Levy positions the Internet and the World Wide Web as the road to information Nirvana—a combination of book, radio, magazine, mailbox, conversation parlor, bulletin board, and television set. The

American Memory site of the Library of Congress is changing the way knowledge is shared around the world. Everything from papyri to photographs from the Civil War is available on-line. England's Public Records Office is creating a catalogue of all of Britain's public documents and records going back a millennium. History can now come directly to the home. Individuals will no longer be victims of geography. The interactive nature of these technologies adds to their empowering properties. If the local library was a passport to the world, the new technologies would bring the sights and sounds of that new world directly to you.

If society's behavioral patterns after the Second World War were shaped by the automobile, our lives in the early years of the next millennium will evolve around the Net. Today, if we need something, we either reach for the telephone or jump in the car and head for the nearest shopping mall. Microsoft founder Bill Gates says that in a few years our first impulse in similar circumstance will be to turn to the Net.

Esther Dyson, author of an insightful book entitled *Release 2.0*, says the Net, above all, is a "home for people." The Net's underlying rules are in the spirit of classic eighteenth-century liberalism: freedom of choice, freedom of speech, honesty, and disclosure. Dyson predicts the Net will "suck power away from central governments, mass media and big business."[8] If information is power, and if that power in recent years has been concentrated in the hands of a political/media elite, then the Net most certainly has the potential to redefine who is, or isn't, "informed."

My Freedom Forum colleague David Shenk raises a valid concern when he argues there is risk in these ascribed properties in terms of leveling hierarchies and dispersing power. The Net, says Shenk, "encourages cultural splintering. It fosters tribes, and sub-cultures, not communities."[9] The Net is certainly a decentralizing force and is inherently transnational. In time, Netizens will be a constituency in and of themselves, and will have more interests in common than citizens who may live next door to each other. The Net's transnational properties may point to a critically important role for the Net in the news process of the future.

Earlier, I referred to the way news gathering is organized around institutions, from Parliament to City Hall. Political news in particular is organized around national, provincial, or state governments, even as our political scientists are questioning the future viability of the nation-state. And the Net, with its transnational capability, may be the most effective way of organizing new patterns to news coverage, a coverage that isn't hostage to national boundaries and the increasingly narrow definition of what constitutes the national interest. In today's world of geopolitics, there is the United States and the rest. When President Clinton decides to launch Operation Desert Fox against Iraqi president Saddam Hussein, governments in the Western world go along to get along. Canadian prime minister Jean Chrétien, shackled to some extent by treaty obligations, stands as one with his NATO and NORAD ally. Chrétien's Foreign Affairs minister, Lloyd Axworthy, keeps his counsel. And as far as the world is concerned, that's the news from Canada. The Net has the power to change the equation. Ordinary citizens articulate their position and share those views with people from Baghdad to Birmingham.

Today's transnational corporations are arguably where the true political power lies. Sovereign states are increasingly subject to the corporate agenda of companies that will shift a plant or a research facility from one continent to another if the policy climate is more favorable. Yet news organizations still devote a disproportionate amount of their resources to covering the government being led by the corporation, rather than the corporation doing the leading.

Like most powerful tools, the Net can be used for both good and bad. Dyson cites the example of individual privacy: once it is breached, it can be breached worldwide. People-finder services can be found on search-engine sites, the Net equivalent to a telephone book for the world. Lost loves, college roommates, and itinerant siblings can be found for a modest fee. But what if one doesn't want to be found?

There is a certain irony in the Net's libertarianism, and its origins as a place without rules or boundaries for personal expression. The Net is, after all, a creation of government, specifically the U.S. government seeking to establish an effective underground system of communication in the event of nuclear holocaust. The Net's inspiration, therefore, was the inspiration of the freedom fighter, the rugged individual, the survivor.

The economies of the Net are hostage, to some extent, to its libertarian soul, and the disinclination of users to pay fees for information. As the Net gets more organized, there will be some weave of advertiser presence, transaction fees, or even membership fees for Net communities. This "commercialization" will irritate its first users to no end, but is a likely precondition if it is to become as dominant a medium as television has been in the past thirty years.

The Internet is in the revolutionary tradition of American activist Thomas Paine, say its apostles. Just as the hackers who built the first PCs in their garages in the 1970s set out to transform the world with a communications populism, today's surfers see the Net as an exciting vehicle of empowerment.

UCLA professor Philip Agre says there is something particularly American about this view of the Internet and its focus on "community." America, after all, was colonized by communities, each determined to exist unfettered and free. From the first Pilgrims at Plymouth to William Penn's Quakers to Joseph Smith's Mormon community, America's story is one of emancipation and independence. For Americans the Net is but the latest opportunity to redefine community.

The Net is particularly empowering for those segments of society that have, through the years, been marginalized by the mainstream media: visible minorities, women, young people, the economically disadvantaged, and the politically disenfranchised. Freedom Forum new-media expert Adam Clayton Powell, III says, "For the first time in human history, every consumer, every reader, and every viewer can be a global publisher, with free and instantaneous world-wide distribution on the Net."[10]

Television journalist Pamela Wallin, host of *Pamela Wallin Live*, tells audiences they can no longer complain about media "because the media is you."

There are no entry barriers for users or information providers. As Levy suggests, anyone can set up a new channel or a storefront on the virtual highway for free, asking permission of no one and accepting income directly over the wire. The trade term used to describe the phenomenon is "antimedia activism." Jesse Hirsch, of Toronto's anti-hierarchical Media Collective, which promotes freedom of expression as a right of every citizen, says the Net questions corporate control. Old media, with its top-down, one-way flow approach to information dissemination, is straining under this idea of empowerment. Hirsch states: "The notion of an authoritative source like a newspaper telling you the news of the day is gone."[11] The Net generation challenges the premise that people should be told what's news. In that sense, the Net generation believes everyone should have access to the marketplace of ideas. Television news mattered because television news told us what to think about. Political and media elites duked it out in an effort to determine what it was we were thinking about. The Net creates the potential to reverse the process, to create a dynamic whereby citizens can tell society's leaders what the leaders ought to be thinking about. The world of politics and journalism, quite simply, could be turned upside down.

At this stage, the Net is still longer on promise than it is on product. A reality check is in order. *Globe and Mail* columnist Jack Kapica has written authoritatively about extravagant claims that have been made about the Internet's potential to deliver news faster than newspapers and television channels can. There is no denying the marketing challenge television's "all news" channels face when a big story breaks away from a camera's all-seeing eye and viewers wait with growing frustration for the latest developments.

The key to Net information is that it is cheap to store and, because of digitalization, can take any form. Consequently, even traditional newsgathering organizations are increasingly multimedia. *Maclean's* magazine's editorial offering includes a weekly television show, books featuring archival material, and a wide range of Web-based products. The *New York Post* invites readers to watch the traditional Christmas tree-lighting ceremony from Rockefeller Plaza live on its Web site. During one of the frequent eruptions during the Clinton impeachment saga, CNN broke into its regularly scheduled programming to relay images from *Roll Call* magazine's Web site for a scoop that new House Speaker Bob Livingston had admitted to a series of extra-marital affairs.

The technology facilitates tailoring of information to suit personal interests and tastes. Nicholas Negroponte's group at MIT have been talking about the "Daily Me" for a decade. Now even Dow Jones offers a personal journal.

Former *Chicago Tribune* publisher Jack Fuller says these new media hold much promise in part because they have the "soul" of reading, that, in contrast to television, Net use is interactive and therefore is inherently more stimulating.

Frank Daniels, III, publisher of the *News and Observer* in Raleigh, North Carolina, has been saying for years: "I think newspapers are a failing business and we'd better figure out what to do next." Daniels predicts, "Ten years from now, we won't publish a daily newspaper."[12] His company's response is Nando, an on-line system—a daily newspaper with instant updates of news and sports, searchable classified ads, an on-line game room, a software library, as well as a learning and reference center and user forums where readers can talk to each other. While I have no trouble containing my enthusiasm for Daniels's version of a chat room, the idea of instant updates for classified ads and stock tables would seem a prerequisite for future viability.

Esther Dyson says that, for the past half-century, news organizations have been in the business of selling the mass audience; the new business will involve creating and selling relationships. Dyson believes journalists of the future will mediate community conversations, that instead of simply telling readers what is going on, news organizations will collaborate with readers to discover the truth. This view of journalists as social animators is not entirely new; specialty channels such as C-PAC and C-SPAN now produce the style of journalism Dyson is describing. News anchors hosting "Town Hall meetings" are an example. But Dyson's model is a radical departure from the traditional view of journalist as detached observer.

The revolution that is the world of commingled bits will render the television set as we know it obsolete. The convergence of a television set, a computer, and the telephone in one new box is somewhere between three and ten years away, depending on where you live. These "teleputers" will be capable of processing the full range of digital bits, whether in the form of a movie or a piece of music, a business file, or a bank statement.

Emerging technologies have also already forced established television networks to rethink their methods of news gathering. For starters, the concept of a single evening or nightly newscast is hopelessly dated.

Today's news cycle is, in the words of the radio advertising jingle, "all news, all the time." CBC correspondents now file repeatedly through the day to *Newsworld*. NBC correspondents now have to feed MSNBC. These real-time deadlines mean reporters have less time to prepare news stories. The hot-house atmosphere can result in a rush to air with information that, subsequently, turns out to be inaccurate. All-news channels mean more talk to fill air time. More talk means more spin.

Two giant video news agencies—Reuters TV and Associated Press TV News—now supply many of the world's news images, which reduces foreign news bureaux's need for the traditional networks. Photojournalism, as a result, is less likely to reflect a uniquely Canadian, British, or American perspective. And television's agenda-setting properties will now be the semiprivate domain of two news agencies.

Satellites, computers, and linked cell phones have changed the way the reporting game is played in the field. There are fewer editors, reporters, and field producers. Former ABC correspondent Barry Dinsmore says the next war will be live, recorded by a one- or two-person crew armed with a camera and satellite uplink that can pack into two suitcases. Digital equipment will give us an editing deck that will fit in an attaché case. In the not-so-old days, as a correspondent covering the Contra war in Nicaragua, for example, I sometimes spent more time worrying about how to get the story back to the *Toronto Star* than I did crafting the story itself. And having hauled a forty-four-pound "portable" computer through too many airports, even the heaviest laptop seems like a luxury.

Television networks reacting to these new technologies are also moving into a new business. In November 1998, CBC president Perrin Beatty said the public broadcaster is entering the portal wars and is determined to become Canada's leading destination for news on the Web. Beatty said the CBC will create a new media unit to challenge Canoe, Canada's most successful news Web site.

"The Internet augurs massive changes for broadcasters, and those broadcasters that live in the past will die," Beatty said. "Our business is content, whether it's new media or traditional media."[13] Beatty's announcement lost some of its oomph, however, when he said the CBC now spends less than 1 percent of its $1.1-billion annual budget on new media. His pledge to "double" the CBC's new media budget still seems to leave the public broadcaster well behind the curve.

"By the year 2005, Americans will spend more hours on the Internet (or whatever it is called) than watching network television,"[14] says Negroponte. He predicts consumers in the near future will act as their own censors by telling the receiver what "bits" to select.

Multimedia products are the future, and Negroponte says "multimedia will someday be as subtle and rich as the feel of paper and the smell of leather."[15] Yet for all the excitement of the Post-Information Age, Negroponte warns, "the next decade will see cases of intellectual property abuse and invasion of our privacy."

Media theorists say the old model of media involved a limited supply of product with homogeneous content delivered to a passive mass audience with an undifferentiated reception and effect. The new media model will involve many different sources, with diverse content, delivered to fragmented active users or audiences with varied and unpredictable reception and effect. Brother Shenk worries we are creating the electronic equivalent of the Tower of Babel. Consensus may be more difficult to achieve. But more voices, with more information, from more sources will force the mainstream media to share the agenda-setting role in society.

Kapica argues that the Net has yet to deliver on its promise, in part because of the prohibitive cost of creating a viable news-gathering operation. Kapica says the real product of the on-line world is, in fact, yesterday's news, an editorial product that has already been crafted by an outside source. Kapica's observations are sound. But what if the new technologies make "journalists" of us all? If a hand-held Sony or Panasonic "Palm-corder" can record events with visuals that are comparable to those shot by an experienced photojournalist armed with an expensive ENG camera, how long will it take networks' news divisions to decide the originators of *America's Funniest Home Videos* may be on to something? Citytv's journalists routinely pack their own cameras.

The electronic emancipation potential of the Net does raise a number of questions of serious consequence to mainstream journalism. For openers, the information superhighway will force media companies to acknowledge that the fundamental economic paradigm of the news business for the last century—the assembly of mass audiences for interests with paid messages to convey—may not sustain itself into the millennium.

Mainstream media with on-line services and Web sites seem to be looking to some form of subscriber base to secure economic viability. Industry insiders insist it's not a real business until you have a secure way to make people pay for the content you are offering.

The mainstream media, therefore, will invest significant amounts of money in a bid to shape cyberspace case law in a way that safeguards "intellectual property" that could—contrary to the spirit of Paine— result in market domination for the huge conglomerates that preoccupy Kitman and company. A silencing of voices of dissent is a risk in this scenario, with all that implies for democracy.

There are emerging moral issues as well. Separating the real from the virtually real in photographic terms has always been tricky. In 1917, two young girls in England took pictures, using a "primitive" Kodak camera, that they used to buttress their claims that fairies actually existed. So convincing were Frances Griffiths and Eloise Wright that leading intellectuals of the day, including Sir Arthur Conan Doyle, creator of the super-sleuth Sherlock Holmes, believed the pictures real. A film entitled *Fairy Tale: A True Story* that tells the enchanting tale of the English school girls premiered at the 1997 Toronto Film Festival to the delight of audiences young and old. Alas, the girls' snaps turned out to be false.

Even in the mainstream media the problem exists. *National Geographic* used technical tricks to move one of the Pyramids so that a demanding editor who wanted two Pyramids in a certain alignment on a 1982 cover could be appeased.

There was also extensive media coverage of *Time* magazine's decision to run a digitally altered version of O.J. Simpson's mug shot following his arrest for the murders of his wife, Nicole Brown Simpson, and Ron Goldman. What was even more newsworthy was *Time* art director Arthur Hochstein's candid admission that the magazine has run "scores" of digitally altered cover photos. Hochstein's rationale was that *Time*'s cover should be considered a sales tool—like a poster or an advertisement. His response begs the question: Should a newsmagazine's art director be a photojournalist or not?

With the emergence of increasingly inexpensive digital technology, faking reality is easy. *Toronto Star* special correspondent Gary Blackwell states, "Rolling your own photo is a relatively simple, three-step process."[16]

Virtual reality is not a phenomenon whose genesis is found in technology or the on-line world. The Celtic myth of "shape-shifting" allowed the Irish to believe that gods, Druids, poets, and others in touch with the "other world" could take different shapes. The Celtic tradition is echoed in the legends of the Cree and the Navaho. These legends are neatly compartmentalized in a world of reason. It remains to be seen whether that compartmentalization holds fast in the virtual world of the future.

The problems of the Net are readily identified and less readily resolved. Champions of the new medium must figure out how to protect children and undesiring adults from potentially offensive material. Efforts to date have been a spectacular failure. In 1996, the U.S. Supreme Court struck down the Communications Decency Act as unconstitutional. In November 1998, a Philadelphia federal court judge issued an order temporarily suspending the effect of a new federal law restricting free speech on the Net. The Child Online Protection Act was part of an omnibus budget bill pushed through Congress prior to the 1998 midterm elections. The bill sought to prevent access to material "deemed harmful to minors." The definition could have included R-rated and other nonpornographic material. Significantly, the legislation didn't apply to people who actually sell X-rated material because their requirement of a credit-card number for purchases is considered a deterrent for children.

Net users will also have to determine how to protect intellectual-property rights and which country's laws have jurisdiction over the Net. A debate is unfolding in Canada as to whether the Canadian Radio-Television and Telecommunications Commission should have jurisdiction over the Net.

The experience in the U.S. is instructive. Efforts have been made by the U.S. Senate to eliminate free-speech provisions in the Constitution from applying to the Net. An amendment to the Telecommunications Bill, moved by former senator James Exron, would have made anyone using a single four-letter word on the Net—a word now published routinely in the *Globe and Mail*—liable to a fine and/or imprisonment. John Perry Barlow, co-founder of the Electronic Frontier Foundation, described the U.S. legislators' attempt succinctly: "They are a government of the completely clueless, trying to impose their will on a place they do not understand, using a means they do not possess."[17]

Esther Dyson says more troubling than the "indecency" issue is the issue of what to do about dangerous information, such as bomb-making instructions.

Netizens predict laws about content, either in terms of community standards or national content, cannot ultimately be effective. Current Canadian laws obliging radio stations to play a fixed percentage of material from Canadian artists cannot be sustained on the Net. "Government censorship is unlikely to be effective in the long run, even though governments will keep trying,"[18] Dyson writes. She cites the example of France, which outlawed the publication of polling information in the run-up to national elections. The Royal Commission on Electoral Reform here recommended Canada consider a similar law. But as Dyson points out, French citizens who wanted the data simply pulled it down from the Net from French-language sources in neighboring Switzerland. In Canada, a court-ordered publication ban on details from the Paul Bernardo trial led to similar disclosures and dissemination from nearby American news sources.

Then there are the "content" issues. Ellen Hume, in a thoughtful paper entitled "Tabloids, Talk Radio and the Future of News," argues that the news story of the future must retain its editorial integrity across different media: in text, audio, video, and multimedia formats.

Technology certainly made it easier for writers to get books published. In 1947, *Books in Print* reported that 357 publishers had 85,000 titles in print. Today, according to Cynthia Crossen of the *Wall Street Journal*, 49,000 publishers offer 1.3 billion titles, with an estimated 140,000 titles appearing annually. "Truly, technology has lowered the barriers," Crossen concludes. I try not to take Crossen's point personally.

The Web world also raises serious questions for the creators of editorial products in the on-line age. For example, how does the information consumer satisfy himself or herself as to the quality, accuracy, and objectivity of the information being posted on a Web site? Or does that even matter any more?

The journalism of Thomas Paine, to borrow a phrase from Canada's other official language, was "un journalisme engagé." Should journalism's existing code of professionalism, built as it is on the twin tenets of objectivity and fairness, be set aside in favor of a new form of information that reflects our own values, biases, and beliefs?

Negroponte talks of the "Daily Me"—a personalized journal of information culled from a variety of sources reflecting interests we have preprogrammed. We already have GOP-TV—a network that offers editorial content shaped by the Republican party's view of the world. It looks, sounds, and is presented in a format that mirrors network television, but reflects the party line. GOP-TV is in effect a step back into the past, when the press was largely partisan. News traditionalists worry about the implications for governance in a world of tailored, personalized information. Carleton University professor Elly Alboim summarized the risks: "We will have pools of people with different sets of agendas, different sets of expectations, different sets of standards for government performance, different sets of policy demands, and different levels of attachment to traditionally common institutions and values."[19] David Shenk shares Alboim's concerns about the inherent dangers to a society where shared culture is lost, posing a threat to our continued ability to govern ourselves.

Mine is a more optimistic view. Politics and political reporting practices in the past two decades have left the public feeling marginalized. They have, themselves, looked to alternative forms of communication to create a dialogue and work to a consensus. Reform Party supporters, for example, could not attract the attention of the mainstream national media. They were forced to rely on direct mail, community television, and audiotapes to spread the word. Mainstream-media attention followed Reform's electoral success, but it was very much a case of the media catching up to the story. The consensus was forged without the benefit of mainstream journalism.

Consumers also will be hard-pressed to satisfy themselves about the professional qualifications of Net information providers. CBC radio host Ian Brown in an interview with the *Toronto Star* expressed the frustration of many when he noted that Net critics can say whatever they want on a subject without having to back up their assertions with any evidence. "You can't do that in public discourse in any other medium but the Internet."[20] Listeners to talk radio may challenge the accuracy of Brown's assertion, but his broader point stands.

There is a risk the digital revolution will increase choice to the point of paralysis. Information consumers may look to the past for suggestions as to how best to categorize the authenticity of the information being shared.

Ellen Hume's formula addresses Negroponte's new world of bits as opposed to the old world of atoms. Schools of journalism may have to consider a similar paradigm shift. As a master's-level student at Carleton, I was expected to choose a concentration—print, broadcast, or the more traditional stream of journalism and society. Journalists in the future will have to be trained in all media forms. The career section of the *Globe and Mail* now routinely includes ads for professors of new media at community colleges.

Journalism education in the multimedia age will have to ensure graduates are as competent technically as they are creatively. In New York City, reporters for Channel One take their own pictures. Global Television has followed suit. *Maclean's* writers are expected to appear on the magazine's weekly television program. In the journalism of the near future, the union contracts establishing clear distinctions in tasks will be job threatening rather than job securing.

The Net will accelerate the decline of the central-authority nation-state as we know it. If the future is virtual communities, how will these communities be represented in legislative assemblies that, at present, gather law-makers selected according to geographic boundaries?

The Net will add impetus to the move toward proportional representation. Political interests who define themselves on a basis other than geography will be allowed to field a slate of candidates with some assurance that individuals speaking to their agenda will sit in Parliament.

News consumers in the world of new media will have to place value on information distributed digitally at low cost. And we will have to satisfy ourselves as to the professional qualifications of the information providers. Alboim writes: "The privileged status of the journalist as quasi-certified professional will be eroded and may disappear altogether as anyone with the technical skill set will be able to assemble and transmit journalism from virtually anywhere." Alboim says, "much of the journalism of the future is going to be in-house journalism whose organizations and institutions hire journalists to manage their information flow."[21]

Corporations, political parties, service clubs, and neighborhood groups have been publishing newsletters and the like for decades. But the Net has opened an exciting new world of possibilities for in-house journalism.

News Theatre, owned and operated by former CTV executive producer Jack Fleischmann, describes itself as a corporate video center; combining a news conference setting, a full television studio, and a state-of-the-art system to distribute signals via microwave link, satellite, or the Net. News Theatre can, and does, bring the production standards of network news to events at its downtown Toronto studio facility. A year ago, Fleischmann and his colleagues were working on ways to move live television pictures down the Net in real time—a quantum leap forward from the Max Headroom capability of the day. Today, the images can move to a desktop computer anywhere. The possibilities from this single advance are endless. Corporations, for example, can be their own news service, producing editorial products for distribution directly to their target audiences.

Publicly traded companies briefing analysis can do so with multi-media presentations and live interactive news conferences from a single venue. A company wanting to communicate with its regional offices can do the same. Even the National Security Agency in the United States prepares a classified news conference for the American intelligence community. The newscast cannot be watched by the general public, but presumably tailors all reports to address the concerns and interests of the intelligence community.

Alboim suggests there may not be a need or demand for centrally organized or centrally housed media centers. I am less convinced of this latter point, in part because I share Alboim's view that the digital revolution will increase choice to the consumer "to the point of paralysis for most." Freedom Forum colleague David Shenk coined the phrase "data smog" to describe the phenomenon. Shenk says we used to consider information overload a minor nuisance. But today the average business manager is expected to process a million words a week. "We thrive on information, but we can choke on it as well,"[22] Shenk says.

In the post-Gutenberg world, the Church of Rome offered guidance to its followers with the introduction of the papal *imprimatur*—offering the seal of St. Peter to texts to reassure the faithful that the ideas presented were consistent with the teachings of the Roman Catholic Church as interpreted by the Vatican. It may well be that the on-line world will create a market for information products with an *imprimatur* of their own.

Differentiating between data and information, we may be predisposed to seek out information provided by traditional news sources such as the *New York Times*, the *Financial Times*, or *Maclean's*. And in the on-line world, the best journalism from the best news operations is literally available by tapping a couple of keys on a terminal. It remains to be seen whether enough of us will be prepared to pay a premium for such information or to allow existing "national" news organizations to sustain large reporting staffs. But reportable news organizations may find their future is in the "editing" of quality content.

If, instead, we are headed inexorably to the empowered world of the freelancer, will we demand some code of professional standing as we do from medical doctors, lawyers, or chartered accountants? Will journalism have to accelerate its transition from craft to profession? And will there be, as Alboim speculates, an emerging need for Robert Heinlein's "Fair Witness"—a trusted observer of events, the on-line answer to the Sennachies of Celtic lore?

Journalism schools will need to train a new brand of journalists—information synthesizers—people who assimilate vast quantities of information and boil it down, draw meaning from it, and order it for news consumers by placing it in some context.

The notion isn't particularly new, Alboim says; wire-service editors have been doing it for years. And network television correspondents in foreign bureaux routinely file "meltdown" news reports. Meltdowns involve pulling down taped images from various network feeds and churning out a script that is little more than a précis of the morning's newspaper headlines. The correspondent then "fronts" the piece with a standup in front of a universally recognized landmark, from Big Ben to the Eiffel Tower, Downing Street to the White House. The problem with meltdowns is that the news item doesn't involve original reporting, but is television's equivalent to a précis.

Increasingly, newspapers are following suit, reinforcing the connection with their readers by having local reporters write about major international events, even if the reporter never actually sets foot in the city where the story in question is playing itself out. The result is closed-circuit news, information recycling rather than an exercise of discovery.

This trend to "information synthesis" alarms James Fallows, who describes the phenomenon as "nexus journalism." With a fax, a telephone, and access to the Net, reporters can cover stories from the newsroom or their home office. Fallows concedes there is a place for this kind of "data crawl," but posts a major concern that "the temptation of the nexus age is for all journalists to write stories that they didn't report."[23]

Pack journalism reaches an entirely new plane in the wired world of computers. Alboim, however, is describing a more sophisticated version of the New Age journalist than the type Fallows fears. The "integrated editors" of today's paginated newspapers are one such example, involved as they are in writing, editing, design, and technology.

Alboim says his colleagues at journalism schools of the future "need to train people in true observation and dispassionate reporting. We need to marry intellectual substance with issue expertise."[24] Alboim's ideal would reduce the likelihood of the kind of journalistic excess that characterized the early coverage in the Airbus affair.

The futurists will busily predict the end of much of the mainstream media as we know it today as the inevitable consequence of the Net explosion. For example, electronic tabloid publishing, based on liquid-crystal, flat-panel technology, is supposed to replace the print media by the year 2005. This should keep the brains' trust at the Canadian Pulp and Paper Association up late at night.

Negroponte talks about the day when computers are implanted in our bodies. Conversations will be controlled by the participant who has the quickest trigger finger on the keyboard calling up bits of supportive information—just like the gunslingers of the Old West. Insufferable bores will continue to dominate dinner parties, but they'll be insufferable bores with lightning-quick reflexes.

The exact form of the new media landscape will be determined at warp speed. But even the new media forums we have been exposed to already point to a decidedly different political journalism from what we are used to.

MSNBC, the network of NBC and Microsoft, is illustrative. MSNBC is talk television, but the new "pundits" aren't schooled in the art of reportage. MSNBC's talking heads are bankers, law professors, political consultants, and rappers. Marcia Clark may have fizzled as an assistant district attorney before a national television audience, but her celebrity status secured a new gig as television host.

The emergence of any new medium invariably is accompanied by predictions of the imminent demise of another. So it is with the emergence of the Net. But NYU professor Mitchell Stephens points out that, with a few notable exceptions (such as eight-track tapes), the appearance of a new medium does not, in fact, result in the disappearance of old media forms. Network radio was as big in the 1940s as network television was in the 1970s. Radio may be less dominant today, but it has hardly disappeared. Even within the medium, when FM radio emerged as the music listeners' band of choice, AM simply reinvented itself as talk radio. So it will be with network television.

Network television has lost its stranglehold on our attention. The comedian Jerry Seinfeld's weekly prime-time comedy series was the most-watched program of the 1990s. Yet in the 1970s, before cable ushered in the era of audience fragmentation, Seinfeld's "monster numbers" would have placed his show near the bottom of the list of the twenty most-watched programs. News junkies celebrate the proliferation of news and current-affairs programs that dot the prime-time schedule. But Don Hewitt, executive producer of *60 Minutes*, says the new programs are mostly about filling air time. "Behind every news magazine, there is a failed sitcom,"[25] Hewitt says.

What is clear, however, is the fact that the Net has inalterably changed the face of journalism, particularly political journalism. And the prime-time soap opera between President Bill Clinton and former White House intern Monica Lewinsky proves the point.

8

Clinton

The front-page story in the February 1, 1998, edition of the *Tampa Tribune* began with a simple but unsettling query: "What if he is telling the truth?" Readers didn't have to be told who "he" was—"he" was William Jefferson Clinton, forty-second president of the United States.[1]

But the story, by Associated Press staff writer Mike Feinsilber, suggested America's mainstream media were scrambling to find the pause button on the saga that overshadowed every other political, social, and economic development in the world for ten days following.

President Clinton stood accused of conducting an Oval Office affair with White House intern Monica Lewinsky, and then compounding the alleged indiscretion to full-blown criminal activity by attempting to suborn perjury. The latter, an indictable offense, was deemed serious enough to bring down the president. And in the world of American political reporting, there is no bigger story than the death—literal or figurative—of a president.

The story, dubbed "Tailgate" or any number of variations on the theme, triggered the most intense media "feeding frenzy" since Watergate. Played out against a public-opinion backdrop of a president with an acknowledged "zipper" problem, the story was more lurid in detail than a locker-room exchange.

The story, said the *Washington Post*'s Bob Woodward, had all the elements—sex, power, and the abuse of same. And to give the furor some historical symmetry, Monica Lewinsky spent the early days of the scandal at her mother's apartment at the Watergate. Because of the story's political setting, observers were quick to clarify that the issue wasn't infidelity, but rather counseling someone to lie about infidelity.

The Lewinsky scandal would create a media maelstrom of significantly more intensity than Canada's Airbus scandal because the press's quarry was a sitting president. However, there were parallels between the two dramas to be sure. Both involved prominent newsmakers—in Clinton's case, the dominant news figure in the world. Both stories grew from "congenial truths." In Mulroney's case, it was public perception of a government plagued by sleaze and corruption; in Clinton's case, a perception of the president as philanderer. These congenial truths were so pervasive that even long-time associates of the two men were reluctant to offer a public defense in the early days of the scandal.

Both the Airbus and the Lewinsky affairs had been the subject of press-club gossip for months as investigative reporters probed for proof. But in the end, there was one fundamental difference between the stories. Mulroney knew he had never taken the alleged $5-million kickback and so did his advisers. Like poker players in a game of "Chicago," they knew they had the "buried spade." Clinton's advisers were denied the ultimate defense of truth, though it would be months before their suspicions would be confirmed by the president himself.

Clinton's dominant news frame on the "character" issue was most definitely a factor in the Lewinsky affair. As Ed Rollins told Larry King, "If these charges had been made against President Carter—the last Democratic president—they would have been laughed away."[2] Carter, the Baptist from Plains, Georgia, is perceived as a straight arrow, an image reinforced by his "candid" admissions in a *Playboy* interview of having been guilty of "lusting in his heart." The public's perception of Clinton was decidedly different. Indeed, during the 1992 campaign, backroom operatives, in private conversation, would acknowledge Clinton's appeal to a certain demographic group because of his "jumpability."

The Lewinsky story was about sex, lies, and audiotape, and a perceived abuse of the power of the Oval Office. But "Tailgate" is also a story about the press; the pressures of competition; the clash of journalistic culture between new media and old; the tabloidization of news and the rush to judgment of the pundit class; and, most important, the ever-widening chasm between the press and the public it purports to serve.

Major Hollywood studios released two motion pictures—*Wag the Dog* and *Primary Colors*—with storylines built around a philandering president, only to discover, to their horror, that their creative efforts suffered in comparison with the real-life version. The news bulletins, updates, and front-page headlines from Bangor to Burbank proved once again that truth really is stranger than fiction. Or is it? *Primary Colors* is based on a novel by *Newsweek* columnist Joe Klein, who wrote the book after a stint covering Clinton's 1992 campaign. Television producer Danny Schechter states that Klein had to turn his hand to fiction to tell what he saw as the true story of the Clinton years because in fiction, you don't have to be caught in the act.

Behind the scenes lurked the shadowy figure of a literary agent with an acknowledged political agenda and a determination to ensure that the supporting cast achieved the ultimate media accolade—a seven-figure book advance as the *pièce de résistance* for Andy Warhol's celebrated fifteen minutes. At center-stage stood a defiant First Lady, Hillary Rodham Clinton, Cardinal Richelieu to her husband's King Louis, and the archrival, independent counsel Kenneth Starr.

In its early days, the Lewinsky story evolved around the issue of whether Bill Clinton's presidency could survive, but in time it became obvious the president's wasn't the only career hanging in the balance.

The Lewinsky saga, whatever its dénouement, is an important signpost in the evolution of North American reporting practices. An analysis of the coverage suggests America's mass media have ushered in a new era of news coverage—an era when even the most intimate details of life are now lead news items on suppertime shows.

Rumors that the president was carrying on an affair with someone on the White House staff began circulating in Washington more than a year earlier. *Newsweek* correspondent Michael Isikoff, acting on a tip from one of Paula Jones's lawyers, worked the leads and pieced together most of the story, in *Newsweek*'s own description, "largely on an off-the-record and background-only basis."[3] Isikoff talked to a number of the principals, including former White House staffer Linda Tripp and literary agent Lucianne Goldberg.

In July 1997, Internet reporter Matt Drudge's newsletter revealed the fact that Kathleen Willey had received a subpoena to testify to

Tripp's assertion that Kathleen had emerged from an Oval Office meeting with the president flushed and disheveled. But the story remained unreported in the mainstream press for another six months.

By Saturday, January 17, 1998, *Newsweek*, in its own words, faced a difficult decision. The issue was whether or not to publish the information that Starr was looking into allegations that Clinton was carrying on an affair with a former White House intern. Further, there were suggestions that Clinton and his close friend and adviser Vernon Jordan had urged the intern about to be subpoenaed by Starr to lie about the affair under oath. Two days before, Isikoff had contacted Starr's office for comment. The prosecutors, in turn, said the report could destroy their investigation. They asked for a day to plead with Lewinsky to agree to be their witness. *Newsweek* agreed to the pause. The next day the newsmagazine's reporters were allowed to listen to a tape of a conversation between Tripp and Lewinsky that included Lewinsky's detailed descriptions of her alleged affair. Still the magazine decided against publication. Editor-in-chief Richard Smith held off because, apart from Tripp's accusations, the newsmagazine "had no independent confirmation of the basis for Starr's inquiry on the subject."[4] Editors were also concerned *Newsweek* reporters had not had an opportunity to speak to Lewinsky directly to establish her credibility. They decided, responsibly, to continue digging.

Matt Drudge had no such hesitation. His Internet-based newsletter, *The Drudge Report*, is the wired world's equivalent of *Frank* magazine. What makes Drudge's site even more appealing is the fact that he facilitates access to America's leading commentators by including their columns on his Web page. Drudge is one-stop shopping. Visitors to his Web site can access Drudge's latest "scoop." The irony in this is the fact that Drudge hasn't figured out a way to get paid for his work. There is no charge for a "hit" on Drudge's Web site.

Drudge's status as a "player" in the Lewinsky affair is underscored by the fact that there were 115 million visits to *The Drudge Report* Web site last year, with 1,162,553 hits when special prosecutor Kenneth Starr issued his report on September 10, 1998. Drudge is a journalistic bottom-feeder by his own admission. Having graduated near the bottom of his high-school class, the self-styled apostle of legendary columnist

Walter Winchell, Drudge writes scoops that, according to *Slate* editor Michael Kinsley, are usually stories the mainstream press have declined to cover. His sources tend to be from within news organizations themselves. In the Lewinsky case, Drudge issued a "red alarm" and reported that *Newsweek* was investigating allegations of a presidential affair with a White House staffer. Drudge himself lays claim to a modest 80 percent accuracy rate. Here in Canada, the satirical review *Frank* sets a more modest benchmark of 60 percent accuracy. Drudge is facing an aggressive $30-million libel lawsuit from White House staffer Sidney Blumenthal, having apologized for a story suggesting Blumenthal had physically abused his wife. Yet Drudge's Internet reporting led directly to news reports in the *Washington Post* and the *Los Angeles Times* and forced *Newsweek* to post the coverage its editors had originally put on hold on its own Web site.

Asked to comment on *Newsweek*'s decision to withhold publication of the Lewinsky story, on CNN's *Larry King Live*, former *Washington Post* editor Ben Bradlee said, "You can't get more responsible than not running it."[5] Bradlee then underlined the cost of that responsibility when he added, "Let's face it, they [*Newsweek*] have done a wonderful job on the story after they got beat on it."[6]

The *Drudge–Newsweek* conundrum is the most spectacular, though characteristic, example of the clash between new and old media over traditional news values.

In a column carried in the February 2 issue of *Time*, Kinsley argues, "The Internet made this story. And the story made the Internet. 'Clinterngate,' or whatever we are going to call it, is to the Internet what the Kennedy assassination was to TV news: its coming of age as a media force. Or some might say media farce."

Drudge's Net scoop triggered a media feeding frenzy. In the post-Watergate era, experts such as Larry Sabato argue the press is "far more interested in finding sleaze and achieving fame and fortune than in serving as an honest broker of information between citizens and government."[7]

White House spokesman Mike McCurry, a press secretary his entire professional life, said in such a charged atmosphere there is a tendency "for opinion to masquerade as fact,"[8] a tendency intensified by competition.

The journalism of the Internet exacerbated the problem. The White House press secretary cited the example of one of America's most prestigious newspapers—the *Wall Street Journal*. The *Journal* put a story out on its Web site that didn't check out by the time the paper went to press. The story in question never ran in the newspaper itself, but did enjoy wide circulation through the Internet.

Real scandals—from Canada's tainted-blood scandal to the savings-and-loan debacle in the United States—go unreported for years.

Sabato believes a certain sad conclusion is inescapable: "The press has become obsessed with gossip rather than governance; it prefers to employ titillation rather than scrutiny; and as a result, its political coverage produces trivialization rather than enlightenment."[9] Sabato, Tom Patterson, and a host of other students of the press's role in democracy believe strongly the future quality of American democracy at least depends in no small measure on our collective success in reversing the recent deterioration in political reporting standards.

These scholars are quick to acknowledge the shortcomings of past practices, particularly at a time when reporters were generally more deferential to powerful interests, whether in the world of politics, business, or professional sport. Old-time sports writers remember the days when young reporters covering the Toronto Maple Leafs hockey club received meal money from the club's general manager. How reasonable is it to expect any individual to consistently bite the hand that feeds it— literally? Similarly, old Quebec hands tell anecdotes of the Duplessis era, when reporters covering a news conference left their trench coats hanging prominently on hooks at the back of the hall to facilitate the distribution of envelopes containing cash.

Predictably, these coverage patterns produce a certain cynicism among the general public. Initially, the public's cynicism is directed toward the politician in the news. But a public fed a steady diet of cynical editorial content will, ultimately, become cynical about the news organization itself.

Sabato describes the "domino" effect of lowest-common-denominator journalism. Purveyors of political smut seek out the weak media link—in terms of traditional journalistic standards—and count on the mainstream media falling in line. *Frank* magazine regularly reminds readers of stories that first surfaced in the pages of their gossip-driven publication that were recycled as major news stories in daily newspapers. With its characteristic degree of cheek, *Frank* tweaks its traditional competitors for any failure to attribute the "scoop" to *Frank. Drudge* and other Net news sources serve a similar purpose.

My Freedom Forum colleague Jeffrey Toobin, whose coverage of the O.J. Simpson trial for *The New Yorker* led to his best-seller *The Run of His Life*, reflected on the feeding frenzy phenomenon following the bombing incident at the Atlanta Olympics in 1996, when the press all but convicted security guard Richard Jewell. "These days, the sheer numbers of reporters chasing a hot story—print, broadcast, cable, on-line, freelance and infotainment—can create for their targets a chamber of horrors."[10] In these circumstances, Toobin said, "reputation is more easily wrecked than rescued."[11]

Sabato further suggests these media feeding frenzies follow certain patterns; for example, they tend to occur during quiet times. The Lewinsky story broke when official Washington was still trying to work off the effects of the holiday hiatus and was slowly gearing up for the president's State of the Union address. In the case of Canada's Airbus affair, the story broke as the national media was catching its collective breath after the 1995 Quebec referendum campaign.

These feeding frenzies are also usually triggered by a self-inflicted wound. Back in 1988, Gary Hart reportedly challenged the media to probe his private life, though Hart himself takes exception to this assertion. Reporters, however, were happy to oblige. The photos of Hart and model Donna Rice relaxing on the deck of a yacht named *Monkey Business* ended his presidential candidacy before the spring snow had melted in most primary states.

Clinton, in turn, had a history of "bimbo eruptions," as his staff took to describing them. The 1992 furor over Gennifer Flowers, who nearly scuppered Clinton's candidacy with claims of a long-standing affair, may have been the most spectacular example, but it was not an isolated case.

Trash TV and publications such as *People* magazine condition news consumers to think about the private lives of public figures. Celebrity politics is the inevitable result. As any number of media analysts have observed, John F. Kennedy may have represented the dawn of image politics in the television era, but Clinton represents the apex. It is politics as soap opera.

This predisposition on the part of the American press to seek out information about the seamier side of political life isn't particularly new. George Washington condemned the American press as savage, and Thomas Jefferson concluded that "even the least informed of the people have learned that nothing in a newspaper is to be believed."[12] In his work *Democracy in America*, published in 1835, Alexis de Tocqueville observed "the journalists of the United States [possess] a vulgar turn of mind."[13]

With the coming of age of the penny press, journalism in America went through definable phases, including the "yellow journalism" of the penny press and the "muckraking" traditions of the early twentieth century.

During Franklin Delano Roosevelt's time in the Oval Office, the rule of thumb for press coverage was simple: the private life of a public figure should stay private and undisclosed unless it "seriously impinged on his or her public performance," Sabato says.

Presidential dalliances were overlooked by the press, even when, as reported by Seymour Hersh in *The Dark Side of Camelot*, the president was dallying with a woman who was also involved with a "made" mobster. Hersh goes so far as to suggest John Kennedy's preoccupation with extramarital sex was a contributing factor to the Cuban missile crisis.

The new rule of political coverage was as open as its predecessors had been closed. Since any aspect of private life is relevant to an official's public performance, the reasoning went, everything is fair game—personal relationships, private behavior, and any matter exhibiting an official's "character" or "judgment." Furthermore, literally anything that affects the political players and outcome—including unproven rumor and innuendo—can be made public in the process.

Sabato breaks the evolution of journalistic coverage patterns into three distinct eras: the "lapdog journalism" that prevailed from 1941 to 1966, the "watchdog journalism" of 1966 to 1974, and the "junkyard dog journalism" from 1974 to the present. The watchdog journalism era of Vietnam, Chappaquiddick, and Watergate was a high-water mark for American journalism. But the canonization of "Woodstein" gave rise to a generation of journalists that see themselves as avenging angels who will sanitize American politics, in the view of former ABC correspondent Sander Vanocur. A bitter Gary Hart insists that "rumor and gossip have become the coin of the political realm."[14]

Since Sabato's book *Feeding Frenzy* appeared in 1991, political reporters in Canada and the United States have held innumerable seminars and discussions with a view to reasserting their commitment to an editorial product that appeals to a constituency other than "inquiring minds."

And then along comes word of a Gennifer or Paula or Monica, or the cost of a hotel suite in Paris, or the size of a prime-ministerial clothes closet, or the refurbishing of an official residence, or whether or not the prime minister is addicted to NyQuil, and once again the "inquiring minds" rule the day.

When there is a hint of scandal in the air, reporters rarely err on the side of caution. Overplaying a story is a more forgivable sin than missing the next Watergate. And when a scandal breaks, reporters are happy people, camouflaging their enthusiasm for the chase with ritualistic expressions of dismay that such events ever come to pass. The fact is, the press loves scandal stories. And the bigger the name of the person involved in the scandal, the more the press likes the story.

Crisis or issue, management is an integral part of media relations for any public figure. Hugh Segal offered a Canadian variation on the theme with his observation that, "in politics, you dig your grave with small shovels."[15]

There are certain absolutes about a crisis in politics, the first being the media will decide what is or isn't a crisis and the exercise will be completely subjective.

Clinton's press secretary, Mike McCurry, began one White House briefing during the Lewinsky affair with the words: "Welcome, ladies and gentlemen, to the theater of the absurd."[16] McCurry and his colleagues, understandably, were hoping the controversy swirling around them was just another "bimbo" eruption. But the mainstream media had already decided otherwise.

The Washington-based Center for Media and Public Affairs conducted a survey and concluded the "Monica story" constituted the biggest feeding frenzy in recent memory, exceeding even the coverage patterns for the tragic death of the Princess of Wales in August 1997.

From the graphics used to introduce network news items, to the overlines on newspaper stories, to the "Bills" introducing radio talk-show programming, the media declared the president to be in crisis. *Newsweek*'s headline "Clinton in Crisis" was typical, but other news organizations brought the language of the locker room into the nation's living rooms with repeated references to "Tailgate," "Oralgate," or "Fornigate." CTV Ottawa bureau chief Craig Oliver, in a standup from the White House lawn, was prepared to discuss the specifics of the alleged affair in some more detail than news anchor Sandi Rinaldo seemed comfortable with. Others showed less restraint. Maureen Dowd noted in her *New York Times* Liberties column, under the subhead "Not Suitable for Children," "the palaver about whether a 21-year-old White House intern had a particular kind of sex with the president has gotten so graphic that CNN's 'Inside Politics' Friday featured a warning that the segment might not be suitable for young viewers."[17]

Over on ABC, Ted Koppel's opening statement on one edition of *Nightline* began with the observation that Clinton's presidency may "ultimately come down to the question of whether oral sex does or does not constitute adultery."[18] Back on CNN, Gennifer Flowers, the original "other woman," at least in terms of media disclosure, was telling Larry King and his viewers that the answer to Koppel's question, as far as Clinton was concerned, is an emphatic no, and the Bible tells him so.

Print coverage was, if anything, even more explicit, prompting comedian Jay Leno to observe: "There is so much sex in the media that even *Newsweek* comes in a plain brown wrapper."

The competitive pressures, fueled by access to news Web sites, put "information" into circulation that didn't hold up as fact for long. The Texas newspaper the *Dallas Morning News*, for example, reported that a secret-service agent had witnessed Lewinsky and the president in a compromising situation. The news was repeated on radio and television newscasts for hours, at least until the *Dallas Morning News* did a roll-back, describing their story in later editions as "essentially" correct. There were reports of a dress Clinton had given the young intern as a present, a dress said to include stains of the president's semen, a dress said to be on its way to a forensic lab for DNA testing.

Literary agent Lucianne Goldberg admitted to Cox News Services that she was the one who leaked the story about the semen-soiled blue dress. "I had to do something to get their [the media's] attention. I've done it. And I'm not unproud of it."[19]

Neiman Foundation director Bill Kovach says: "There was a time when there was a kind of standard that most journalists lived by, that you had to verify a piece of information about which you had no real knowledge with at least one source, maybe two. But that day is gone in the competitive world. When Matt Drudge puts it up on the Internet and everyone in town is talking about it, it's difficult to resist at least trying to match what he's put out. So each judgment maker in each news organization is left to design his or her own standards."[20] *Washington Post* media critic Howard Kurtz agrees, telling CNN "we seem to have graduated from the two-source rule to the no-source rule."[21]

The public is certainly aware of the competitive pressures reporters face, but reflects little sympathy for this plight. A CNN/*Time* poll conducted during the Lewinsky affair suggested 77 percent of respondents believed the media had been more interested in getting the story first than in getting it right. And more than half of the respondents believed the media acted irresponsibly in their coverage.

American University communications professor Lewis Wolfson acknowledges the inherent risk of the integrity of the press in situations such as the Lewinsky affair. "It happened in Watergate as well," Central Michigan University professor John Hartman told the *Globe and Mail*. "Now, as then, reporters have shown a willingness to lower their standards of attribution because they expect they will be vindicated."[22]

The spicy revelations of the Lewinsky affair pushed every other major news story to second-tier status. The news anchors from ABC, NBC, and CBS had all traveled to Cuba to host newscasts from Havana during Pope John Paul's historic visit. Seconds after signing off the first night, Peter Jennings, Tom Brokaw, and Dan Rather were on chartered flights back to Washington. As *Globe and Mail* columnist Jeffrey

Simpson observed, "So Washington, a city with relentless self-fascination, has jacked up the narcissism, proof of which was the speedy return of the poster boys of the U.S. television networks—the anchors—from Cuba where what's his name was meeting what's his name."[23]

Appearing on a Freedom Forum/CNN news special later in the week, Rather explained, "We were faced with two choices: get back to Washington to cover this big breaking story, or ask for [permanent] assignment to Cuba."[24]

Castro had devised a strategic media-relations plan for the papal visit with a geopolitical objective worthy of Disraeli. The Cuban dictator agreed to allow the leader of the Roman Catholic Church to be sharply critical of certain practices of the Castro regime. In exchange, however, the Pope would explicitly denounce the American economic boycott of Cuba as immoral. The Pontiff did, in fact, denounce the U.S. sanctions as "oppressive, unjust, and ethically unacceptable." Such strong language would have led the network newscasts in any other circumstances, particularly with the anchors from the three major networks on location in Havana. Instead, Castro's gamble came up craps; the Pope's statement was carried "inside" most U.S. dailies behind further allegations of the White House sex scandal.

Similarly, Israeli prime minister Benjamin Netanyahu and PLO chairman Yasser Arafat were sitting in the Oval Office, meeting with the president in an attempt to work out a resolution to the current difficulties of the Middle East. In other circumstances, the meeting would have constituted a major news story. In the context of this feeding frenzy, the two Middle East leaders might as well have been on the dark side of the moon.

McCurry says he had heard rumblings *Newsweek* was pursuing the Lewinsky story weeks earlier. He was literally heading out the door one Tuesday night after a long day of preparing for Netanyahu's visit when "someone handed me the Internet version of the *Washington Post* story. I knew we would have to respond." McCurry's immediate reaction, however, was to go home "and get some sleep. A wise choice as it turned out."[25]

Canadian news organizations were equally quick to respond to the "crisis" in Washington. Both CTV and CBC dispatched anchors Lloyd

Robertson and Peter Mansbridge to the U.S. capital. Though the Canadian dollar may have been falling to record low levels against its U.S. counterpart at the time, that story was afforded also-ran status. Mansbridge would win a Gemini Award for his work from Washington.

The *Toronto Star*'s January 23, 1998, edition was typical of the approach of Canadian newspapers to the Clinton story. The *Star*'s front page included two staff-written pieces and a front-page readers' guide read as follows: "Excerpts from Tapes, Pg. 6, Clinton Compromised, Pg. 6, Impeachment Possible, Pg. 7, Flowers Feels Vindicated, Pg. 17, Portrait of a 'Chatty Kid,' Pg. 18." A story recounting the guilty plea of Unabomber Ted Kazinsky, by contrast, was run on page 2. The stories on the *Star*'s inside pages appeared under the overline "Crisis for Clinton," and a series of photos arranged in a special "box" identified all of the principal players for readers. Columnist Richard Gwyn, with his usual perspicacity, rounded out the *Star*'s offering with a piece that concluded: "Whatever the truth, Clinton is no longer fit for office."

Editors at *Maclean's*, Canada's newsmagazine, in an act of raw courage stuck with the proposed merger of the Royal Bank and the Bank of Montreal on the cover of their February 2 edition. Lewinsky and Clinton were reduced to thumbnail photos on the top righthand corner under a small headline that read "Sex and the Presidency: the threat of impeachment." When I offered *Maclean's* editor Robert Lewis congratulations on his team's decision, Lewis conceded the decision to go with the more substantive Canadian story probably cost the magazine in terms of newsstand sales.

In the early days of the Lewinsky affair, Clinton's media team violated certain of the rules of crisis management. The White House was slow to designate a lead spokesperson and ignored the rule of thumb that the more serious the crisis, the more senior the spokesperson should be. They also let the legal perspective prevail. Lawyers, invariably, prefer the "no comment" route. They argue they need more time to assemble facts, that there is no need to be panicked into precipitous action, that there are legal implications that have to be carefully considered, that any public pronouncement should be delayed until a solution to the problem presents itself.

Lawyers intuitively instruct their clients to maintain strict silence in such circumstances. They are dead wrong. For a political figure, the court of public opinion is as important as a court of law. Lawyers chafe at the idea that a nonlawyer should ever offer legal advice. Yet lawyers routinely think they can offer sophisticated media-relations advice. They are mistaken.

McCurry says that, in any normal situation, a press secretary has to assume he or she has 100 percent of the information needed to do the job. But he told a Harvard community gathering: "In this matter, things have been turned upside down." McCurry says he did not have all the information available to legal counsel, and he didn't want it. "I was reluctant personally to become an original finder of fact," McCurry said, out of concern he might then be subject to subpoena by special prosecutor Ken Starr. McCurry concludes: "It is a wholly unsatisfactory way to do business."[26]

In the Lewinsky case, Clinton's lawyers had an additional card to play: the threat of subpoena from Starr's team of prosecutors. The president's lawyers, therefore, decided the only people in the "loop" should be those who could claim lawyer–client privilege.

As a result, Clinton's supporters were slow to mount a defense, and designated spokespersons such as McCurry seemed curiously tentative in their denials. On the talk-show circuit, former Clinton adviser Mandy Grunwald explained that, on occasion, "you have to sacrifice your short-term public relations strategy for your long-term legal strategy." Starr's team, on the other hand, felt no such constraint and was leaking like sieves.[27]

Republican political consultant Ed Rollins, appearing on *Larry King Live*, said Clinton operatives such as James Carville and Paul Begala, who had been so effective in the past, weren't allowed to tell their story this time. "You get diminished ... if you don't get out there and tell your own story,"[28] Rollins said.

Australian golfer Greg Norman, playing the first week of February in the international tournament in Sydney that bears his name, fielded queries over two separate days as to whether Monica Lewinsky had accompanied the president when Clinton visited Norman's Hobe Sound, Florida, home. Norman told the press he couldn't say whether Lewinsky was in Florida, but he emphatically denied the former White House intern had ever been in his home. Reports persisted that Starr had subpoenaed television footage from a Florida TV station, forcing Norman to field questions a second day. Exasperated, Norman urged the press, "Let it go, guys. What he does in his private life is his business." Norman admitted the media press over Clinton's visit had thrown the Australian off his game.[29]

Clinton's normal Praetorian Guard—Paul Begala, James Carville, and others—could not run the risk of becoming targets for the subpoena-waving prosecutors from Starr's team. White House staffers had incurred exorbitant and extraordinary legal expenses as a direct consequence of Starr's previous incursions and, as Begala told Larry King, "I can't expose myself and my family to that risk." Begala says the tension among Clinton's advisers was not dissimilar to the tension that gripped the nation's newsrooms. "One group wants to get it right, one group wants to get it right away."[30]

Peter Mansbridge was struck by a particular similarity between Clinton's travails and Canada's Airbus affair. In the early days, longtime associates of Clinton and Mulroney were equally reluctant to come forward and defend their beleaguered leaders.

Other "friends" were decidedly less helpful than Greg Norman. The president's former pollster Dick Morris, whose access to the president was curtailed when Morris was caught up in his own sex scandal, was particularly insensitive and crass in this public comment: "Let's assume, okay, that his [Clinton's] sexual relationship with Hillary is not all it's supposed to be, let's assume that some of the allegations that Hillary ... [is] sometimes not necessarily ... into regular sex with men ... might be true." Morris went on to suggest that, in such circumstances, the president might just be forced to explore other avenues of satisfaction. What is extraordinary is not simply that the media reported Morris's statement, but rather that he had begun his musings with the disclaimer: "None of what I am about to say is necessarily fact." As Maureen Dowd pointed out, "The revolution always eats its own." Morris sought to defend his former client by smearing the First Lady.[31]

In a crisis, any vulnerability may be, and likely will be, exploited by the competition, by dissatisfied associates, disgruntled employees past or present, and real or self-proclaimed experts. All of these factors were in evidence during Clinton's January travails.

The story was triggered by a pair of disgruntled former White House employees: Tripp and Lewinsky. Former Clinton staffers Dee Dee Myers and George Stephanopoulos made comments that were less than helpful. Myers, who served as Clinton's official spokesperson, told Larry King, "I'm glad I'm not the press secretary today," thereby creating the impression that she was happy she wasn't being called on to defend the indefensible.[32] Stephanopoulos was even less helpful, and was the first commentator to invoke the dreaded "i" word—impeachment. Stephanopoulos's answer was the correct response for an individual who has crossed over to the land of pundit, but it was devastating for Clinton. The president's political rivals, from that point on, could invoke the impeachment question and attribute the question to one of Clinton's most trusted former aides.

Of equal significance, in the land of media wall posters, was the fact that the Democratic party leadership went missing in action in the early hours. Most conspicuous by his absence was Vice-President Al Gore. Gore, who harbors presidential aspirations of his own, ultimately mounted a spirited public defense of the president, but not before assessing the opportunities and risks to his own political future.

As any crisis escalates, every aspect of an individual or organization's past will be closely examined by everyone from the cab driver hauling fares from the airport to family friends. No bit of personal dirt remains unearthed when someone becomes famous, according to Howard Kurtz. And sex is no longer off limits to the mainstream press.

Both the Clinton and Starr camps have learned that bare-knuckle media manipulation works, even if the headlines on occasion suggest the strategy has backfired. And each side has accepted the soundness of the assertion that mud-slinging makes for better copy when both sides are involved.

This phenomenon was particularly problematic for Clinton. In 1992, during the New Hampshire primary that would determine the legitimacy of his campaign for president, Clinton sought out an interview with the top-rated public-affairs program *60 Minutes* on CBS. Clinton and Hillary agreed to answer allegations regarding whether he had conducted an affair with Gennifer Flowers while governor of Arkansas. The interview was to air on Super Bowl Sunday, ensuring maximum ratings for the program. While admitting he had caused pain to his marriage, Clinton told interviewer Steve Kroft that Flowers's claim to a twelve-year affair was false. With Hillary providing a firewall with her presence, Clinton struck a deal with the electorate that suggested he had outgrown his wandering ways.

Clinton had offered similar explanations when pressed about other issues from his past. Asked about drug use, he claimed he didn't inhale. And his explanation as to how he managed to avoid the draft during the Vietnam War was creative if less than forthcoming.

The print press, including the *Globe and Mail*, helped readers track the wiggle disclosures with "Media Watch" columns that listed in single-paragraph form the "scoops" of news organizations from the *Portland Oregonian* to CNN. From Clinton's perspective, one of the most damaging wiggle disclosures was a report in the *Washington Post* to the effect that the president had admitted in his deposition that he had, in fact, had an affair with Flowers.

In the context of Marlin Fitzwater's two kinds of truth, the kind you prove in court and the kind any damn fool can plainly see, Clinton clearly opted for the former. Clinton used precision of language, including verb tense, to lead the viewer inexorably to a conclusion that wasn't the whole truth, but stopped short of a bald-faced lie. Flowers claimed her affair with Clinton lasted twelve years. If the actual duration was only eleven years and a few months, her assertion, strictly speaking, was false.

Clinton's cleverness, in terms of precision of language, set the benchmark for the subsequent media interrogation on Lewinsky. When the president shifted verb tenses in an interview with PBS anchor Jim Lehrer, the press pounced.

As was the case in 1992, Hillary Clinton assumed the lead role in the counterattack. The First Lady sallied forth to the media capital of America—New York City—to what the tabloid press described as "the ultimate test of her poise under fire." Appearing on network television programs, Mrs. Clinton had her elbows up, denouncing the right-wing cabal that was out to destroy her husband's presidency and insisting her husband was a victim of "evil."

The Clintons made effective use of a photo-op to have the president himself issue an unequivocal denial, and followed up with a strong

State of the Union address. Their attack force, led by Carville, picked up the First Lady's reference to the right-wing cabal. Their comments were deliberately over the top. Carville in particular was aggressively advancing an image of whisky-swilling, right-wing fanatics making up all manner of unsubstantiated allegations about the president and then leaking them to lazy reporters disinclined to establish whether the tip was fact or fiction.

On the Sunday after the scandal broke, the Clintons arranged a photo opportunity outside a Methodist church in D.C. The president, toting his favorite Bible, was talking with the church's pastor as Mrs. Clinton looked on. The message was unmistakable. God and Mrs. Clinton have obviously forgiven the president his transgressions, who are you to sit in judgment?

Political operatives in my circle winced at the transparency and phoneyness of the photo-op, but in conversation were willing to concede its likely effectiveness with middle America beyond the chattering classes of Washington.

In any crisis, the media constituency is much broader than the mainstream press. ABC news correspondent Ann Compton once observed that America's political agenda is not set on the evening news shows, but in the opening monologues of the late-night talk shows hosted by, for example, Jay Leno and David Letterman. Here in Canada, a Rick Mercer moment on *This Hour Has 22 Minutes* can have more impact on public opinion than a learned editorial in one of Canada's national newspapers.

Journalists fancy themselves as individuals who provide the initial record of what will become history. But, as *Time* magazine states, in today's wired world it is "the comics who truly write the first draft of history."[33]

Five days in, the Clinton crisis-management team finally hit its stride. Attack lines had been honed ("This is an ongoing campaign of lies and leaks").

The use of the leak as a strategic tool is a factor in any crisis. *Newsweek* bureau chief Evan Thomas, participating in a panel discussion on *Larry King Live*, said simply, "The way the world works in Washington is that people leak." *Time* managing editor Walter Isaacson agreed: "In a war like this, leaks and sources are the weapons." The same ground rules apply in Ottawa, London, Canberra, or any other capital of a Western liberal democracy.[34]

Media scholar Kathleen Hall Jamieson says news consumers should know more about sources, especially if these sources are leaking selectively for partisan advantage. Marvin Kalb agrees. "Give me some idea where the person is coming from; whether he or she has a special agenda." Former *Washington Post* editor Ben Bradlee told ABC News, "Everybody who talks to you has a reason, and it is the first job of the journalist to figure out what that reason is." Later, on CNN's *Capital Gang*, syndicated columnist Robert Novak stated a fundamental truth when he said, "In this town, if you have contacts in the media, you can really destroy someone."[35]

There were media voices sounding a note of caution even at the height of the frenzy. *New York Times* columnist William Safire, a former speech writer for President Richard Nixon, suggested Americans should presume Clinton innocent "not merely on high-minded judicial principle, but because it's hard to conceive of this deft politician being so reckless as to carry on an 18-month affair with a White House intern a few years older than his daughter, and then to raise it to the level of federal crime by suborning perjury."[36]

The overwhelming majority, however, were offering variations on a theme struck by *Sun* columnist Peter Worthington, who declared flatly, "He's finished. Bet on it." Veteran ABC correspondent Sam Donaldson took the same aggressive line during various appearances on the ABC "loop" and as a guest commentator on rival network CNN's *Larry King Live*. Worthington's son-in-law, columnist David Frum, offered one explanation: after years of being lied to and manipulated by Clinton, the Washington press corps were sick of him.

The people, apparently, were not. At the height of the media frenzy, various news organizations were polling public opinion. To their surprise, Clinton's approval ratings shot up to record heights after his State of the Union address. The Neilson Company reported the audience for the address was 29 percent higher than it had been the year before for two reasons. First, the media's fixation with the Lewinsky affair heightened interest. Second, the president wasn't competing with a decision in the O.J. Simpson case, as he was in 1995.

With a large number of Americans tuned in, Clinton made effective use of the powers of television to connect directly with the people. Published polls suggest the president succeeded beyond his handlers' fondest hopes.

An ABC news poll released January 30, 1998, afforded Clinton a 68 percent approval rating, up 11 percent in a week, and four points above the previous high recorded in August 1997. A CBS poll published in the same timeframe put the president's approval rating at 73 percent. Further, the polls indicate women were sticking by Clinton in greater numbers than were men. Clinton may be the "Animal House president," as Maureen Dowd dubbed him, but as the Lewinsky affair reached its high-water mark in terms of media coverage, the press and the public found themselves in decidedly different places.

Peter Donolo, one of Canada's most perceptive political observers, raised an important point about public opinion in a discussion we had in early February 1998. Acknowledging President Clinton's record-high approval ratings, Donolo wondered: "What is going to happen when the public is confronted with real evidence?"[37] Donolo, and the rest of us, would get an answer to this question in November 1998, when Americans trooped to the polls for Congressional mid-term elections. Donolo, like most observers "inside the Beltway," had concluded the president's public declarations to that point constituted something less than the whole truth. The longtime Liberal party activist was convinced the judicial process would uncover evidence that Clinton had done more than lie about a sexual relationship. Donolo had been struck by one commentator's observation that Americans weren't troubled their president would lie about sex, because people in America would lie about sex themselves. What might prove more problematic for American public opinion was if it was established that the president's mendacity extended beyond the nature of his relationship with Monica Lewinsky. Donolo's observations were remarkably prescient, as the world would discover on August 17, 1998.

With his infectious laugh puncturing each sentence, Donolo quipped: "There are two rules that apply in this type of crisis. The first rule is, it isn't the act that gets you in trouble, it's the decision to try to cover it up. The second one is, people forget the first rule."[38] The

PMO's communications director talked of the conflicting streams of advice that surface in any political crisis—between the legal and the communications advisers, on the one hand, and the inside political "fixers" and the communications advisers, on the other hand.

At that point the media frenzy seemed to pause, perhaps due to a dearth of new revelations, perhaps because the media do not like to be offside. Political operatives have long asserted that there is a direct correlation between the media's aggressiveness and a politician's standing with the electorate.

Mike McCurry's crisis checklist is a little longer than Donolo's. The first, golden rule for any official spokesperson, is: Thou shalt not lie. Any breach, says McCurry, would be near fatal for the press secretary and would do great damage to the presidency. McCurry's second and somewhat surprising rule is: Thou shalt not spin. He acknowledged a media handler's stock-in-trade is the attempt to shape a story, but says the Lewinsky story didn't lend itself to that. "People want to know *factually* what happened." The third rule is to recognize that there are contrary voices in the media—individuals less influenced by the pack—and to seek those voices out. The fourth rule is to try to slow everything down, particularly in this digital age. And the fifth rule is to maintain a sense of humor.

McCurry cites two important factors in the news-gathering process in Washington that, in his opinion, place the institution of political journalism in some peril. The first flows from the global information revolution, which has drastically transformed into the proliferation of information services that transmit news bulletins around the world in literally an instant. "There is no such thing as a news cycle any more." There is no longer any "rhythm" to news coverage. The Nixon White House practice of announcing "the lid is on" by way of signaling to news organizations that it was time to stand down is, like so many other statements from that particular White House, inoperative.[39]

The competition across news disciplines compounds the problem, McCurry says. Newsmagazines, via the Net, compete with daily newspapers. Newspapers then turn their print reporters into talking heads on their television networks. The cumulative effect is a further intensification of the competitive pressure.

The second factor, in McCurry's view, is the search for "context"—an observation that is somewhat ironic, given the number of experts who consider "context" the primary purpose of political journalism in particular. McCurry's argument is that in this search for context journalism's five Ws—who, what, when, where, and why—increasingly give way to why. There is less reporting of the hard facts. "The strategic thinking behind a decision or event is more important than the substantive detail," McCurry said. In such a climate, "opinion can quickly outrun fact."[40] And because of the never-ending news cycle, the average citizen often gets an opinion about a policy pronouncement without the benefit of ever hearing the factual basis for the policy. Newspapers, anxious to put a new "top" on a story to move it along from television newscasts the previous night, are particularly vulnerable to McCurry's charge. Invariably, the front page of any policy pronouncement fractures a new lead—often opposition reaction to the initiative.

This preoccupation with strategic thinking is reflected in the language of political journalism itself, says the White House press secretary. The use of "insider baseball" terminology results in a political/public discourse that is ever more remote from the average citizen. "We are becoming more and more insular in Washington," McCurry says. "Inside the Beltway has taken on a whole new meaning."[41] "Inside the Beltway" is, of course, a prime example of Washington-speak. The reference is to the ring road around the Capitol, which is used to differentiate the reaction of the cognoscenti, who live in places like Georgetown, Bethesda, Alexandria, or Foggy Bottom, from the great unwashed of the far Maryland 'burbs.

As a consequence, McCurry says the "Washington story" is becoming less interesting. When the Associated Press compiled its list of the top-ten news stories for 1997, no Washington story cracked the top five.

In an essay sponsored by the Twentieth Century Fund that analyzed President Clinton's first year with the press, Los Angeles Times critic Tom Rosenstiel was prescient in setting out the clash of news values between the old and new media that would later be played out in the Lewinsky affair.

"Instead of continuing to move in the direction of becoming more policy oriented than before, the press has resumed the course of moving further away from objective reporting and becoming quicker to make judgments, interpret and analyze," Rosenstiel states. "At the same time, Old Media have allowed their journalistic standards to decline in the face of New Media. Both of these changes are a mistake, and they are based on false choices the traditional news media are making about how to survive economically."[42]

Rosenstiel conducted a two-month study of the front pages of the *New York Times*, *Washington Post*, and *Los Angeles Times* to test the hypothesis of a more subjective tone to news reporting. Only slightly more than half of the 1,332 stories carried by these three prestigious newspapers in the spring of 1993 could be classified as straight news. Nearly 40 percent of the stories were analytical or interpretive treatments of news events or trends. And what is alarming is that nearly 80 percent of these analytical stories had *no* label to identify them as analysis, interpretation, or opinion. *L.A. Times* White House correspondent John H. Broder refers to the trend as "soufflé journalism"—the recipe is one part information mixed with two parts attitude and two parts conjecture. Former ABC correspondent Jeff Greenfield captured the spirit with his story on the number of journalists who had filed pieces declaring the Clinton administration a failure—ten days into Clinton's first term.

As a result of the old media's ill-advised response to new-media pressures, rumor and innuendo have found their way into public discourse more easily, Rosenstiel states. He warned that the great risk of tabloidization is its corrosion of the public trust. "The only truly valuable commodity that the press has is its credibility. If in the short term it compromises that, in the long term it will destroy itself."[43] Rosenstiel's point is critically important if the press is to maintain its relevance to the political process. If the mainstream media opts for an editorial product that is sensational rather than substantive, its relationship to news will be akin to pro-wrestling's relationship to sports.

As the torrent of "revelations" in the Lewinsky affair slowed to a trickle, American news organizations began a collective examination of conscience before articulating the obligatory "mea culpa." Shorenstein Center director Marvin Kalb, a distinguished network correspondent for thirty years, watched the carnage and concluded that "it's one of the most sorry chapters in American journalism; from the story that exploded a week ago, we have a storm of half-baked, unsubstantiated gossip, innuendo and rumor coming out with very little hard facts. We live in a new journalistic culture in which everything is out of the can instantly and picked up by others ... using very few sources. Everything goes, everybody's an expert, and no one knows anything."[44]

There are many significant lessons for the pundit class in the Lewinsky affair. Media scholars fret about the consequences to democracy inherent in the media's shift from covering matters of importance to covering matters of interest. Yet Clinton's experience through the winter and spring of 1998 suggests the news-consuming public is perfectly capable of making the distinction. Kurtz attributes Clinton's popularity to "a carefully honed media strategy—alternately seducing, misleading, and sometimes intimidating the press."[45]

On March 15, 1998, former White House volunteer Kathleen Willey appeared on the CBS public-affairs program 60 Minutes to repeat allegations that she had been sexually groped by the president during a November 29, 1993, meeting in the Oval Office. Willey, whose husband, Edward Willey, Jr., committed suicide the same day over his impending financial ruin, was deemed a more credible witness than either Lewinsky or Jones because of her party connections and social standing. Her story, that she had come to the White House to plead for help only to be confronted with unwanted sexual advances, was so compelling, even the president's steadfast supporters, such as NOW president Patricia Ireland, were rattled.

The interview resulted in 60 Minutes, rated as the most popular network television program of the week, eclipsing even Seinfeld. It was the first such ranking for 60 Minutes in four years, and the viewing public most certainly got the message. A CBS poll discovered 67 percent of respondents said they thought the president's personal conduct left a lot to be desired. Yet the same poll also suggested Clinton's approval ratings were an impressive 67 percent, a finding that was reinforced in a Gallup poll conducted at the same time. The high approval ratings reflect satisfaction with the president's perceived stewardship of the nation's business. Fully 78 percent of respondents to the CBS poll said Clinton was doing a good job on the economy.

Clinton's difficulties built to a crisis on August 17, 1998, when the tape of his testimony to special prosecutor Kenneth Starr was finally released, and aired on prime-time TV. What unfolded was the sorry saga of a beleaguered president and his trailer-trash ways.

In January, when the scandal first broke, Clinton used the intimacy of the television-camera lens to look America in the eye and say: "I want to say one thing to the American people. I want you to listen to me. I'm going to say this again. I did not have sexual relations with that woman, Miss Lewinsky."[46]

Cornered by a subpoena-wielding Ken Starr, Clinton admitted to ten sexual encounters in a study, in a hallway, and in a White House bathroom, each but a few steps from the Oval Office. The president's legal counsel David Kendall argued Clinton did not technically perjure himself in January when he swore under oath that he did not have a sexual relationship with Lewinsky because, in the presidential definition, oral sex doesn't count.

In the best tradition of Sunday television evangelists, Clinton summoned leading clergymen to the White House to declare: "I have sinned. The sorrow I feel is genuine."[47]

Yet the president would not let go of his claim that he had been "legally accurate" in prior testimony. Presidential adviser James Carville, the self-described Ragin' Cajun, was on the set of *Larry King Live* when the president's address was televised. Carville looked as if he would be physically ill, and beat a hasty retreat, pleading a prior commitment. California senator Dianne Feinstein was speaking for many of Clinton's friends and supporters when she said of the president: "My trust in his credibility has been badly shattered."[48]

Television news shows replayed clips from a cabinet meeting in January. Cabinet secretaries, led by Secretary of State Madeleine Albright, emerged from the session to defend Clinton against the charges he was involved sexually with Lewinsky. Albright looked into the camera and said the president had assured cabinet there was nothing to the allegations, and she believed him.

Clinton's act had serious ramifications for the ongoing spin wars that are at the center of political culture in any national capital. Harvard professor Tom Patterson says we are at our most vulnerable, in a political context, when we are subjected to a deliberate lie. But what Clinton put in motion was even more potent than a lie: it was a lie told with the conviction of an individual—in this case Albright—who believes he or she is telling the truth. That Clinton would use his unwitting cabinet secretaries in such a brazen bluff is staggering. That his action did not result in a single resignation from his cabinet is revealing.

Setting aside the moral issue involved in a head of state knowingly and deliberately sending a cabinet secretary out to lie, what are the implications for such a decision for diplomacy? Why wouldn't world leaders pause any time Albright spoke in the president's name?

Ken Starr would later insist Clinton used the same technique throughout the Whitewater/Jones/Lewinsky affair. Starr claims the president lied to potential grand jury witnesses, knowing they would then be in a position to repeat the lie under oath.

Clinton, his wife, Hillary, and daughter, Chelsea, headed out to Martha's Vineyard for a few days off. The ever-present cameras recorded the strain between the president and his wife, as Chelsea acted as intermediary and spokesperson for the assembled scribes.

Two days later, on August 19, Clinton cut his Cape Cod sojourn short and returned to Washington, where he ordered cruise-missile strikes against reputed terrorist hideouts in the Sudan and Afghanistan, the latter strike aimed at alleged terrorist Osama bin Laden.

It was life imitating art. The storyline from the Hollywood film *Wag the Dog* was now national security policy. Evening newscasts featured "streeters" as average Americans reflected the pervasiveness of pop culture, linking the visuals of the missile attack with the action on cassette at their local video store. And they did so in perfect "clip."

Clinton's *True Confessions* outing on national television set the stage for an even more spectacular media event weeks later.

In early September, Special Prosecutor Ken Starr released a 445-page report on the Clinton affair on the Internet, which *New York Times* columnist Maureen Dowd likened to "a Harold Robbins novel." In fact, the heated prose of the author of such bestsellers as *The Carpetbaggers* seemed decidedly straightlaced by comparison. Starr alleged Clinton committed eleven impeachable offenses, including abuse of power, obstruction of justice, and witness tampering. Starr shipped thirty-six boxes of evidence and even more lurid material than that contained in his report to Congress.

Starr's report underscored the fact that the Internet had emerged as the information medium of choice in the Lewinsky affair. The entire report was posted on the Internet on the Friday, and was released in paperback a few days later. Americans literally raced to their neighborhood cyber café to download the story. There were predictions of massive communications snarls, but the Net held up quite well.

The paperback edition sent the Starr Report to the lofty heights at the top of the *New York Times* bestseller list. The most oft-repeated word used to describe Starr's accounts in news stories was "lurid." Starr provided surfers and readers alike with graphic detail on Clinton's sexual liaisons with Lewinsky, ironically without a single reference to Whitewater.

The report dominated magazine covers from *Time* and *Newsweek* to the supermarket tabloids. Late-night show hosts thought they'd died and gone to heaven.

Clinton's confession was the number-one topic of conversation in America. Dinner parties, coffee klatches, bar talk, the family supper were given over to detailed analysis of Clinton's prevarication.

There was the whiff of impeachment in the air—an irony, given the fact that both Clinton's and the political generation they came to represent cut their collective teeth on the Watergate scandal that drove Richard Nixon from office.

As was the case with Watergate, the media consensus held that the issue threatening Clinton's presidency was not the relationship with Lewinsky, but rather the orchestrated attempt to cover it up. Clinton himself admitted: "I certainly didn't want this to come out, if I could help it. I was embarrassed about it. I knew it was wrong."[49]

The pundit class moved into high gear. *Larry King Live* served as a national water cooler. *Washington Post* media icon Bob Woodward sat next to King, reinforcing the link to Watergate. Former Clinton staffer Dee Dee Myers struggled to find a balance between loyalty to the president and professional integrity. Bush administration spokesperson Marlin Fitzwater drew the link back to the Gennifer Flowers incident in the 1992 presidential campaign. Carville's wife and Republican strategist, Mary

Matalin, enjoyed his obvious discomfort and denounced Clinton as a man with the morals of an alley cat. The scene was played out on every other network and cable station, from ABC's *Evening News* to *Nightline* to Chris Matthews's *Hardball* on CNBC. Matthews, a former chief of staff to Democratic Speaker Thomas P. "Tip" O'Neill, had his show increased from thirty minutes nightly to a full hour as a direct consequence of viewer interest in the Lewinsky affair.

Myers and Stephanopoulos were in particularly awkward positions. They had served the president as senior communications advisers, but in the revolving door of today's political journalism they were now employed by news organizations: Myers as the political editor at *George* magazine and Stephanopoulos at ABC. Their old boss and his supporters expected them to provide the same kind of firewall Hillary had during the famous *60 Minutes* interview during the 1992 presidential primaries. Their new bosses expected some journalism, including word from the inside.

Both wanted to show the president some empathy; both had to protect their credibility. The two demands, in certain instances, were irreconcilable. Myers, in an essay carried in the August 24 edition of *Time*, described the president's relationship with Lewinsky as "so reckless as to seem pathological." Drawing on her personal experience as White House spokesperson, Myers said of Clinton: "Too often, he meant exactly what he said—and no more." But in the end, Myers had to concede: "I never believed that Bill Clinton would actually risk his presidency—a job he had studied, dreamed about, and prepared for since he was a kid—for something so frivolous, so reckless, so small."[50]

Canada's chattering classes were equally addicted to the talk TV shows. Anecdotal evidence would suggest the political advisers in my circle of friends and acquaintances were down on Myers and Stephanopoulos for their perceived disloyalty.

The president's defense, articulated by designated spokespersons on talk radio and TV, was relatively simple. Clinton's private mistakes do not constitute an impeachable offense. As Maureen Dowd wrote in her September 13 column: "These are not grounds for impeachment. These are grounds for divorce."[51]

The pundits focused on the November midterm elections. They insisted that while the furor over the sex scandal at the White House was overshadowing the Congressional elections, the fallout was most certainly to impact the outcome, as well as the presidential race in the year 2000. Control of the House of Representatives was touted as key to any move to impeach Clinton. And conventional wisdom suggested the Lewinsky affair would have a significant impact on the November result.

Former Reagan speechwriter Tony Dolan was one voice of restraint, telling the *New York Times*: "It's madness to predict where we are at this point. You can't strategize about chaos. And we are just entering chaos."[52]

Through September and October, media coverage trumpeted Clinton's woes, suggesting he was closer to becoming the second American president ever to be impeached. (Nixon resigned before an impeachment vote could be held.)

Then, on the first Tuesday in November, the pundits paused for air and the people spoke. Contrary to all expectations, the president's party could claim victory. When the votes were counted, the Senate standings remained unchanged: the Republicans held 55 seats and the Democrats 45. But, in the House, the Democrats picked up 5 seats, leaving the current standings at 223 Republicans and 211 Democrats. With these results, much of the air went out of the impeachment balloon. Republican Speaker Newt Gingrich quickly fell on his sword to appease an angry GOP, resigning his seat and relinquishing the reins of leadership. If someone had held up a photo of Clinton and Gingrich on March 10 and said that, on November 10, only one of these men will still have his job, how many pundits would have picked the president? Writing in the November 8 edition of the *New York Times*, Janny Scott stated: "If Gingrich is the big loser, political pundits are running a close second." Added George Stephanopoulos: "The pundits are remarkably better on autopsy than they are at prophecy."[53]

The pundits, not for the first time, missed the people's message. They knew the Lewinsky affair was interesting, and consistent with their new news approach, proclaimed it important as well. The people knew the Lewinsky affair was interesting, but they knew it wasn't important. The economy was important.

Monica Lewinsky drew ratings. Weekly ratings for all news television networks spiked each and every time there was a significant development in the Lewinsky affair. In fact, for the week ending August 23, after Clinton admitted having a series of sexual liaisons with the young woman, the all-news networks—CNN and MSNBC—had their highest ratings of the year.

Newsmagazine sales also improved when Lewinsky revelations were featured on the cover of *Newsweek, Time*, and *U.S. World and News Report*. People did want to know the intimate details of each presidential tryst, but they didn't equate their voyeuristic inclinations with the important. My Freedom Forum colleague Rob Snyder, editor of the *Media Studies Journal*, said that, for the Washington press corps, the Clinton story was a story of betrayal. For the general public, the story was about a man lying about something of limited consequence in the context of the country's interests.

The Clinton scandal story line lurched back toward impeachment in early December. Once again, the president reverted to his role as commander-in-chief of America's armed forces and launched another missile strike—this time against Iraqi president Saddam Hussein.

The Republicans in the Congress claimed the timing of Operation Desert Fox was no coincidence; the House of Representatives was poised to vote in favor of impeachment. The sorry saga seemed headed for the floor of the U.S. Senate. The Republicans tried to cloak their actions in the constitution, but under questioning, they admitted their real agenda was to placate Christian conservatives—a core constituency for the GOP.

A majority of Americans opposed impeachment; the moral majority did not. The politics of the issue for Republicans couldn't have been more clear.

But the American public has given the Washington press corps its biggest wakeup call of this decade. The voters have established that they can differentiate between the interesting and the important. It remains to be seen whether the pundits can as well.

At year's end, *Time*'s cover proclaimed Kenneth Starr and Bill Clinton "Men of the Year" for 1998. Rival *Newsweek*'s special double issue summarized Clinton's year in a single word—Impeached.

Readers who made it past the Monica quiz at the front end of the "book" read a detailed account of how Clinton became the first president in 130 years to face a legal trial in the Senate, formally accused of perjury and obstruction of justice. *Newsweek* reported the president was impeached by the U.S. House of Representatives one year to the day after Lewinsky received a subpoena to testify in the Paula Jones case.

As the U.S. Senate prepared itself for Clinton's trial, Matt Drudge was reporting another "scoop" in his Net Report—that Hillary had slugged the president the day the House of Representatives voted to impeach.

9

Notions

In recent years, as I thumbed through various learned treatises, columns, and articles on media matters, I came across an artful putdown of Washington's chattering classes for their use of the term "notion" in conversation rather than the more straightforward noun "idea." The writer—I want to say William F. Buckley, Jr., but it may have been William Safire—dismissed the practice as an affectation. To me, the term is wonderfully precise, an accurate reflection of the end-product at the nexus of press, politics, and public policy. *Idea* implies finality, clarity, precision of thought. *Notion* suggests a work in progress, something evolutionary and, occasionally, illusionary. Much of public policy, and the press coverage of it, can only be considered a work in progress, subject as it is to the vagaries of events large and small that can shift a nation's economic and social priorities. Public opinion, in particular, is a work in progress. Notion, therefore, works for me.

The media, as media-relations specialists incessantly repeat to their clients, are not a monolith. Even individual news organizations will offer readers, listeners, or viewers a range of opinion. But peer pressure is a serious issue in today's political journalism. *Washington Monthly* seer Charles Peters says, "There is nothing the average journalist fears more than ridicule." Peters believes "one of the most important reasons for the vicious pack mentality in journalism is that people are so afraid of ridicule from their peers."[1]

Brian Mulroney and Charles Peters, to the best of my knowledge, have never met. And if Peters's extraordinary body of work over the years is at all reflective, it isn't likely the two men would agree on much, save for a shared belief in the promise of John Kennedy's New Frontier. But they are of a mind on the issue of pack journalism, or the intense pressure on individual reporters to conform with the consensus of their peers, a pressure reinforced by news desks back home.

The "pack" is very much a fact of life in the journalistic hot-house atmosphere of the parliamentary press gallery. Once the group comes to a position, dissenting voices are raised at some personal and professional risk. The protective coloration of choice for too many reporters here is cynicism and negativity. The same holds true in Washington. As one ABC reporter put it, "If you are going to say something remotely positive, you'd better be 150 percent right or you're going to be accused of rolling over."[2]

The Canadian press corps, particularly the parliamentary scribes, have been markedly less critical in their coverage of the Chrétien government through the first term. To some extent, the media have been accused of rolling over by Opposition parties. Part of the explanation lies in the fact that Chrétien and his colleagues were highly skilled in managing what my friend Elly Alboim describes as "government by risk avoidance."

The strategy recognizes the media's preoccupation with gossip instead of governance. The modern equivalent of the Roman circus, the media are used by the government of the day to deflect attention from the business at hand. You make a point of telling the media you've parked the prime-ministerial Cadillac permanently, and your prime minister is perfectly content to be ferried around in a Chevy. You slide over the fact the old Cadillac has been bought and paid for several times over and, therefore, isn't actually costing the taxpayers a dime. You certainly don't tell anyone the new "Chevy" is going to cost the taxpayers upwards of $400,000 once it is rendered bullet- and bomb-proof. You see, it's about optics. As you do in the childhood game of scissors/paper/rock, you set out to wrap the rock with paper.

Alboim, a veteran Ottawa media sage, says if an issue is "important" but doesn't fit the new mandate of "interesting," then it won't get covered. The consequence, he says, is that "the governors can routinely operate publicly, but essentially in private, interacting only with elites and the powerful because what they are engaged in attracts no attention, fits none of the new models, or criteria for political coverage."[3] In other words, presidents or prime ministers skilled at managing the media toward lifestyle or personal habit issues can now preside over policy development away from the distracting glare of the media searchlight. By diverting the media's attention toward the limited ministerial use of government air-craft, the Chrétien government managed to avoid media scrutiny of their decision to shift the financial burden of Canada's health-care system to the provinces through massive cuts to federal transfer payments.

Chrétien's media managers have been demonstrably less successful in their second term of office in this regard, in part because the parliamentary press gallery has reverted to its more traditional adversarial role and in part because PMO spin doctors have been less successful in managing the "interesting" aspect of the media–politics relationship. Peppergate is but one example.

When I think about why former prime minister Brian Mulroney's relations with the press soured so completely during his term as prime minister, my response lacks sound-bite succinctness.

Mulroney enjoyed a good relationship with working reporters in his earlier incarnation as source. The relationship remained positive when he first became a candidate. Part of the reason, in my view, is that, in these earlier stages, the relationship was mostly with print journalists, and Mulroney's store of information and insight made him a valuable contact. The dominant media "frame" began to change, however, when Mulroney became Conservative party leader. Because Canadian politics is so leader-focused, the media searchlight settled on the boy from Baie Comeau to the virtual exclusion of everyone else in the caucus or cabinet. This wasn't Mulroney's fault, or the fault of anyone in his cabinet. It was, quite simply, a direct consequence of the evolving nature of news gathering and news reporting. Mulroney's political ascendancy coincided with the apex of television's power as the information medium of choice. Mass audiences were being assembled nightly on relatively few networks.

Mulroney, while a natural orator, is not a child of the television era. His epistemology, to use Postman's term, is print. He was raised in an era when the few hundred souls who trooped out to a community center or parish hall to hear the leader speak were the focus of the leader's attention. Anyone who has traveled with Mulroney can attest to the effort and energy he would expend to provide the assembly with a top-caliber performance worthy of the stage at Stratford. The problem, of course, is that the performance required to woo audiences at Stratford is most likely over-the-top for television audiences. Though intellectually Mulroney knew the 400 people in the hall weren't representative, they were simply a backdrop for the larger, national television audience; emotionally and personally, Mulroney was incapable of keeping a distance. He needed to connect with the people on a one-to-one basis, and sought to do so with rhetorical flourishes that drew standing ovations from those present, but were ultimately counterproductive when stripped of context and used as a sound bite on the evening news. This emphasis on the "live" performance gave rise to what Mulroney's party stalwarts began to refer to as the "blarney" factor. The former Tory leader's ability to use humorous exaggerations for effect worked in front of partisan audiences, but caused certain concerns in the broader population. A constituency grew within Tory ranks that insisted Mulroney tone down the rhetoric. Mine was a minority view because I argued against such a change. Mulroney's oratorical style was very much a part of his public persona. For better or worse, the electorate had, by now, factored it into the equation. The "tone it down" faction ultimately prevailed, however, though to Mulroney's detriment in my opinion. By forcing the prime minister to curb his natural tendencies, the advisers inadvertently created a persona that appeared contrived on television. Television is effective in communicating character, but since the viewers were being presented with an image that did not strike them as authentic, the consequential negative impact on Mulroney's standing was inevitable.

As a child of partisan politics, Mulroney's every instinct was to race to the defense of any cabinet colleague in trouble. The subsequent visual image of this inevitably linked Mulroney directly to the controversy in question. The decision to partially deindex pensions was recommended by the Department of Finance, pushed by the minister, and ratified by the entire cabinet. Yet when Solange Denis poked her forefinger into Mulroney's chest in the celebrated confrontation on Parliament Hill, the message to voters was unmistakable: this guy is taking money out of the pockets of our seniors. When the subsequent decision to exempt seniors was taken, the same cameras once again portrayed Mulroney as the villain, this time, for the bankers on Bay Street, preoccupied with deficit reduction.

The media focus on travel, costs, and executive perks exacted a huge price, as did the recurring accusations of wrongdoing on the part of the government. Again, the structure of the television news reports laid all blame squarely at Mulroney's feet. In 1984, Canadians, collectively, were on a roll. Mulroney epitomized success, a self-made man with a beautiful life partner, given to good work, with an approachable manner, and an engaging and extraordinarily photogenic family. A few years later, we were mired in recession, half-convinced much of the economic slowdown could be attributed to free trade, a policy Mulroney personified. Canadians were hurting, and suspected Mulroney wasn't. Suddenly, the government jets and the Cadillac limousine took on a larger significance.

Then the "congenial truth" took hold that Mulroney presided over a government that had lost its moral compass. Supported by the rumors and innuendo being promulgated by a number of journalists, political opponents—particularly the Liberals and Reform—seized the political advantage of this congenial truth, even as the Liberals assumed Mulroney's policy platform for their own. Mulroney then committed an unpardonable sin: he left public life before Canadians could vent their collective anger upon him. The voters, their attitudes shaped by years of negative media coverage, never had an opportunity to knock Mulroney off his electoral perch, and even when they reduced his party and his successor to rubble, there was an element of unfinished business to it all.

The Airbus affair resonated with the population precisely because it was consistent with the dominant media "frame" around Mulroney that had developed over a decade. In English Canada, Mulroney was "the man we love to hate," according to then *Sun* columnist Bob Fife. The early Airbus coverage reflected Mulroney's "presumed" guilt, to paraphrase William Kaplan. In French Canada, where the RCMP has a certain history of political involvement, the media was predisposed to a presumption of innocence, in sharp contrast to the situation in English

Canada, where, legally, the burden of proof fell to the accusers. The French-language media alone quickly determined the charges set out in the letter to the Swiss lacked substantiating evidence.

Ironically, the trauma of Airbus also gave Mulroney the opportunity to begin to alter his dominant media frame once again. Ours is a society directed by mass communication. In fact, communications theorists argue the central function of media is the creation of community. When the mass media seizes upon scandal, thereby creating a community seized by scandal, the potential for excess is pronounced. In a review of the book *Scandal* by Suzanne Garment, Amy Waldman refers to "the modern scandal production machine": "What starts as a reasonable inquiry snowballs into something akin to the Salem witch trials." What begins as a legitimate investigation into allegations of criminal activity "gives way to a potent alchemy of gossip upgraded to news by an eager press, an easily manipulated investigatory process, and an artfully crafted political theater."[4] So it was with Airbus. Not surprisingly, in this era of spin, Mulroney's counteroffensive included artfully created political theater as well as full legal recourse.

The Airbus affair may signal the end of an era in political journalism. Airbus was the direct result of a particular media, political, and public opinion climate. That climate was created by a convergence of forces not likely to occur again. Television's emergence as the information medium of choice, its entertainment narrative voice, the passive nature of the audience, and the way television news items finger one individual as responsible for the problem set out in the news report, are key. Of equal importance is the fact that, through the 1970s, 1980s, and most of the 1990s, relatively few media voices ever reached an overwhelming majority of the population. The media coverage shaped public opinion, and as public opinion turned increasingly negative, an emboldened press made certain that opinion was mirrored in its coverage. The ensuing vortex proved to be an irresistible force.

In today's new media environment, it is unlikely a similar situation could be recreated as easily. More media choices mean more media voices. More media voices should result in a diversity of opinion, less uniformity of thought, more challenges to conventional wisdom, and less acceptance of a "top-down" news model.

The impetus for new media and this diversity will most likely come from both traditional and nontraditional forces. The more forward-looking of federal Liberals, for example, are already expressing concern about the reordering of ownership of Canadian newspapers. These Liberals believe a small "c" conservative view is now dominant in Canadian newspapers. Citing Conrad Black's *National Post* as an example, they argue the ownership's editorial bias is reflected in the news coverage. With the rapid expansion of the Sun Media Corp., the merger with Quebecor, and the *Globe and Mail*'s position as a national newspaper, these Liberals wonder how the center/center-left perspective in Canadian politics will get a fair hearing, the *Toronto Star* notwithstanding. These concerns tend to amuse Conservatives, who have long believed the mainstream media reflect a small "l" liberal bias. But seeing as how there aren't many newspapers left to buy in Canada, it would seem reasonable to assume the Liberals will look to Net-based opportunities to further express their voice.

Similar impulses will motivate business and labor leaders. Today's mainstream media rarely provide sufficient detail in news reports for businesses or professional bodies with a particular interest in a public-policy issue. Even sophisticated sections such as the *Globe*'s Report on Business cannot provide the level of detail insiders require without boring the subscriber to tears. Again, the Net looms as an answer.

Technological breakthroughs in the past—including television—have contributed significantly to societal change. Television coverage of desegregation efforts in the American South in the 1950s and early 1960s provided important momentum for the Civil Rights movement. Television placed the Vietnam War at the top of America's political agenda. The creation of Radio-Canada, anticipated as a force for Canadian unity, in fact allowed Quebec nationalism to flourish. Images of the economic, social, and political progress in the former Federal Republic of Germany helped bring down the Berlin Wall.

The Internet affords similar opportunities in the developing world. Paul Simon's lyrics proclaim these as the "days of miracle and wonder." The diaspora of troubled African nations—from the Democratic Republic of the Congo (which is neither) to Robert Mugabe's Zimbabwe—use the Net as a lifeline of communication.

The forms and business models for these new voices are still taking shape, and are, in the main, beyond the imagination of people such as myself, hopelessly rooted in the tradition of print. Colleague Mitchell Stephens makes the telling point that whenever a new medium appears, early efforts to develop its full potential are stifled by people in positions of power wedded to the old format. When television first appeared, for example, it sounded like radio and looked like the stage. It took a later generation of creators to begin to realize the medium's true potential, and to find new business models for it, from pay-TV to cable-subscriber-funded specialty channels.

These emerging media forms will raise larger issues about the future of political reporting and the mass media in general. Recently, a U.S. congressional committee that included Joseph Kennedy tried to come up with a more modern definition of news, with a view to stripping First Amendment protections from such infotainment programs as *Hard Copy*. *Electronic Media*, a new media trade publication, sneered at the committee's attempts, insisting news was "new information about anything." As media observer Daniel Schechter concludes, the logical extension of the argument is that freedom of speech protection is afforded everything from the *New York Times* to *Jerry Springer*. Springer's talk show is to current-affairs programming what wrestling is to sports.

There is comfort in the lament that the crass commercial Philistines of the money markets have corrupted today's journalism. The problems of today's political journalism, however, are not simply and narrowly the problems of the marketplace. The market-driven argument may mask a deeper truth. The current sorry state of the nexus of press, politics, and public policy can be attributed to the excess and errors of modern journalism's golden era—that period from the mid-1950s to the mid-1980s when mainstream journalism was relatively free of market pressures.

Journalism's code of professionalism, with its middle-class values and its dominant male voice, is as elitist as it is exclusionary. Noam Chomsky may overstate the case, but today's mainstream media do advance a preferred social, political, and economic order. The "new journalism," which began with the tequila-fueled "gonzo" insights of Hunter S. Thompson, may be unacceptable to media traditionalists precisely because it questions the established order.

Kiku Adatto has charted the silencing of candidates' voices in political discourse through the ever-shrinking sound bite. But again, the problem is broader than the media's predisposition to reduce everything to snappy one-liners and shorter sound bites. Brevity, in and of itself, need not signal a lack of substance. The socio-judicial structure of democracies with a Judeo-Christian tradition flow from ten commandments that in total do not amount to 100 words of text. And Descartes's assertion "I think, therefore I am" is no less profound for its brevity.

Neil Postman has identified the real problem with truncated political discourse: the sound bites and one-liners of today's journalism are offered up for consumption without any context, either historical or ideological.

The news media, in the main, have become the chroniclers of Boorstin's world of pseudo-events and image. *Globe and Mail* columnist Rick Salutin says this evolution has given a whole new meaning to image politics. "Cultivating an image used to be a means to an end in politics. Now image itself is at the end of the road. We aren't choosing because of an image, we're choosing the image itself. We're not choosing a government, we're choosing the guys who play government in the TV show about it."[5] In our postmodern cynicism, as sociologist Todd Gitlin has observed, we debunk image and image-makers, yet in the end, we accept them as the only reality we have left.

Traditionally, news is afforded importance and place in any democratic society. Swedish researcher Jörgen Westerståhl believed news must be factual and impartial if it is to provide a foundation for independent and rational decision making.[6] Political scientists assert the quality of public debate depends on the quality of the information available. And as the influence of political parties wanes, the media's role in keeping people informed grows in importance.

Walter Lippmann made the point that "the quack, the charlatan, the jingo and the terrorist can flourish only where the audience is deprived of independent access to information."[7]

News is a powerful instrument of social control because news defines the reality on which people act. And as Lippmann observed, "All that the sharpest critics of democracy have alleged is true if there is no steady supply of trustworthy relevant news. Incompetence and aimlessness, corruption and disloyalty, panic and ultimate disaster must come to any people which is denied assured access to facts. No one can manage anything on pap. Neither can a people."[8]

These conclusions about the inadequacies of current political journalistic practice would appear to apply equally to political coverage of public-policy issues. Policy problems lack the novelty a reporter needs. Journalism is a world of absolutes, a world of assertion, of fact, of stark choices. Government is mostly a world of gray, a world of consensus, a world of qualifiers, a world of allocating increasingly scarce resources to a longer list of worthy initiatives than can be accommodated. These policy discussions do not lend themselves to the sound bites and angry journalists of the current media market. Yet the fact remains, without reliable information, self-government becomes impossible.

The communication between governments and the citizenry broke down in the 1990s. Public servants tend to shrug off the crisis by assuming the dissatisfaction and disaffection is directed at elected officeholders, and not at the institutions themselves. That view is mistaken. Governments are the product of a democratic exercise. That exercise is predicated on the active participation of the populace. Every policy pronouncement by government, whatever its form, is value-laden. Unless there is an understanding of those values and how the policy gives effect to those values, the policy thrust is doomed to failure.

Today's candidates and reporters alike converse in the political equivalent of "insider baseball," a dialogue that excludes the very public both are dependent on. Having spent a generation consciously or unconsciously excluding the public from their worlds, politicians and the press alike have finally tumbled to the fact that the public in the end did get the message. Seizing the opportunities presented by emerging technologies, that public is actually starting to move on.

By supporting populist politicians such as Preston Manning or Ross Perot and new media outlets, from talk radio to *Larry King Live*, the public in a very real sense has tried to retrieve political dialogue from the mainstream press. People may be disillusioned when they discover that alleged reformers such as Manning are simply using the same image techniques. But the success of *Pamela Wallin Live* on CBC

Newsworld and *The Lead* hosted by Allison Smith suggests people do understand the need to change the nature of public discourse.

The mainstream media will never again enjoy the mass audiences of the 1970s. Like the politicians who came to rely on that access, the mainstream press will have to reinvent itself, seizing the opportunities emerging from the information revolution as well.

Political leaders with complex public-policy options to advance rely on today's news assembly culture to promulgate their view at some peril to themselves, their political formation, and their policy options. Tomorrow's leaders will have to apply the same sophisticated thinking to their communications strategies as they brought to the development of the policy itself. Photo-ops and snappy one-liners cannot by themselves advance public understanding of or support for sound public policy. Like Nero, political leaders who are prepared to indulge in the pyrotechnics of sound-bite public discourse face a certain, unhappy political future.

Political communication is increasingly a multimedia exercise conducted on the Internet, community cable channels, weekly newspapers, and talk radio. An Internet newsletter report culminated in William Jefferson Clinton's impeachment. *Hustler* magazine broke the news that destroyed the political career of would-be speaker Bob Livingston. *This Hour Has 22 Minutes* is shaping public opinion as effectively as any editorial page.

The days of a stump speech delivered to a largely partisan gathering timed to connect to a daily news cycle are over. All-news networks, the laptop computer, the cell phone, and satellite links have made traditional news timelines obsolete. In the world of the wired, political communication is instantaneous.

These improvements in the delivery system serve only to underscore the need for a substantive storyline—as James Fallows describes it, a "master narrative."

Political reporters would be mistaken in assuming this requirement for renewal does not apply to their craft. As Larry Sabato reports, the public has already signaled its unhappiness with the current state of press–politics relations and has concluded it is being manipulated by both sides. The public's message to both sides is, basically: Grow up, the game is over.

Media scholars who see the press as a public utility and not just a business have advanced ideas to improve the sorry state of today's political journalism. Advocates of public journalism, including NYU professor Jay Rosen, propose a new journalism that seeks to engage citizens in public life while reconnecting journalists to the community they serve. Newspaper editor Buzz Merritt further suggests that it's time reporters understood that journalism's self-interest—both intellectual and economic—is inextricably linked to the well-being of public life. Merritt's rather novel argument is that a journalist's credibility should not flow from some contrived detachment, but rather from a new alignment forged by a shared commitment with citizens to improve their lot. Journalism, in and of itself, cannot create and sustain healthy public life, Merritt says, but it can be the gravity that keeps society from flying apart.

The operating premise of this movement is that, for journalism to remain viable, public life must remain viable. Public journalism is about coming to public judgment. It is civic participation in a wider, broader sense than elections or election campaigns. Public journalism sets up a deliberative dialogue rather than a debate, a politics of public learning. Merritt was inspired, in part, by a 1993 Yankelovich Monitor survey which reported that, in a time of declining trust in all institutions, journalism's decline was by far the steepest.

Merritt has an interesting description of journalism as "industrial art," as much a product of the industrial revolution as a tin can. What he is saying, in effect, is that as we move into the postindustrial, information economy, it is time to fashion a journalism that is more in keeping with the era.

E.J. Dionne, one of the most widely respected journalists in America, wrote an important book in 1992 entitled *Why Americans Hate Politics*. Yet in an afterword for a later edition, Dionne wrote: "Americans want a politics they don't have to hate. And therein lies our hope. Democracies are uniquely open to change, and if citizens want politicians to move beyond false choices, it is in their power to demand it." Dionne's assertion can be taken a step further. Citizens equally have it in their power to demand more "content" from news organizations.

Public journalism also involves a fundamental shift in the business side of the news business in that, instead of seeing subscribers, listeners, and viewers as consumers, it sees them as active participants in the search for solutions to public problems.

Public journalism may be too much of a reach for media properties traded as part of a larger corporate holding on the New York Stock Exchange, at least in the short term. And even one of America's most respected journalists, former *New York Times* managing editor Eugene Roberts, sees it as a "public-relations hoax." Says Roberts: "The best public service a newspaper can provide is to tell people what is going on."[9]

Roberts's more traditionalist view is appealing to a certain demographic to be certain, aging boomers in particular. *New York Times* publisher Arthur Sulzberger, Jr. says his news organization is "going to be making money for years to come based on what we do on paper."[10] Newspaper publishers, he says, should be putting their money into newsrooms today if they want to ensure their prosperity in the media world of tomorrow. "He or she who has the best news will win this war," Sulzberger told a Neiman Conference at Harvard.[11]

One cannot help but wonder how a publisher is to invest in his or her newsroom, given the ethos of Bay Street or Wall Street where success is measured not in the quality of journalism, but in EBITDA— earnings before interest, taxes, depreciation, and amortization.

We in Canada, with our tradition of a public broadcaster, would seem to be well placed to move toward Merritt's objectives, with a CBC that could lead the journalistic pack by example. That said, a public broadcasting system is of limited value if the state expects it to operate according to the profit-seeking dictates of the marketplace. Nor is there significant value to a public broadcaster's news and current-affairs programming if the journalism slavishly follows Gans's "paraideology" of North American reporting with its exclusionary, elitist ways. Public broadcasters that embrace the spirit of public journalism can resist the tabloid tendencies of today's market-driven newscasts, but only if they are free of the market pressures.

Governments in most Western democracies, including Canada, have deemed the airwaves to be a resource owned by the people.

Governments, including Canada's, owe it to the people to invest in that resource. CBC news anchor Peter Mansbridge summarized the conundrum succinctly in a May 1994 speech at the University of Manitoba. Mansbridge concedes there is a place for tabloid TV, just as there is a place at neighborhood newsstands for the *National Enquirer*. "But that place should not be in public broadcasting." Mansbridge added, "We exist to do something different from the private sector, not to try and mimic it."[12] The CBC will have to move more aggressively into new media than the timetable set out in its current business plan if it is to be relevant in the future.

George Gilder, in his book *Life After Television*, says television was a superb technology for its time, but is now obsolete: "the age of television, for all its intents and purposes, is over." "Television will not readily disappear," Gilder says. "The corpse will linger in American living rooms for many more years, but its fate is foreordained."[13] The future market will see a peer network replace the broadcasting pyramid. "People will order what they want rather than settling for what is there. In the world of teleputers, broadcasters, educators, investors, and film-makers who thought they could never go broke underestimating the intelligence of the American people are going to discover that they are wrong."[14] TV networks, says Gilder, are today's *Look* magazine.

Of equal significance is Gilder's prediction of a shift in the economies of the businesses, with less for distributors than is the case today and more for the writers and creators—whether the business is film, television, or magazines.

For that reason, newspapers may actually enjoy a more secure future in the wired world. "The computer is the perfect complement to the newspaper," Gilder writes. "It enables the existing news industry to deliver its product in real time."[15] Newspapers are better at collecting, editing, filtering, and presenting information. Computers are the technology that can eliminate the disadvantages of distribution. Gilder's prognosis is encouraging for those of us who cling to the descriptive "ink-stained wretch" even as we acknowledge the ink-stained wretch of the future isn't likely to have to deal with paper or printer's ink and will instead have to develop multimedia skills.

The Net's fans liken it to the birth of a solar system; search engines such as Yahoo! will likely emerge as the media powers of the next millennium. There is considerable hope that emerging technologies will lead us to a higher journalistic plane. Much of the hope for the future lies with the Net generation, the 88 million computer-savvy kids born in North America after 1977. According to technology guru Don Tapscott, this new generation is more dynamic, confident, and even assertive. They have been as profoundly influenced by digital technology as the Boomers were by television. But the interactive nature of the Net means the "nerds" are a more well-rounded, intellectually stimulated generation than their couch-potato parents. Citizens will have direct access to information sources via computers, says writer Michael Schudson, and, as a result, "they are as easily disseminators as recipients of news." Telegraphy, as Postman says, created the concept of information stripped of context, either historical or ideological. In the post-Information Age, news consumers will be looking for context rather than content in news coverage. Emerging technologies will be about communication and not just information. The new media point to a new form of journalism with a future based on an editing function rather than an information-relay function, with the consumer doing the editing. The old truism that journalism is about accuracy, not veracity, will be reversed. Reporters, says Esther Dyson, will evolve from news filters to news curators. Journalists of the future, she says, will mediate community conversations. Publications will no longer purport to tell readers what went on yesterday, but will collaborate with readers in a "joint venture" to discover truth—the truth being something other than the product we call news.

Newsweek columnist Steven Levy seems to be heralding a high-tech return to the era of the pamphleteer, with the World Wide Web serving as a liberating technology that empowers literally anyone to set up a news channel, a 'zine, or a storefront on the virtual highway.

The world will continue to be divided into "haves" and "have nots." Economic standing will continue to be the litmus test, but computer literacy and access to information will be the determinant.

Ironically, these technological advances in mass media may presage a return to Lazarsfeld's two-step flow theory of communications, where most of us will assimilate political information, values, and attitudes from friends or associates, and community "leaders" with extensive, even obsessive, media-consumption habits.

Nancy Maynard Hicks, in a 1996 article entitled "Where Is Page One in Cyberspace?" said, "Good journalism is like farming; it requires constant effort, seemingly disproportionate to its yield."[16] The media, whether new or old, must resist the creeping anti-intellectualism that threatens the *raison d'être* of the fourth estate. Otherwise, current feelings of detachment and disenchantment with our democratic institutions will harden.

Nobel Prize-winning author Gabriel García Márquez, through the Foundation for a New Latin American Journalism, recently assembled a group of distinguished writers, editors, and designers, including *Kitchener-Waterloo Record* editor Lou Clancy, to consider a newspaper for the future—*El Periodico Ideal*. The group's point of departure is that people still like to read and are, in fact, reading more than ever. The working group also concluded: "... there is something enduring about this old physical medium."[17] Through two days of intense discussion, the working group concluded that "newspapers need to get away from the journalism school dictums of bland objectivity and inject passion and narrative into reports." Participants agreed that the best storytelling in most newspapers today can be found on the sports pages. The opportunity lies in the emotional edge of print over other media, that is, the ability to connect intimately the writer and the reader. The newspaper will feature reporting that connects with people, writing that tells great stories, and design that gets attention. And the going-in intention is to present this reporting and storytelling in a newspaper that looks like a newspaper.

The group noted that, in the past, local newspapers tended to have their own typefaces, just as local towns had their own beers. Looking ahead, the group believes the future belongs to big national newspapers and strong local newspapers, that traditional metro dailies, like telephone books, are doomed. Clancy argues any newspaper reader should know what city he or she is in even if the paper's masthead has been cut off. "The successful newspapers, like police departments, have gone back to their roots, the beats,"[18] the report states.

Gabriel García Márquez is convinced the unique selling point of the paper of the future will be the quality of the editorial work, and the impact of a design that helps make the important interesting. The approach is expensive but in the "value-added" economy of the post-information era, it may represent journalism's last, best hope.

Since their designation as the "fourth estate," the media have been positioned as an important institution in Western democracies. Yet this assumed status has no standing in law. Constitutions present the principle of free speech; they are silent as to form.

The media emerged as a primary site of political discourse because the media circulated information that had societal value. As the economic foundation of the news business shifted, so did its primary "product"—with the audience replacing editorial content. As technological innovation and emerging media heightened the challenge through audience assembly, the content became increasingly sensational and less substantive.

"Spin" was an inevitable byproduct of this evolution. The acceptable and honorable quest to advance an idea or an individual to advantage gave way to a troubling belief in certain circles that spin could solve any or all problems. The predators among us became convinced that any transgression could be camouflaged provided the "story" was given the right spin. Treasury-looting despots, charlatan televangelists, criminal pugilists, and ever-repentant presidents operated on the premise that people would overlook a multitude of sins if their venal acts could be situated in a big picture—with spin.

The multimedia universe of the future holds the promise of a more constructive dialogue. A billboard in downtown Toronto points to a new media age. Touting the value of an education at Seneca College, the advertisement proclaims twenty-first-century careers for the twenty-first-century economy. Seneca and its sister community college, Sheridan, are leading the digital revolution. Its graduates will shape the multimedia universe, where political discourse will occur. They will not be bound by artificial barriers between media and entertainment. After all, the prophets spoke in parables. And the life lessons of fables transcend the storybook settings.

Like the revolutionary clerics in Central America in the early 1980s, the members of the Net generation will give effect to "liberation technology." They will end the age of passivity, ushering in a new period of dialogue and political discourse *predicated* on interactivity. They will know content matters, but will better appreciate technology's criteria to strengthen the narrative with other sign systems—from music to sound, from typeface to presentation. Linear thinking will be as dated as Latin. The deconstructionisms of postmodern thought will achieve full expression.

In recent years, spin doctors have positioned themselves as the stage managers of politics. Carefully coiffed, nattily attired in Armani or Brooks Brothers, they often appear on current-affairs programs to share their insights, crowding their clients for face-time. They are the self-declared masters of the universe of the pseudo-event, and their days are numbered.

"Spin" wars, as practiced over the past three decades, will be remembered as an artifact of an earlier media culture, a period piece of possible interest to future anthropologists.

The spin *meister* of the future will be a policy wonk or a believer in a cause. My son Graham, who spent the summer of 1998 as press secretary to Conservative party leadership hopeful Hugh Segal, is one example. Paternal pride notwithstanding, Graham proved an effective intermediary precisely because of his policy background.

A 1998 pre-Christmas issue of the *New York Times Magazine* offered an insight into how the Web world works for radical movements as well. Craig Rosbraugh, a twenty-six-year-old spokesperson for the vegan, fur-free anarcho-cause is the media contact for the Earth Liberation Front. The environmental group claims it burned down a ski resort in Vail, Colorado, to preserve a lynx habitat. Rosbraugh is a classic 1990s radical, dressed in black clothing, free of animal hair and skin. His job is to position an act of terrorism as "an act of love for the environment." And he does his job without speaking directly to his audience. Rosbraugh is understandably vague as to whether the underground communiqués he distributes to the press reach him by fax or e-mail.

But if America is on-line, so is spin, and like space itself, cyber-spin will be out there.

Notes

Chapter One:

1 Freedom Forum Media Studies Center Fellows for the 1995–1996 academic year included: Lord Asa Briggs, chancellor of the Open University, London, England; Michael Janeway, former editor of the *Boston Globe*; Al Gollin, former vice-president of the Newspaper Association of America; Orville Schell, dean of the school of journalism, Berkeley; *New Yorker* writer and ABC legal affairs correspondent Jeffrey Toobin; New York University professor Mitchell Stephens; *Philadelphia Inquirer* editor Hank Klibanoff; *Spy* magazine columnist David Shenk; former *USA Today* reporter Margaret Usdansky; University of Maryland professor Marjorie Ferguson; and University of Calgary professor Edna Einsiedel.

2 The Fellows met for a formal discussion each week, with a leading journalist or academic as an invited guest. Invitees ranged from CBS *60 Minutes* host Mike Wallace to Harvard's Thomas E. Patterson, author of *Out of Order*.

3 Postman, Neil. *Amusing Ourselves to Death: Public Discourse in the Age of Show Business*. New York: Penguin Books, 1985, Pg. 107.

4 Iyengar, Shanto, and, Donald Kinder. *News That Matters: Television and American Opinion*. Chicago: University of Chicago Press, 1991, Pg. 1.

5 Leonard, Thomas C. *The Power of the Press: The Birth of American Political Reporting*. New York: Oxford University Press, 1987.

Chapter Two:

1 Davey, Sen. Keith. *The Rainmaker: A Passion for Politics*. Toronto: Stoddart, 1986, Pg. 184.

2 Hess, Stephen. *The Government/Press Connection. Press Officers and Their Offices*. Washington, D.C.: The Brookings Institute, 1984, Pg. 37.

3 Fitzwater, Marlin. *Call the Briefing! Reagan and Bush, Sam and Helen: A Decade with Presidents and the Press*. New York: Times Books, 1995, Pg. 4.

4 Ibid., Pg. 11.

5 Ibid., Pg. 74.

6 Chrétien, Jean. *Straight from the Heart*. Toronto: Key Porter Books, 1985, Pg. 46.

7 Patterson, Tom. *Out of Order*. New York: Vintage Books, 1994, Pg. 59.

8 Fallows, James. Brown Bag lunch, Shorenstein Center on Press, Politics and Public Policy, Havard University, April 18, 1995.

9 Crouse, Timothy. *The Boys on the Bus*. New York: Random House, 1972, Pg. 29.

10 Cronkite, Walter. *The First Annual Theodore H. White Lecture*. Shorenstein Center on Press, Politics and Public Policy, John F. Kennedy School of Journalism, Harvard University, November 15, 1990.

11 *New York Times*. "An Old Hand's View of TV News: Not Good." March 22, 1998, Pg. 41.

12 McGinniss, Joe. *The Selling of the President*. New York: Penguin Books, 1969, Pg. 26.

13 Crouse, Timothy. *The Boys on the Bus*. New York: Random House, 1972, Pg. 34.

14 Boorstin, Daniel J. *The Image: A Guide to Pseudo-Events in America*. New York: Anthenum, 1978, Pg. 37.

15 Ibid., Pg. 42.

16 Fraser, Graham. *Playing for Keeps: The Making of the Prime Minister 1988*. Toronto: McClelland & Stewart, 1989, Pg. 16.

17 Lee, Robert Mason. *One Hundred Monkeys: The Triumph of Popular Wisdom in Canadian Politics*. Toronto: McFarlane, Walters and Ross, 1989, Pg. 42.

18 Ibid., Pg. 80.

19 Ibid., Pg. 138.

20 Fraser, Graham. *Playing for Keeps: The Making of the Prime Minister 1988*. Toronto: McClelland & Stewart, 1989, Pg. 336.

21 Boorstin, Daniel J. *The Image: A Guide to Pseudo-Events in America*. New York: Anthenum, 1978, Pg. 44.

22 Weaver, Paul. "Is Television News Biased?" *The Public Interest* 27 (1972), Pg. 69.

23 Rosen, Jay, and Paul Taylor. *The New News v. the Old News: The Press and Politics in the 1990s*. Politics' Vision and the Press Agenda for Journalism. A Twentieth Century Fund Paper, New York, 1993, Pg. 5.

24 Patterson, Tom. *Out of Order*. New York: Vintage Books, 1994, Pg. 26.

25 Goar, Carol. *Toronto Star*. January 10, 1998, Pg. E-2.

26 *The Toronto Star*. January 10, 1998. Carol Goar column, Pg. E-2.

27 Frizzell, Alan, and Jon H. Pammett. *The Canadian General Election of 1997*. Toronto: Dundurn Press, 1997. *Securing Their Future Together: The Liberals in Action*, by Stephen Clarkson, Pg. 51.

28 Anderson, Rick. Personal Interview, February, 1998.

29 Ibid.

30 Chrétien, Jean. *Straight from the Heart*. Toronto: Key Porter Books, 1985, Pg. 215.

31 Hall Jamieson, Kathleen. *Dirty Politics: Deception, Distraction and Democracy.* Oxford University Press, 1992, Pg. 62.

32 Patterson, Tom. *Out of Order.* New York: Vintage Books, 1994, Pg. 89.

33 Kurtz, Howard. *Spin Cycle: Inside the Clinton Propaganda Machine.* New York: The Free Press, 1998, Pg. xix.

34 Ibid.

35 Merritt, Davis "Buzz." *Public Journalism and Public Life: Why Telling the News is Not Enough.* Hillsdale, N.J.: Laurence Erlbaum Publishers, 1995.

36 Rosenstiel, Tom. *The Beat Goes On: President Clinton's First Year with the Media.* A Twentieth Century Fund Essay, Pg. vii.

37 Bagdikian, Ben. *The Media Monopoly.* 4th edition. Boston, MA: Beacon Press, 1992, Pg. xxvii.

Chapter Three:

1 Schramm, Wilbur. *The Nature of News.* 1949, Pg. 288.

2 Davey, Sen. Keith. *The Rainmaker: A Passion for Politics.* Toronto: Stoddart, 1986, Pg. 155.

3 McManus, John H. *Market-Driven Journalism: Let the Citizen Beware.* Thouand Oaks, CA: Sage Publications, 1994, Pg. 25.

4 Gans, Herbert J. *Deciding What's News: A Study of CBS Evening News, NBC Nightly News, Newsweek and Time.* New York: Vintage Books, 1980, Pg. xii.

5 Patterson, Tom. Brown Bag Discussion, Shorenstein Center on Press, Politics and Public Policy, John F. Kennedy School of Government, Harvard University, February 27, 1995.

6 Gans, Herbert J. *Deciding What's News: A Study of CBS Evening News, NBC Nightly News, Newsweek and Time.* New York: Vintage Books, 1980, Pg. 234.

7 Ettema, James S., and Theodore L. Glasser. *On the Epistemology of Investigative Journalism.* U.S.A.: Gordon and Breach, Science Publishers Inc., 1985, Pg. 187.

8 Greenfield, Jeff. "When facts alone won't do." *The New York Times,* November 2, 1998, Pg. A-27.

9 Postman, Neil. *Amusing Ourselves to Death: Public Discourse in the Age of Show Business.* New York: Penguin Books, 1985, Pg. 80.

10 Ibid., Pg. 156.

11 Gans, Herbert J. *Deciding What's News: A Study of CBS Evening News, NBC Nightly News, Newsweek and Time.* New York: Vintage Books, 1980, Pg. 116.

12 Sigal, Leon. *Who? Sources Make the News. Reading The News: A Pantheon Guide to Popular Culture.* Eds. Manoff and Schudson. New York: Pantheon Books, 1986, Pg. 81.

13 Gans, Herbert J. *Deciding What's News: A Study of CBS Evening News, NBC Nightly News, Newsweek and Time.* New York: Vintage Books, 1980, Pg. 118–9.

14 Epstein, Edward Jay. *Between Fact and Fiction: The Problem of Journalism.* New York: Vintage Books, 1975, Pg. 9.

15 Ibid., Pg. 10.

16 Hess, Stephen. *The Government/Press Connection: Press Officers and Their Offices.* Washington, D.C.: The Brookings Institute, 1984, Pg. 76.

17 Crosbie, John C. *No Holds Barred: My Life in Politics.* Toronto: McClelland & Stewart, 1997, Pg. 422.

18 Weston, Greg. Telephone Interview, March 27, 1998.

19 Calamai, Peter. Personal Interview, February 9, 1998.

20 Merritt, Davis "Buzz." *Public Journalism and Public Life: Why Telling the News Is Not Enough.* Hillsdale, N.J.: Laurence Erlbaum Associates Publishers, 1995, Pg. 58.

21 Calamai, Peter. Personal Interview, February 9, 1998.

22 Reston, James "Scotty." *New York Times,* December 7, 1995.

23 Weston, Greg. Personal Interview, March 27, 1998.

24 Report of the Senate Committee.

25 Corcoran, Terrence. "The $1B Pearson Scandal." *Globe and Mail,* May 17, 1997. Pg. B-2.

26 *Globe and Mail,* December 10, 1997. "A supposedly managerial government is mishandling helicopters." Jeffrey Simpson, Pg. A-26.

27 Nankivell, Neville. "Pearson." *The Financial Post,* April 28, 1998, Pg. 21.

28 Fallows, James. *Breaking the News: How the Media Undermine American Democracy.* New York: Pantheon Books, 1996, Pg. 7.

29 Ibid., Pg. 91.

30 Rosen, Jay, and Paul Taylor. *The New News and the Old News: The Press and Politics in the 1990s.* A Twentieth Century Fund Paper, New York, 1992, Pg. 25.

31 Dowd, Maureen. *The New York Times,* June, 1994, Pg. 1.

32 McManus, John H. *Market-Driven Journalism: Let the Citizen Beware.* Thousand Oaks, CA: Sage Publications, 1994, Pg. 192.

33 Gans, Herbert J. *Deciding What's News: A Study of CBS Evening News, NBC Nightly News, Newsweek and Time.* New York: Vintage Books, 1980, Pg. 312.

34 Ibid., Pg. 320.

Chapter Four:

1 Iyengar, Shanto, and Donald Kinder. *News That Matters: Television and American Public-Opinion.* Chicago: The University of Chicago Press, 1991.

2 Statement by Rt. Hon. Kim Campbell. Rideau Hall, September 8, 1993.

3 Greenspon, Edward. "Leaders Focus on the Economy: Campbell Stresses Deficit, Chrétien Zeroes in on Jobs." *Globe and Mail,* September 9, 1992, Pg. A-1.

4 Jamieson, Nancy. Personal Interview, January 24, 1994.

5 Greenspon, Edward. "Leaders Focus on the Economy: Campbell Stresses Deficit, Chrétien Zeroes in on Jobs." *Globe and Mail,* September 9, 1992, Pg. A-1.

6 Iyengar, Shanto, and Donald Kinder. *News That Matters: Television and American Public-Opinion.* Chicago: The University of Chicago Press, 1991, Pg. 46.

7 Stewart, Edison. "Jean Charest: A Man at the Crossroads." *Toronto Star*, March 15, 1998, Pg. 1.

8 Entman, Robert M. "Framing: Toward a Clarification of a Fractured Paradigm." *Journal of Communication* 43.4 (1993), Pg. 55–56.

9 Iyengar, Shanto, and Donald Kinder. *News That Matters: Television and American Public-Opinion.* Chicago: The University of Chicago Press, 1991, Pg. 1.

10 Donolo, Peter. Personal Interview, February 10, 1998.

11 Ibid.

12 Ibid.

13 Tucher, Andie. *Froth and Scum: Truth, Beauty, Goodness and the Ax Murder in America's First Mass Medium.* Fellows' Seminar, Freedom Forum Media Studies Center, Columbia University, December 5, 1995.

14 "Seatmate Clears Scott on APEC." *Toronto Star*, October 7, 1998, Pg. A-1.

15 Tucher, Andie. *Froth and Scum: Truth, Beauty, Goodness and the Ax Murder in America's First Mass Medium.* Fellows' Seminar, Freedom Forum Media Studies Center, Columbia University, December 5, 1995.

16 Fitzwater, Marlin. *Call the Briefing! Reagan and Bush, Sam and Helen—A Decade With Presidents and the Press.* New York: Times Books, Random House, 1995, Pg. 329.

17 Ibid., Pg. 131.

18 Ibid., Pg. 198.

Chapter Five:

1 *New York Times.* Obituary Page, October 2, 1995, Associated Press.

2 Neuharth, Al. *Confessions of an S.O.B.* New York: Doubleday, 1989, Pg. 110.

3 Squires, James. *Read All About It: The Corporate Takeover of America's Newspapers.* New York: Times Books, 1993, Pg. 24.

4 Ibid., Pg. 8.

5 Ibid., Pg. 57.

6 Bagdikian, Ben. *The Media Monopoly.* 4th Edition. Boston, MA: Beacon Press, 1992, Pg. 252.

7 Jurkowitz, Mark. *Boston Globe.* Brown Bag lunch, Shorenstein Center on the Press, Politics and Public Policy, Harvard University, March 21, 1995.

8 Davies, Robertson. *New York Times*, December 4, 1995.

9 *American Journalism Review.* October 1995, Pg. 15.

10 Auletta, Ken. *Three Blind Mice: How the Television Networks Lost Their Way.* New York: Random House, 1991, Pg. 16–17.

11 Ibid.

12 Ibid., Pg. 475.

13 Ibid., Pg. 34.

14 Ferguson, Rob. "Hollinger rejects call for inquiry." *Toronto Star*, May 22, 1998, Pg. E-3.

15 *Toronto Star*. "Critics crank up pressure over Black's newspaper play." May 23, 1998, Pg. C-1.

16 Ibid.

17 The Campaign for Press and Broadcasting Freedom. *Diversity and Quality in the Monopoly Press: A Content Analysis of Hollinger Newspapers*. April 1997.

18 Ibid.

19 Ibid.

20 McKenzie, Jim. *Content Analysis of the Regina Leader-Post under Hollinger Ownership*. Prepared for the Council of Canadians and the Campaign for Press and Broadcasting Freedom, December 1996.

21 Ibid.

22 Ibid.

23 Ibid.

24 Ibid.

25 Hayes, David. "Fear Itself." *Toronto Life*, October, 1998, Pg. 120.

26 *New York Times*, January 11, 1998, Pg. 3-D.

27 Dennis, Everette. *Reshaping the Media: Mass Communication in an Information Age*. Newbury Park: Sage Publications, 1989, Pg. 60.

28 Auletta, Ken. *Three Blind Mice: How the Television Networks Lost Their Way*. New York: Random House, 1991, Pg. 85.

29 Squires, James. *Read All About It: The Corporate Takeover of America's Newspapers*. New York: Times Books, 1993, Pg. 106.

30 Gunther, Marc. "All in the Family." *American Journalism Review*, October, 1995, Pg. 36.

31 *American Journalism Review*. October, 1995, Pg. 38

32 *New York Times*. November 19, 1998.

33 Baker, Russ. "Murdoch's Mean Machine." *Columbia Journalism Review*, May/June 1998.

34 *Daily Herald*. Thursday, 28 November 1995.

35 Squires, James. *Read All About It: The Corporate Takeover of America's Newspapers*. New York: Times Books, 1993, Pg. 78.

36 Tape of Proceedings, American Magazine Conference, Phoenix, Arizona, 1997.

37 Ibid.

38 Ibid.

39 Squires, James. *Read All About It: The Corporate Takeover of America's Newspapers*. New York: Times Books, 1993, Pg. 78.

40 Ibid., Pg. 74.

41 Bogart, Leo. *Preserving the Press: How Daily Newspapers Mobilized to Keep Their Readers*. New York: Columbia University Press, 1991, Pg. 272.

42 Squires, James. *Read All About It: The Corporate Takeover of America's Newspapers*. New York: Times Books, 1993, Pg. 120.

43 Ibid., Pg. 145.

44 Ibid., Pg. 189.

45 Ibid., Pg. 210.

46 Cronkite, Walter. Speech, University of South Dakota, October 27, 1989.

47 Barron, Jerome. Fellows' Seminar, Freedom Forum Media Studies Center, November 16, 1995.

48 Squires, James. *Read All About It: The Corporate Takeover of America's Newspapers.* New York: Times Books, 1993, Pg. 221.

49 Roberts, Eugene. Fellows' Seminar, Freedom Forum Media Studies Center, January 10, 1996.

50 Ibid.

51 Ibid.

52 Kovach, Bill. "Hamburger Helper if the Worldwatch." *Neiman Reports,* Fall 1995.

53 Shepard, Alicia C. "Denver Post—Rocky Mountain News locked in an old fashioned newspaper war." *American Journalism Review,* October 1995, Pg. 31.

54 Hayes, David. "Fear Itself." *Toronto Life,* October, 1998, Pg. 116.

55 McManus, John H. *Market-Driven Journalism: Let the Citizen Beware.* Thousand Oaks, CA: Sage Publications, 1994, Pg. 85.

56 Hallin, Daniel C. *We Keep America on the Top of the World: Television Journalism and the Public Sphere.* New York: Routledge, 1994, Pg. 88.

57 McManus, John H. *Market-Driven Journalism: Let the Citizen Beware.* Thousand Oaks, CA: Sage Publications, 1994, Pg. 107.

58 Ibid., Pg. 134.

59 Ibid., Pg. 8.

60 Lichtenberg, Judith. *The Politics of Character and the Character of Journalism.* Shorenstein Center on the Press, Politics and Public Policy, Discussion Paper C-2, October 1989, Pg. 7.

61 Dionne, E.J., Jr. *They Only Look Dead: Why Progressives Will Dominate the Next Political Era.* New York: Simon and Schuster, 1998, Pg. 238.

62 Merritt, Davis "Buzz." *Public Journalism and Public Life: Why Telling the News Is Not Enough.* Hillsdale, N.J.: Lawrence Erlbaum Associates Publishers, 1995, Pg. 58

63 Hume, Ellen. "Campaign Lessons for '92." Study, Shorenstein Center on the Press, Politics and Public Policy, John F. Kennedy School of Government, Harvard University, Pg. 24.

Chapter Six:

1 Bradlee, Ben. *NBC Today,* September 25, 1995.

2 Klapp, Orrin E. *Symbolic Leaders: Public Dramas and Public Men.* Chicago: Aldine Publishing Co., 1964, Pg. 195, *op. cit.* Gibney, Frank. *The Operator.* New York: Harper, 1960, Pg. 195.

3 Ibid.

4 Ibid., Pg. 101.

5 Ibid., Pg. 102.

6 Ibid., Pg. 113.

7 Ibid., Pg. 195.

8 Mulroney, M. Brian. Testimony at Examination for Discovery, Palais de Justice, Montreal, Quebec, April 17, 1996.

9 Translated version of the communiqué to Swiss authorities was available to a number of sources, including Karl-Heinz Schrieber's lawyer, Robert Hladun.

10 Ibid.

11 Heinrick, Jeff. "Mulroney failed to hush allegations, Well connected lawyers couldn't put lid on probe." *Montreal Gazette*, November 23, 1995, Pg. 1.

12 Kaplan, William. *Presumed Guilty: Brian Mulroney, The Airbus Affair and the Government of Canada*. Toronto: McClelland & Stewart, 1998, Pg. 105.

13 Lavoie, Luc. Personal interview, February 24, 1998.

14 Ibid.

15 Ibid.

16 Ibid.

17 Ibid.

18 Text of a fax signed by Andrew Phillips, then national editor, *Maclean's* magazine, dated Thursday, November 16, 1998.

19 Kaplan, William. *Presumed Guilty: Brian Mulroney, The Airbus Affair and the Government of Canada*. Toronto: McClelland & Stewart, 1998, Pg. 125.

20 Lavoie, Luc. Personal interview, February 24, 1998.

21 Ibid.

22 Twain, Mark.

23 Mulroney, M. Brian. Personal interview. N.B. Through the "Airbus Affair," the author was in regular contact in person and by telephone with Mr. Mulroney and also conducted a lengthy interview February 23, 1998.

24 News release issued Saturday, November 18, 1995.

25 Nickerson, Colin. "Mulroney sues Canadian government, Ex-prime minister asserts he was libelled by inquiry." *Boston Globe*, November 21, 1995, Pg. 1.

26 Feschuk, Scott. "Western Voices." *Globe and Mail*, November 24, 1995.

27 Ibid.

28 *The New York Times Company v. L.B. Sullivan, Ralph D. Abernathy et al.* The Supreme Court of the United States. Argued January 6 and 7, 1964. Decided March 9, 1964.

29 Ibid.

30 Heinrick, Jeff. "Mulroney failed to hush allegations, Well connected lawyers couldn't put lid on probe." *Montreal Gazette*, November 23, 1995, Pg. 1.

31 Kaplan, William. *Presumed Guilty: Brian Mulroney, The Airbus Affair and the Government of Canada*. Toronto: McClelland & Stewart, 1998, Pg. 250.

32 Lavoie, Luc. Personal interview, February 24, 1998.

33 Ibid.

34 Ibid.

35 Ibid.

36 Ibid.

37 Donovan, Kevin. "FBI dismayed by lack of Airbus probe. Surprised Mulroney's name surfaced: source." *Toronto Star*, November 28, 1998, Pg. 1.

38 Fitzwater, Marlin. Telephone interview, February 12, 1996.

39 Mulroney, M. Brian. Personal interview, February 24, 1998.

40 Quigley, Supt. Tim. "Big deal gets even bigger." *Toronto Star*, November 20, 1995, Pg. 2.

41 Lavoie, Luc. Personal interview, February 24, 1998.

42 Ibid.

43 Koring, Paul. "Gray knew Rock's tack with RCMP." *Globe and Mail*, December 12, 1995, Pg. 1.

44 Delacourt, Susan. Personal interview February 11, 1998.

45 Ibid.

46 Ibid.

47 Ibid.

48 Ibid.

49 Ibid.

50 Ibid.

51 Ibid.

52 Ibid.

53 Mulroney, M. Brian. Personal interview.

54 Ibid.

55 Ibid.

56 Ibid.

57 Ibid.

58 Mulroney, M. Brian. Testimony, April 17, 1996.

59 Mulroney, M. Brian. Personal interview.

60 Ibid.

61 Ibid.

62 Ibid.

63 Ibid.

64 Ibid.

65 Ibid.

66 Ibid.

67 Ibid.

68 Ibid.

69 Ibid.

70 Ibid.

71 Ibid.

72 Ibid.

73 Weston, Greg. Telephone interview, March 27, 1998.

74 Ibid.

75 Ibid.

76 Ibid.

77 Ibid.

78 Fife, Bob. Telephone interview, March 26, 1998.

79 Ibid.

80 Ibid.

81 Ibid.

82 Ibid.

83 Ibid.

84 Ibid.

85 Ibid.

86 Ibid.

87 Mulroney, M. Brian. Testimony at Examination for Discovery, Palais de Justice, Montreal, Quebec, April 17, 1996.

88 Ibid.

89 Mulroney, M. Brian. Personal interview.

90 Unnamed source. Personal interview, April 17, 1996.

91 Sheppard, Claude-Armand. Elevator scrum, April 17, 1997.

92 Segal, Hugh D. Personal interview.

93 Mulroney, M. Brian. Personal interview.

94 MacDonald, Neil. Personal interview, February 23, 1998.

95 Mulroney, M. Brian. Testimony at Examination for Discovery, Palais de Justice, Montreal, Quebec, April 17, 1997.

96 MacDonald, Neil. Personal interview, February 23, 1998.

97 Ibid.

98 Mulroney, M. Brian. Personal interview.

99 Ibid.

100 Ibid.

101 Ibid.

102 Lavoie, Luc. Personal interview, February 24, 1998.

103 Ibid.

104 Ibid.

105 Ibid.

106 Ibid.

107 Ibid.

108 Ibid.

109 Ibid.

110 Fitz-James, Michael. "The Law." *Financial Post*, November 19, 1997, Pg. 17.

111 Ibid.

112 Ibid.

113 Kaplan, William. *Presumed Guilty: Brian Mulroney, The Airbus Affair and the Government of Canada.* Toronto: McClelland & Stewart, 1998, Pg. 272.

114 Wilson, Michael. CBC's *The Magazine*, January 9, 1997.

Chapter Seven:

1 Kitman, Marvin. Fellows' Seminar, Freedom Forum Media Studies Center.

2 Kitman, Marvin. "The Big Get Bigger." *The Marvin Kitman Sunday Show: FANFARE*, September 3, 1995.

3 Levy, Steven. "How the propeller heads stole the electronic future." *New York Times Magazine*, September 24, 1995.

4 Fulton, Katherine. "A tour of our uncertain future." *Columbia Journalism Review*. March/April 1996.

5 Ibid.

6 Powell, Adam Clayton, III. "Diversity in cyberspace." *Freedom Forum Media Centre Studies Paper*, 1995.

7 Maynard, Nancy Hicks. "Where is page one in cyberspace?" *Global Business Review*, 1996.

8 Dyson, Esther. *Release 2.0. A Design for Living in the Digital Age.* New York: Broadway Books, 1997, Pg. 6.

9 Shenk, David. Fellows' Seminar, Freedom Forum Media Studies Center, January 17, 1996.

10 Powell, Adam Clayton, III. "Diversity in cyberspace." *Freedom Forum Media Centre Studies Paper*, 1995.

11 Cribb, Robert. "The Fourth Medium." *Toronto Star*, September 1, 1997, Pg. H1

12 Daniels, Frank, III. "Public interest journalism: Winners and losers in the on-line era." Neiman Foundation Conference, Cambridge, MA, May 4, 1995.

13 *Globe and Mail*. "Beatty pursues new TV, internet services for CBC." November 13, 1998, Pg. A-11.

14 Negroponte, Nicholas. *Being Digital.* New York: Alfred A. Knopf, 1995, Pg. 58.

15 Ibid.

16 *Toronto Star*. "Roll your own photos." November 20, 1997.

17 *Newsweek*. "A bad day in cyberspace. The senate takes a sledge hammer to our communications future." June 26, 1995, Pg. 47.

18 Dyson, Esther. *Release 2.0. A Design for Living in the Digital Age.* New York: Broadway Books, 1997, Pg. 51.

19 Alboim, Elly. "Covering the Suits." Speech to the Canadian Association of Journalists, April 11, 1994.

20 Cribb, Robert. "The fourth medium." *Toronto Star*, September 11, 1997, Pg. H-1.

21 Alboim, Elly. "Covering the Suits." Speech to the Canadian Association of Journalists, April 11, 1994.

22 Shenk, David. Fellows' Seminar, Freedom Forum Media Studies Center, January 17, 1996.

23 Fallows, James. *Breaking the News: How the Media Undermine American Democracy.* New York: Pantheon Books, 1996, Pg. 148.

24 Alboim, Elly. "Covering the Suits." Speech to the Canadian Association of Journalists, April 11, 1994.

25 *New York Times*. "An old hand's view of television news: Not good." March 22, 1998, Pg. 41.

Chapter Eight:

1 Feinsilber, Mike. The Associated Press. "Tide could be turning for Clinton." *The Tampa Tribune*, February 1, 1998, Pg. 1.

2 Rollins, Ed. "Larry King Live." *CNN*, January 26, 1998.

3 *Newsweek*. Editor's Note, January 22, 1998.

4 Ibid.

5 Bradlee, Ben. "Larry King Live." *CNN*, January 26, 1998.

6 Ibid.

7 Sabato, Larry J. *Feeding Frenzy: How Attack Journalism Has Transformed American Politics*. New York: The Free Press, 1991, Pg. 2.

8 McCurry, Mike. Presidential spokesperson, transcript. Brown Bag Session, Shorenstein Center on the Press, Politics and Public Policy, February 9, 1998.

9 Sabato, Larry J. *Feeding Frenzy: How Attack Journalism Has Transformed American Politics*. New York: The Free Press, 1991, Pg. 6.

10 Toobin, Jeffrey. "Comment: Courtroom v. Newsroom." *The New Yorker*. January 27, 1997, Pg. 6.

11 Ibid.

12 Sabato, Larry J. *Feeding Frenzy: How Attack Journalism Has Transformed American Politics*. New York: The Free Press, 1991, Pg. 27.

13 de Tocqueville, Alexis. *Democracy in America*. Volume 1, Pg. 194.

14 Hart, Gary. Speech Text, Yale University, November 11, 1987.

15 Segal, Hugh D. Personal interview.

16 McCurry, Mike. Press Briefing, The White House, January 22, 1998.

17 Dowd, Maureen. "Not suitable for children." *New York Times*, January 25, 1998.

18 Ibid.

19 Kenna, Kathleen. "Not a period the press can be proud of." *Toronto Star*, February 17, 1998, Pg. E-1.

20 Scott, Janny. "Media push limits on news gathering." New York Times News Service, *Globe and Mail*, January 28, 1998.

21 Kurtz, Howard. "Town hall at the news scrum." *CNN*, January 26, 1998.

22 Hartman, Central Michigan.

23 Simpson, Jeffrey. Column. *Globe and Mail*, January 23, 1998.

24 Kurtz, Howard. "Town hall at the news scrum." *CNN*, January 26, 1998.

25 McCurry, Mike. Presidential spokesperson, transcript. Brown Bag Session, Shorenstein Center on the Press, Politics and Public Policy, February 9, 1998.

26 Ibid.

27 "Larry King Live." *CNN*, January 26, 1998.

28 Ibid.

29 "Golfer Greg Norman thrown off his game." *Toronto Star*, February 7, 1998.

30 "Larry King Live." *CNN*, January 26, 1998.

31 Dowd, Maureen. Liberties Column. *New York Times*, January 31, 1998.

32 "Larry King Live." *CNN*, January 26, 1998.

33 "Truth and consequences." *Time*, August 24, 1998.

34 "Larry King Live." *CNN*, January 26, 1998.

35 Ibid.

36 Safire, William. Column. *New York Times*, January 22, 1998.

37 Donolo, Peter. Personal interview, February 10, 1998.

38 Ibid.

39 McCurry, Mike. Presidential spokesperson, transcript. Brown Bag Session, Shorenstein Center on the Press, Politics and Public Policy, February 9, 1998.

40 Ibid.

41 Ibid.

42 Rosenstiel, Tom. *The Beat Goes On: President Clinton's First Year with the Media*. A Twentieth Century Fund Paper, New York, 1993, Pg. 3.

43 Ibid., Pg. 40.

44 Kenna, Kathleen. *Toronto Star*, January 31, 1998, Pg. 1.

45 Kurtz, Howard. *Spin Cycle: How the White House and the Media Manipulate the News*. New York: The Free Press, 1998, Pg. xvii.

46 Newsclips. January 24, 1998, *NBC, ABC*, etc.

47 Presidential address. August 17, 1998.

48 Berke, Richard. "That woman has turned politics upside down." *The New York Times Week in Review*, August 23, 1998.

49 Presidential address. August 17, 1998.

50 Myers, Dee Dee. "That's where he lost me." *Time*, August 31, 1998.

51 Dowd, Maureen. *New York Times*, September 13, 1998.

52 Berke, Richard. "That woman has turned politics upside down." *The New York Times Week in Review*, August 23, 1998.

53 Scott, Janny. "The pundits, talking heads' post-mortem: All wrong all the time." *New York Times*, November 8, 1998, Pg. A-20.

Chapter Nine:

1 Fallows, James. *Breaking the News: How the Media Undermine American Democracy*. New York: Pantheon Books, 1996, Pg. 180.

2 Ibid.

3 Alboim, Elly. "Covering the Suits." Speech to the Canadian Association of Journalists, April 11, 1994.

4 Waldman, Amy. *The Washington Monthly*, May 15, 1996, Pg. 24.

5 Salutin, Rick. "Viewers Oops, Voters Pick a New Cast." *Globe and Mail*, May 2, 1997, Section C-1.

6 McManus, John H. *Market-Driven Journalism: Let the Citizen Beware*. Thousand Oaks, CA: Sage Publications, 1994, Pg. 192.

7 Lippmann, Walter. *Public Opinion*.

8 McManus, John H. *Market-Driven Journalism: Let the Citizen Beware*. Thousand Oaks, CA: Sage Publications, 1994, Pg. 211.

9 Roberts, Eugene. Fellows' Seminar, Freedom Forum Media Studies Center, January 10, 1996.

10 Sulzberger, Arthur, Jr. "Public interest journalism: Winners and losers in the on-line era." Neiman Foundation Conference, Cambridge, MA, May 4–5, 1995.

11 Ibid.

12 Mansbridge, Peter. Speech to the University of Manitoba, May, 1994.

13 Gilder, George. *Life After Television: The Coming Transformation of Media and American Life*. New York: W.W. Norton and Co., 1994, Pg. 44.

14 Ibid., Pg. 45.

15 Ibid., Pg. 139.

16 Maynard, Nancy Hicks. "Where is page one in cyberspace?" *Global Business Review*, 1996.

17 Clancy, Lou. Draft report, working group, *El Periodico Ideal*, May, 1998.

18 Ibid.

Bibliography

Achar, Mark. *Manufacturing Consent: Noam Chomsky and the Media*. Montreal: Black Rose Books, 1994.

Auletta, Ken. *Three Blind Mice: How the TV Networks Lost Their Way*. New York: Random House, 1991.

Bagdikian, Ben. *The Media Monopoly*. 4th ed. Boston: Beacon Press, 1992.

Bain, George. *Gotcha: How the Media Distort the News*. Toronto: Key Porter Books, 1994.

Benjamin, Burton. *Fair Play: CBS, General Westmoreland and How a Television Documentary Went Wrong*. New York: Harper and Row Publishers, 1988.

Boorstin, Daniel J. *The Image: A Guide to Pseudo-Events in America*. New York: Athenaeum, 1961.

Bradlee, Ben. *A Good Life Newspapering and Other Adventures*. New York: Simon and Schuster, 1995.

Bryant, Jennings, and Dolf Zillman. *Media Effects: Advances on Theory and Research*. Hillsdale, N.J.: Laurence Erlbaum Associates, 1994.

Cameron, Stevie. *On the Take: Crime, Corruption and Greed in the Mulroney Years*. Toronto: Macfarlane, Walter and Ross, 1994.

Chancellor, John, and Walter R. Mears. *The New News Business*. New York: Harper Perennial, 1995.

Chrétien, Jean. *Straight from the Heart*. Toronto: Key Porter Books, 1985.

Christians, Clifford G., Mark Fackler, Keni B. Rotzoll, and Kathy Brittain McKee. *Media Ethics Cases and Moral Reasoning*. 5th ed. New York: Longman, 1998.

Cook, Phillips, Douglas Gomery, and Lawrence W. Lichtz. *The Future of News: Television, Newspapers, Wire Services and News Magazines*. Washington, D.C.: The Woodrow Wilson Press Center, Baltimore and London: Johns Hopkins University Press.

Cooper, Barry. *Sins of Omission: Shaping News at CBC-TV*. Toronto: University of Toronto Press, 1994.

Cronkite, Walter. *A Reporter's Life*. New York: Ballantine Books, 1996.

Crosbie, John. *No Holds Barred*. Toronto: McClelland & Stewart, 1997.

Crouse, Timothy. *The Boys on the Bus*. New York: Random House, 1972.

Dahlgren, Peter, and Colin Sparks. *Communication and Citizenship: Journalism and the Public Sphere*. London and New York: Routledge, 1991.

Davey, Keith. *The Rainmaker: A Passion for Politics*. Toronto: Stoddart, 1986.

Dionne, E.J., Jr. *They Only Look Dead: Why Progressives Will dominate the Next Political Era*: New York: Simon and Schuster, 1996.

Dennis, Everette E. *Reshaping the Media: Mass Communication in an Information Age*. Newbury Park: Sage Publications, 1989.

Dyson, Esther. *Release 2.0: A Design for Living in the Digital Age*. New York: Broadway Books, 1997.

———. *Democracy without Citizens*. New York: Oxford University Press, 1989.

Entman, Robert M. "Framing: Toward a Clarification of a Fractured Paradigm." *Journal of Communication* 43/4 (1993).

Epstein, Edward Jay. *Between Fact and Fiction: The Problem of Journalism*. New York: Vintage Books, 1975.

Fallows, James. *Breaking the News: How the Media Undermine American Democracy*. New York: Pantheon Books, 1996.

Fitzwater, Marlin. *Call the Briefing! Reagan and Bush, Sam and Helen— A Decade With Presidents and the Press*. New York: Times Books, Random House, 1995.

Fraser, Graham. *Playing for Keeps: The Making of the Prime Minister 1988*. Toronto, McClelland & Stewart, 1989.

Frizzell, Alan, and Jon H. Pammett. *The Canadian General Election of 1997*. Toronto: Dundurn Press, 1997.

Fuller, Jack. *News Values: Ideas for an Information Age*. Chicago: University of Chicago Press, 1996.

Gans, Herbert J. *Deciding What's News: A Study of CBS Evening News Nightly News, Newsweek and Time*. New York: Vintage Books, 1980.

Gibney, Frank. *The Operators*. New York: Harper, 1960.

Gilder, George. *Life After Television, Revised Edition: The Coming Transformation of Media and American Life*. New York: W.W. Norton, 1994.

Gitlin, Todd. *The Twilight of Common Dreams: Why America Is Wracked by Culture Wars*. New York: Metropolitan Books, 1995.

Goodwin, Andrew, and Gary Whanel. *Understanding Television*. London: Routledge, 1990.

Graber, Doris. *Processing the News: How the People Tame the Information*. New York: Longman, 1988.

Gratton, Michel. *So What Are the Boys Saying? An Inside Look at Brian Mulroney in Power*. Toronto: McGraw-Hill Ryerson, 1987.

Grossman, Laurence K. *The Electronic Republic: Reshaping Democracy in the Information Age*. A Twentieth Century Fund Book. New York: Vintage, 1995.

Hachten, William A., and Harva Hachten. *The World News Prism: Changing Media of International Communication*. 4th Ed. Ames: Iowa State University Press, 1996.

Hallin, Daniel C. *We Keep America on the Top of the World*. New York: Routledge, 1994.

Haynes, William. *Public Television for Sale, Media, the Market and the Public Sphere*. Boulder, CO: Westview Press, 1994.

Hess, Stephen. *The Government/Press Connection: Press Officers and Their Offices*. Washington, D.C.: The Brookings Institute, 1984.

Hood, Stuart, and Thalia Tabary-Peterson. *On Television*. 4th Edition. London: Pluto Press, 1997.

Innis, Harold A. *The Bias of Communication*. Toronto: University of Toronto Press, 1951.

Iyengar, Shanto, and Donald Kinder. *News That Matters: Television and American Public Opinion*. Chicago: The University of Chicago Press, 1991.

Iyengar, Shanto. *Is Anyone Responsible?* Chicago: University of Chicago Press, 1991.

Jamieson, Kathleen Hall. *Dirty Politics: Deception, Distraction and Democracy*. New York: Oxford University Press, 1992.

Just, Marion R., W. Russell Neuman, and Ann N. Crigler. *Common Knowledge*. Chicago: University of Chicago Press, 1992.

Kaplan, William. *Presumed Guilty: Brian Mulroney, The Airbus Affair and the Government of Canada*. Toronto: McClelland & Stewart, 1998.

Kellner, Douglas. *Television and the Crisis of Democracy*. Boulder, CO: Westview Press, 1995.

Key, V.O. *The Responsible Electorate: Rationality in Presidential Voting, 1936–60*. Cambridge, MA: The Belknap Press, 1966.

Klapp, Orrin E. *Symbolic Leaders: Public Dramas and Private Men*. Chicago: Adline Publishing Company, 1964.

Kurtz, Howard. *Media Crisis: The Trouble With America's Newspapers*. New York: Time Books, Random House, 1993.

———. *Spin Cycle: Inside the Clinton Propaganda Machine*. New York: The Free Press, 1998.

Kurtz, Howard, and Frank Denton. *Reinventing the Newspaper. Prescriptives on the News*. A Twentieth Century Fund Paper. New York: 1993.

Lee, Robert Mason. *One Hundred Monkeys: The Triumph of Popular Wisdom in Canadian Politics*. Toronto: Macfarlane, Walter and Ross, 1989.

Leonard, Thomas C. *News for All: America's Coming of Age with the Press*. New York: Oxford University Press, 1995.

———. *The Power Press: The Birth of American Political Reporting*. New York: Oxford University Press, 1986.

Manoff, Robert Karl, and Michael Schudson. *Reading the News: A Pantheon Guide to Popular Culture*. New York: Pantheon Books, 1986.

McDonald, Marci. *Yankee Doodle Dandy: Brian Mulroney and the American Agenda*. Toronto: Stoddart, 1995.

McGinniss, Joe. *The Selling of the President*. New York: Penguin Books, 1988.

McLuhan, Marshall. *Understanding Media: The Extension of Man*. A Mento Book. New York: The Penguin Group, 1964.

McManus, John H. *Market-Driven Journalism: Let the Citizen Beware*. Thousand Oaks, CA: Sage Publications 1994.

McQuail, Denis. *Media Performance: Mass Communication and the Public Trust*. Newbury Park: Sage Publications, 1992.

Merritt, Davis "Buzz." *Public Journalism and Public Life: Why Telling the News Is Not Enough*. Hillsdale, N.J.: Lawrence Erlbaum Associates Publishers, 1995.

Negroponte, Nicholas. *Being Digital*. New York: Alfred A. Knopf, 1995.

Neuharth, Al. *Confessions of an S.O.B.* New York: Doubleday, 1990.

Neuman, W. Russell. *The Future of the Mass Audience*. New York: Cambridge University Press, 1991.

Noonan, Peggy. *What I Saw at the Revolution: A Political Life in the Reagan Era*. New York: Random House, 1990.

Patterson, Thomas E. *Out of Order*. New York: Vintage Books, 1994.

Postman, Neil, and Steve Pavers. *How to Watch TV News*. New York: Penguin Books, 1992.

———. *Amusing Ourselves to Death: Public Discourse in the Age of Show Business*. New York: Penguin Books, 1985.

———. *Technology: The Surrender of Culture and Technology*. New York: Vintage Books, 1992.

Rosen, Jay, and Paul Taylor. *The New News and the Old News: The Press and Politics in the 1990s*. A Twentieth Century Fund Paper. New York: 1992.

Rosenstiel, Tom. *The Beat Goes On: President Clinton's First Year with the Media*. A Twentieth Century Fund Paper. New York.

———. *Strange Bedfellows: How Television and the Presidential Candidates Changed American Politics*. New York: Hyperion, 1992.

Sabato, Larry J., *Feeding Frenzy: How Attack Journalism Has Transformed American Politics*. New York: The Free Press, 1991.

Sabato, Larry J. and Glenn R Simpson. *Dirty Little Secrets: The Persistence of Corruption in American Politics*. New York: Times Books, Random House, 1996.

Scheckter, Danny. *The More You Watch, the Less You Know*. New York: Seven Stories Press, 1997.

Schudson, Michael. *The Power of News*. Cambridge, MA: Harvard University Press, 1995.

Speakes, Larry. *Speaking Out: Inside the Reagan White House*. New York: Scribners, 1988.

Squires, James. *Read All About It: The Corporate Takeover of America's Newspapers*. New York: Times Books, 1993.

The Oxford Book of Canadian Political Anecdotes. Toronto: Oxford University Press, 1988.

Index